LITERARY MATHEMATICS

STANFORD
TEXT TECHNOLOGIES

Series Editors
Elaine Treharne
Ruth Ahnert

Editorial Board
Benjamin Albritton
Caroline Bassett
Lori Emerson
Alan Liu
Elena Pierazzo
Andrew Prescott
Matthew Rubery
Kate Sweetapple
Heather Wolfe

Literary Mathematics

Quantitative Theory for Textual Studies

MICHAEL GAVIN

Stanford University Press
Stanford, California

STANFORD UNIVERSITY PRESS
Stanford, California

©2023 by Michael Gavin. All rights reserved.

No part of this book may be reproduced or transmitted in any form or by any means, electronic or mechanical, including photocopying and recording, or in any information storage or retrieval system without the prior written permission of Stanford University Press.

Printed in the United States of America on acid-free, archival-quality paper

Library of Congress Cataloging-in-Publication Data

Names: Gavin, Michael, author.

Title: Literary mathematics : quantitative theory for textual studies / Michael Gavin.

Other titles: Text technologies.

Description: Stanford, California : Stanford University Press, [2022] | Series: Stanford text technologies | Includes bibliographical references and index.

Identifiers: LCCN 2022005505 (print) | LCCN 2022005506 (ebook) | ISBN 9781503632820 (cloth) | ISBN 9781503633902 (paperback) | ISBN 9781503633919 (ebook)

Subjects: LCSH: Early English books online. | Digital humanities—Case studies. | Quantitative research.

Classification: LCC AZ105 .G38 2022 (print) | LCC AZ105 (ebook) | DDC 001.30285—dc23/eng/20220222

LC record available at https://lccn.loc.gov/2022005505

LC ebook record available at https://lccn.loc.gov/2022005506

Typeset by Newgen North America in 10/15 Spectral

For related materials please visit: https://literarymathematics.org/

CONTENTS

Acknowledgments vii

INTRODUCTION
The Corpus as an Object of Study — 1

1 Networks and the Study of Bibliographic Metadata — 24

2 The Computation of Meaning — 59

3 Conceptual Topography — 113

4 Principles of Literary Mathematics — 165

CONCLUSION
Similar Words Tend to Appear in Documents with Similar Metadata — 200

Notes 209
Bibliography 241
Index 261

ACKNOWLEDGMENTS

Thanks should go, first of all, to one's teachers. My introduction to digital humanities came from Scott L. Dewitt, whose seminar on new media and composition at Ohio State taught me to see how computers opened new genres of critical writing, a development he greeted with joyously open-minded pedagogical creativity. At Rutgers, Meredith L. McGill modeled passionate curiosity. Her seminar on intellectual property placed humanities computing within a long history of text technology, and her leadership at the Center for Cultural Analysis was personally welcoming and intellectually inspiring. At the University of South Carolina, David Lee Miller's forward-thinking advocacy for innovative scholarship, including his efforts to build and lead the Center for Digital Humanities there, provided support during my formative years as a junior professor. I consider David and Esther Gilman Richey among my best friends and most important teachers—as colleagues in the best of all senses. Thank you!

While researching this book, I enjoyed the privilege of attending two NEH-funded institutes hosted by the Folger Shakespeare Library. My thanks go out to institute leaders Jonathan Hope and Ruth Ahnert and to the many guest instructors, as well as to Michael Witmore and the staff at the Folger, who together created a pitch-perfect environment for creative and critical research at the intersection of digital humanities and early modern studies. I remain astonished by the intellectual energies of the participants, among them Collin Jennings, Brad Pasanek, and Lauren Kersey, who joined with me for our first foray into computational semantics. I had the further privilege of presenting material from this book at the Indiana Center for Eighteenth-Century Studies' annual workshop, in Bloomington, and at the Center for Digital Humanities Research, in College Station, and I thank Rebecca L. Spang and Laura Mandell for organizing those events.

Among my departmental colleagues, Nina Levine was a good friend and a great chair. Ed Madden and Jon Edwards generously read and commented on more pages of my writing than I can guess. Jeanne Britton found time to make invaluable suggestions on a related essay. Cynthia Davis lent her careful eye to a key chapter. Most importantly, Rachel Mann worked with me to test methods on data and topics related to her dissertation, helping usher that research through publication.

This book was written from 2018 through 2020 and revised during 2021. During most of this time, I served as the director of my university's first-year English program, which employs about 100 instructors to teach more than 4,000 students. To manage a large academic program is always challenging, of course, but those challenges were multiplied and amplified by the pandemic. This book simply could not exist without the inspired leadership and brilliant teaching of associate director Nicole Fisk as well as of the graduate assistants who contribute to all aspects of the program's management. Our instructors demonstrated resilience and compassion under terrifying conditions. Our students somehow, despite everything, kept at it. This book is just one minor by-product of their collective effort, courage, and goodwill.

I also received material support from the University of South Carolina's College of Arts and Sciences in the form of a sabbatical and two small grants. Very early in the process, an award from the Office of the Vice President for Research allowed me to spend a summer developing computational methods. Thanks go, too, to editors at *Cultural Analytics*, *Critical Inquiry*, *Textual Cultures*, *Review of English Studies*, and *Eighteenth-Century Studies*, among others, who supported this research by publishing related articles. Echoes and borrowings can be found throughout, especially in chapters 1 and 2, which draw heavily from my earlier pieces, "Historical Text Networks: The Sociology of Early English Criticism" (2016) and "William Empson, Vector Semantics, and the Study of Ambiguity" (2018). Thanks to Paolena Comouche for helping prepare the manuscript for submission and also to editors Caroline McKusick, Susan Karani, and Dawn Hall for ushering it through publication. I am extremely lucky to work with editor Erica Wetter as well as series editors Ruth Ahnert and Elaine Treharne, whose belief in this project never seemed to waver, and to the anonymous readers who gave the manuscript a careful and rigorous read at multiple stages.

Eric Gidal has worked alongside me every step of the way. His curiosity is as boundless as his patience. I cannot imagine a better friend or collaborator.

David Greven and Alex Beecroft opened their hearts and their home during a time when everything else was shutting down. Your kindness has been our saving grace.

To Rebecca I owe everything. I am especially thankful for our children through whom your virtues manifest in new and beautiful forms—for Haley's graceful intelligence, for Hayden's enduring compassion, for Kieran's open-hearted charm, and for Lily's relentless vivacity. Thank you for sharing your lives with me. To my parents and everyone in our families who helped us in ways both large and small, thank you.

During Christmas of 2019, our youngest daughter suffered a burst appendix, developed sepsis, and almost died. She underwent two surgeries and was hospitalized for nearly a month. This book is dedicated to

Dr. Bhairav Shah and to the nursing staff of the pediatric intensive care unit at Prisma Health Children's Hospital in Columbia, South Carolina. If not for your timely intervention, your competence, and your professionalism, I would not have had it in me to complete this book. Nor, perhaps, any book.

Thank you.

LITERARY MATHEMATICS

INTRODUCTION
THE CORPUS AS AN OBJECT OF STUDY

ONLY IN LITERARY STUDIES IS distant reading called "distant reading." In fact, corpus-based research is practiced by many scholars from a wide range of disciplines across the humanities and social sciences. The availability of large full-text databases has introduced and brought to prominence similar research methods in disciplines like political science, psychology, sociology, public health, law, and geography. Henry E. Brady has recently described the situation in terms that humanists may find familiar: "With this onslaught of data, political scientists can rethink how they do political science by becoming conversant with new technologies that facilitate accessing, managing, cleaning, analyzing, and archiving data."[1] In that field, Michael Laver, Kenneth Benoit, and John Garry demonstrated methods for using "words as data" to analyze public policy back in 2003.[2] Scholars like Jonathan B. Slapin, Sven-Oliver Proksch, Will Lowe, and Tamar Mitts have used words as data to study partisanship and radicalization in Europe and elsewhere across multilingual datasets.[3] In psychology the history is even deeper. The first mathematical models of word meaning came from psychologist Charles E. Osgood in the 1950s.[4] The procedures he developed share much in common with latent semantic analysis, of which Thomas K. Landauer, also a psychologist, was a pioneering figure, alongside computer scientists like Susan Dumais.[5] In sociology, geography, law, public health, and even economics, researchers are using corpus data as evidence in studies on topics of all kinds.[6]

At a glance, research in computational social science often looks very different from what Franco Moretti called "distant reading" or what Lev Manovich and Andrew Piper have called "cultural analytics."[7] But the basic practices of quantitative textual research are pretty much the same across disciplines. For example, Laver, Benoit, and Garry worked with a digitized collection of political manifestoes in their 2003 study titled "Extracting Policy Positions from Political Texts Using Words as Data." Their goal was to develop a general model for automatically identifying the ideological positions held by politicians across Great Britain, Ireland, and Europe. In largely the same way that a digital humanist might study a corpus of fiction by counting words to see how genres change over time, these social scientists sort political documents into ideological categories by counting words. "Moving beyond party politics," they write, "there is no reason the technique should not be used to score texts generated by participants in any policy debate of interest, whether these are bureaucratic policy documents, the transcripts of speeches, court opinions, or international treaties and agreements."[8] The range of applications seemed limitless. Indeed, many scholars have continued this line of research, and in the twenty years since, the study of "words as data" has become a major practice in computational social science. This field of inquiry emerged independently of humanities computing and corpus linguistics, but the basic procedures are surprisingly similar. Across the disciplines, scholars study corpora to better understand how social, ideological, and conceptual differences are enacted through written discourse and distributed over time and space.

Within literary studies, corpus-based inquiry has grown exponentially. When I first sketched out a plan for this book in late 2015, it was possible to imagine that my introduction would survey all relevant work. My plan was to cite Franco Moretti and Matthew Jockers, of course, as well as a few classic works of humanities computing, alongside newer studies by Ted Underwood and, especially, Peter de Bolla.[9] Now, as I finish the manuscript in 2021, I see so many studies of such incredible variety, I realize it's no longer possible to sum them up. The last few years have seen the publication of several major monographs. Books by Underwood and Piper have probed the boundaries between genres while updating and better specifying the methods of distant reading.[10] Katherine Bode has traced the history of the Australian novel.[11] Sarah Allison and Daniel Shore have explored the dispersion of literary tropes.[12] Numerous collections have been published and new journals founded; countless special issues have appeared. To these can be added a wide range of articles and book chapters that describe individual case studies and experiments in humanities computing. To offer just a few examples: Kim Gallon has charted the history of the African American press; Richard Jean So and Hoyt Long have used machine learning to test the boundaries of literary forms; and Nicole M. Brown has brought text mining to feminist technoscience.[13] Scholars like Dennis Yi Tenen, Mark Algee-Hewitt, and Peter de Bolla offer new models for basic notions like space, literary form, and conceptuality.[14] Manan Ahmed, Alex Gil, Moacir P. de Sá Pereira, and Roopika Risam use digital maps for explicitly activist purposes to trace immigrant detention, while others use geographic information systems (GIS) for more conventional literary-critical aims.[15] The subfield of geographical textual analysis is one of the most innovative areas of research: important new studies have appeared from Ian Gregory, Anouk Lang, Patricia Murrieta-Flores, Catherine Porter, and Timothy Tangherlini.[16] Within the field of early modern studies, essays by Ruth and Sebastian Ahnert, Heather Froehlich, James Jaehoon Lee, Blaine Greteman, Anupam Basu, Jonathan Hope, and Michael Witmore have used quantitative techniques for describing the social and semantic networks of early print.[17]

This work comes from a bewildering variety of disciplinary perspectives. Although controversy still occasionally swirls around the question of whether corpus-based methods can compete with close reading for the purpose of literary criticism, such debates miss a larger and more important point.[18] We are undoubtedly in the midst of a massive shift in the study of textuality. If economists are studying corpora, something important has changed, not just about the discipline of economics but also about the social realization of discourse more broadly. The processes by which discourse is segmented into texts, disseminated, stored, and analyzed have fundamentally altered. From the perspective of any single discipline, this change is experienced as the availability of new evidence ("big data," "words as data," "digital archives," and such) and as the intrusion of alien methods ("topic modeling," "classification algorithms," "community detection," and so on). But when you step back and look at how this kind of work has swept across so many disciplines, the picture looks very different. Considered together, this research represents an extraordinary event in the long history of textuality. More or less all at once, and across many research domains in the humanities and social sciences, the *corpus* has emerged as a major genre of cultural and scientific knowledge.

To place the emergence of the corpus at the center of our understanding offers a different perspective on the rise of cultural analytics within the humanities. It is often said or assumed that the basic story of computer-based literary analysis involves a confrontation between explanatory regimes represented by a host of binary oppositions: between qualitative and quantitative methods, between close and distant reading, between humans and machines, between minds and tools, or between the humanities and the sciences. This formulation has always struck me as, not quite wrong exactly, but not quite right. Research fields that were already comfortable with many forms of statistical inquiry, like political science, still need to learn and invent techniques for measuring, evaluating, and interpreting corpora. It's not that quantification is moving from one place to another but that researchers across domains have been suddenly tasked with learning (or, more precisely, with *discovering*) what methods are appropriate and useful for understanding these new textual forms. For this reason, what other people call "humanists using digital tools," I see differently: as one small piece of a large and diffuse interdisciplinary project devoted to learning how to use textual modeling to describe and explain society.

Rather than see quantitative humanities research as an intrusion from outside, I think of it as our field's contribution to this important project. Because of humanists' hard-won knowledge about the histories of cultures, languages, and literatures, we are uniquely well positioned to evaluate and innovate computational measures for their study. By interdisciplinary standards, we have the advantage of working with data that is relatively small and that is drawn from sources that are already well understood. Whereas an analysis of social media by public-health experts might sift through billions of tweets of uncertain provenance, our textual sources tend to number in the thousands, and they've often been carefully cataloged by archivists. Select canonical works have been read carefully by many scholars over decades, and many more lesser-known texts have been studied in extraordinary detail. Even more importantly, we are trained readers and philologists who are sensitive to the vagaries of language and are therefore especially alert to distortions that statistical modeling exerts on its sources. As scholars of meaning and textuality, we are in the best position to develop a general theory for corpora as textual objects and to understand exactly how the signifying practices of the past echo through the data. Put simply, we know the texts and understand how they work, so it makes sense for us to help figure out what can be learned by counting them. Such is the task before us, as I see it.

Here, then, are the guiding questions of this book: What are corpora? What theory is required for their description? What can be learned by studying them?

To ask these questions is different from asking, "What can digital methods contribute to literary studies?" That's the question most scholars—practitioners and skeptics alike—tend to emphasize, but it's a very bad question to start with. It places all emphasis on "findings" and "results" while leaving little room for theoretical reflection. It creates an incentive for digital humanists to pose as magicians by pulling findings out of black-box hats, while also licensing a closed-minded "show me whatcha got" attitude among critics who believe they can evaluate the merits of research without having to understand it. I believe this to be unfortunate, because what literary scholars bring to the interdisciplinary table is their robust and sustained attention to textual forms. We have elaborate theories for poetic and novelistic structures, yet cultural analytics and the digital humanities have proceeded to date without a working theory of the corpus as an object of inquiry—without pausing to consider the corpus itself as a textual form. By jumping the gun to ask what corpora can teach us about literature, we miss the chance to ask how quantification transforms the very texts we study. Many impressive case studies have been published in the last ten years, and I believe they have largely succeeded in their stated goals by demonstrating the efficacies of various computational methods. But I do not believe that any provide a satisfactory general answer to the questions (restated from above in somewhat different terms) that have nagged me from the beginning: What are these new textual things? What does the world look like through the perspective they provide? What new genres of critical thinking might they inform or enable? This book represents my best effort to answer these questions and to develop an understanding of corpus-based inquiry from something like the ground up.

The Argument

First, a preview of the argument. In this book, I will argue the following:

Corpus-based analysis involves a specific intellectual practice that shouldn't be called "distant reading" because it really has little to do with reading. I call that practice *describing the distribution of difference*. Across any collection of documents, variations that reflect meaningful differences in the histories of their production can be discovered. Depending on the corpus and the analysis that's brought to bear on it, these variations can be observed at a wide scale, revealing differences across broad outlines, and they can be highly granular, revealing what's particular about any given document or word. However, in order to engage in this practice more effectively, we need a good working theory, a general account of the corpus that is grounded in mathematics but sensitive to the histories of textual production behind its source documents. We also need good middle-range theories to justify the statistical proxies we use to represent those histories. In the chapters that follow, I'll borrow concepts from network science, computational linguistics, and quantitative geography to demonstrate how corpora represent relations among persons, words, and places. But I'll also argue that we have an imperative to innovate. We can't simply transpose ideas from one domain to another without being willing to get down to the theoretical basics and to offer new accounts of key concepts.

In support of this overarching argument, I will put forward two main supporting claims.

The first is an extremely technical claim, the precise details of which will matter to relatively few readers. I will propose a hyperspecialized definition for the word *corpus*. Conventionally, a corpus is defined by linguists as "a set of machine-readable texts."[19] This definition has the merit of simplicity, but I believe it to be inadequate, because it leaves unmentioned the role played by bibliographical metadata. For any corpus-based cultural analysis, whether it involves a few hundred novels or billions of tweets, the key step always hinges on comparing and contrasting different sources. To do this, researchers need both good metadata and an analytical framework for identifying the most relevant lines of comparison and establishing the terms under which they'll be evaluated statistically. I'll argue that any corpus is best defined in mathematical terms as a *topological space with an underlying set of elements (tokens) described under a topology of lexical and bibliographical subsets*. That is admittedly a mouthful. I'll explain what I mean by it in chapter 4. For now, the main point is simply to say that our understanding of the corpus should be grounded in a theoretical framework that anticipates the quantitative methods we plan to apply. To understand what's happening in any collection, we need to be able to describe how words cluster together in the documents, and we need to be able to correlate those clusters with the generic, social, temporal, and spatial properties of the source texts. The first goal of corpus-based cultural analysis is to explain with confidence who wrote what, when, and where. With that goal in mind, we should begin with a theory of the corpus that foregrounds its peculiar ability to blend textual data with contextual metadata and thereby to represent both text and context as a single, mutually informing mathematical abstraction. I will invite you to see words as something other than words—as countable instances that mark the points of intersection between language and history.

The second claim follows from this reconceptualization of the corpus as an object of inquiry. It's a much broader claim and will be of interest, I hope, to all readers of this book. Put simply, I'll argue that corpus-based inquiry works—that to study corpora is an effective way to learn about the world. Why? Because the documents that make up any corpus were written on purpose by people who meant to write them—people who were motivated in many cases because they cared deeply about their topics and believed (or at least hoped) their readers might care just as much.[20] This means that their intentions and their lives echo through the data. If that sounds fanciful, it's not. In fact, if you consider just a few examples, you'll see that this proposition is quite obvious (at least in its most basic formulation): Imagine a collection of American newspaper articles from 1930 to 1950. You don't have to read them to know that articles from 1939 to 1945 will have a lot to say about the topic of war. Similarly, a collection of novels set in New York or Los Angeles will refer to different buildings and streets from novels set in London or Tokyo. The same principle holds for any collection of documents. Food blogs will differ from obituaries; obituaries, from job ads. Essays by one author will differ from those by another; sermons from earlier centuries will differ from those preached today. No matter the axis of differentiation—genre, historical period, geographical place, author, subject, or virtually anything recorded in our bibliographical metadata—differences in the ways we categorize texts will tend to correspond with differences in their contents (that is, in the words they use). And those differences will tend to correspond, in turn, with things that mattered to the authors and their readers, and therefore to their shared histories. Of course, in any large corpus there will be plenty of exceptions—outliers or anomalies that have little to do with larger trends—but the general tendencies usually hold, and this correspondence, I'll argue, is why corpus analysis works.

However, as might be obvious, to say that corpus analysis "works" in this way is to say it does something very different from *reading* or *interpretation*—terms that can be very misleading when used to describe the practices of intellection I'll demonstrate in this book.[21] To read a text critically is to attempt to comprehend its meaning while remaining on the lookout for ideological distortions, to consider the enabling constraints of genre, to imagine or describe their reception by other readers, and to evaluate the texts and their authors for credibility and bias. Although many computational methods can be used to assist with critical reading in various ways, reading is not what those methods most directly involve.[22] (This disjunction has caused a great deal of confusion and frustration, not only among skeptics of corpus-based literary analysis but also, I think, among practitioners who contort their studies while attempting to meet the demands of such critics.) Instead, the main function of corpus analysis is to measure and describe how discourse is situated in the world. Its fundamental question is not, "What does this text mean?" but "Who wrote what, when, and where?"[23] Theodor Adorno once remarked that "topological thinking . . . knows the place of every phenomenon and the essence of none."[24] He meant it in a bad way, but nonetheless I agree. The goal of corpus analysis is not to explain the presumed essence of its object but to describe the observable relations among its parts. Quantitative textual analysis does not ask what words or texts really are; it describes how they're actually situated in relation to each other.

To turn from the real to the actual is a powerful act. Corpus-based inquiry is so effective across so many research domains because documents tend to correspond, one way or another, to the actual lives of their authors and readers. The kind of reasoning it facilitates is fundamentally dialectical. To learn about words, you need to know who wrote and read them, when and where. To learn about people, you need to learn what words they wrote and read, when and where. By aligning biographical, temporal, geographical, and lexical metadata and bringing them to bear as descriptive frameworks for historical documents, corpus analysis provides an extraordinarily powerful set of techniques for identifying correspondences across all these axes of comparison.

For this reason, quantitative textual analysis also draws together insights from other disciplines:

- In network science, the principle of *homophily* suggests that similar people will tend to travel in similar social circles.[25] Doctors are more likely to know and interact with other doctors than they are with, say, police officers. These differences correlate to what we might think of as kinds of people, and the weak ties among them form conduits through which information and influence flow. Robert K. Merton and Paul F. Lazarsfeld are sometimes credited with discovering this principle in 1954, but in fact psychologists, sociologists, and others had been working with similar ideas much earlier, and this principle has been foundational to the study of social networks more or less since the beginning.[26] The idea itself is simple enough to be stated in the terms of an ancient aphorism: "Birds of a feather flock together."
- In corpus linguistics, the *distributional hypothesis* proposes that similar words tend to be used in similar contexts.[27] Medical reports use different words from police reports. These differences correlate to meaning—terms like "pancreatic" and "embolization" will appear together in clusters, separate from but much like "burglary" and "perpetrator." Just as social networks form into cliques, so too words gather into topical clusters. The distributional hypothesis was first formally proposed by the linguist Zellig Harris, but Warren Weaver and other scientists also contributed to its development in the wake of World War II.[28] Indeed, the distributional hypothesis is so similar to the principle of homophily that computational linguists often describe it using J. R. Firth's variation on a similar aphorism: "You shall know a word by the company it keeps."[29]

- In quantitative geography, the principle of *spatial autocorrelation* holds that nearby places will tend to have similar attributes.[30] Neighboring towns will sit at relatively even elevations, have similar annual rainfalls, and share common demographics and cultures. For this reason, global averages are usually less meaningful than local ones. It doesn't tell you much to say that the elevation of Denver is above average, if that average was calculated over the entire United States; city planners need to know whether it's higher or lower than nearby places in central Colorado. As a premise, spatial autocorrelation goes back at least to John Snow's map of the cholera outbreak in 1854. Sometimes this principle is given as Tobler's First Law, which states that, in a geographic system, "everything is related to everything else, but near things are more related than distant things."[31]

Corpus-based inquiry draws together data about words, people, and places, thus bringing the distributional hypothesis, homophily, and spatial autocorrelation into a productive new theoretical relation. Corpora identify that point of intersection between modalities that draws these notions together and reveals them to be variants of a single idea. Reasoning out from these premises, we might ask: What do we actually mean when we say two people, two places, or any two things are similar, except that we use similar words to describe them? What does it actually mean to say that two words are similar, except that they're used by similar people in similar places when talking about similar things? By the end of the book, this will be my central argument: Corpora propose a measurable tautology between language and actuality that subjects the symbolic production of human experience to new forms of mathematical description. This tautology explains why corpus analysis works, why corpora have so much explanatory power, and why they provide so rich a source of evidence across so many research domains. I express this tautology with the phrase, *Similar words tend to appear in documents with similar metadata*.

The most difficult task facing cultural analytics, I believe, is to develop a body of quantitative theory and a general set of procedures for exploring this correspondence. For lack of a better name, I have taken to calling this nascent project *literary mathematics*. By that term I refer to a category of intellectual work at the center of cultural analytics that has received relatively little discussion. Not learning to code; learning the math. When commentators talk about "computational methods" in "digital humanities," they're usually talking about "tools"—about software that can be used to advance the extremely vague ambition of "finding patterns in the data."[32] But the most interesting and important aspects of such work relate only obliquely to the task of managing computer software. Instead, quantitative textual analysis involves sampling ideas from radically different disciplines and folding them into our own ways of thinking, such that we learn to see in our texts, not patterns, but structures that can be defined, described, and evaluated formally using mathematical expressions that name relations among textual parts. Literary mathematics is not a branch of mathematics; rather, it stretches like a loose and fragile cobweb across already existing and much sturdier branches—most importantly among them: graph theory, matrix algebra, and statistics. However, the phrase is also meant to suggest that there remains work to do. The theories and concepts we need aren't already somehow given; we can't take them for granted. The question of which quantitative models are appropriate for describing which textual phenomena remains very much open.

This book's use of mathematics will have different stakes for different groups of scholars. The primary readers I mean to address are those in the field of cultural analytics, including people who might be hoping to learn or are merely curious. For experienced researchers in the field, the mathematical operations I'll describe will all be familiar. In some places, my methods might even seem simple or willfully pared down to their basics. The chapters that follow will make no use of cutting-edge machine-learning algorithms. No topic modeling. No word-embedding models. No neural networks. No black boxes. That's intentional. What's needed for rigorous computational humanities research, I'll argue, is not that it borrows methods from the vanguard of technological advancement, but things altogether more pedestrian: good corpora, accurate metadata, and a clear-eyed attention to their interrelation.

For others—for humanists looking to enter the field or students hoping to learn—the math will be unfamiliar and perhaps even daunting. Math can pose a seemingly insurmountable obstacle to one's own research goals. To these scholars, I hope to show that their fear can be set aside. Armed with a good corpus and a clear sense of what can and can't be accomplished, anyone can learn to perform corpus-based analysis and to write about their work with confidence and clarity. All methods used in this study could be learned in a couple of semesters by graduate students or aspiring faculty. Each case study provides a model to follow, and the final chapter summarizes the most crucial theoretical concepts. Further, this book's online supplement features easy-to-use datasets and easy-to-execute sample code, along with tutorials and student-oriented documentation. Those tutorials provide a walkthrough for each chapter, explaining the mathematical procedures in more detail and providing further examples of my own and samples of student work.[33]

As corpus-based inquiry continues to gain footing across the disciplines, information scientists will continue to advance methods for modeling language-in-use. Humanists and social scientists will continue to evaluate those methods against known cases, every now and then pushing the methods in new directions where needed. Together, whether working in collaboration or (more often) in parallel, such research will advance our shared understanding of how computationally recorded discourse can be studied to tackle big questions that matter. But to be most successful it will require, I believe, a guiding theory, a motivating proposition about how history and society are represented through corpora and about how discourse, measured at scale, reflects the actualities of its production. The purpose of this book is to sketch an outline of such a theory.

The Dataset

The chapters that follow will feature technical demonstrations based on data taken from the *Early English Books Online* (EEBO) corpus, as transcribed and published by the Text Creation Partnership (TCP). The analyses were mostly performed between the years 2016 and 2019, when the corpus was in varying states of public availability. Curatorial work involving that corpus remains ongoing. For this reason, the results presented in this book should be considered neither final nor definitive. Although I hope and expect that they'll "hold up" fairly well, they are offered for demonstration purposes only. The latest publicly available data and updated analyses can be accessed on this book's accompanying website. All analyses for this book were performed, and all visualizations created, using the R program for statistical computing.[34]

The EEBO corpus has a long and complicated history.[35] It began with the first efforts by editors A. W. Pollard, G. R. Redgrave, and Donald Wing to compile authoritative bibliographies of English-language books printed before 1700. Their reference works informed an initiative to photograph the books and create microfilm copies of each title, work that began in the 1930s and continued for decades. The microfilms were scanned and published online in the 1990s. Shortly thereafter, a consortium of scholars called the Text Creation Partnership transcribed a large representative sample of the scanned images, using Standard General Markup Language (SGML) to organize the resulting documents and their contents. This entire process took about a century to complete, and over the decades countless scholars took part—not just the editors whose names we know but also archivists and librarians across England and North America, technical experts working with the TCP, and anonymous coders working for third-party contractors in India. Just over 60,000 volumes were transcribed and published.

When discussing EEBO, specialists in early modern studies understandably emphasize its shortcomings, and their concern is directed primarily toward its problems.[36] These problems occur at many levels. Errors and omissions can be found in the transcripts; many digitized books were not transcribed; many surviving books did not get scanned; and many books did not survive since their first publication. In addition to all of these losses, the total universe of every book published, even if it still existed, would be an incomplete record of early modern life.

Manuscript culture thrived alongside print, as did many forms of oral communication, such as play performance, but none of that discourse can be represented in a print-based corpus. (An important omission, to people who study Shakespeare!) Further, the textual record is biased toward wealthy male writers; the perspectives of women are very underrepresented; the poor and people of color are excluded almost entirely. For all these reasons, it's impossible for any corpus-based analysis (or any other kind of analysis, for that matter) to represent early modern life in anything like its full complexity. This point must be emphasized up front and kept firmly in mind at all times. In the analyses that follow, I'll take EEBO mostly as I find it, but that should not be interpreted as a lack of awareness about any of these issues. The question of how to evaluate EEBO's representativeness is important, and it's understandably most on the minds of experts in the field.[37] But it's not a question with which I will be centrally concerned. Although some details in the case studies might very well require revision as new data becomes available, none of my larger arguments will hinge on issues peculiar to EEBO as such. My emphasis will be entirely on explicating analytical methods.

In any case, the public release of the EEBO dataset, along with a number of other digital initiatives, has sparked exciting new research at the intersection of early modern studies and digital humanities. While writing this manuscript, I participated in two Early Modern Digital Agendas institutes hosted by the Folger Shakespeare Library, where I had the honor of seeing some of this work firsthand.[38] I am not a Renaissance scholar, however. My graduate training focused on eighteenth-century literature and book history, and my dissertation did not address concerns central to the study of the Renaissance. For this reason, the chapters that follow will engage the community of early modernists only obliquely. Although I hope that specialists in that field will consider the case studies interesting and informative in their own right, my true goals are theoretical and are meant to speak to a broader audience of researchers in cultural analytics and other humanists curious about quantitative methods in general.

For this reason, the case studies that follow will not presume more than a passing familiarity with English history in broad strokes. This was the era of the printing press, the compass, and gunpowder. Book production grew, sporadically but exponentially, as England gained economic, military, naval, and political power. The collection goes back to the 1470s, when the printing press was first introduced to London, and extends to 1700, when England had grown to be a major force in the Atlantic world. (A few texts from the eighteenth century slipped into the corpus, but I excluded those from the analyses herein.) EEBO thus describes early English modernity over a *longue durée*, with the first printed editions of Chaucer's *Canterbury Tales* on one side and Dryden's *Aeneid* on the other, and with Shakespeare's First Folio somewhere in the middle. Books were produced almost exclusively in London, where shops and printing houses were often within easy walking distance of each other. Most books were small things, more like pamphlets than "books" as we understand them today. Their printing was often self-financed by authors or funded by patrons, even when booksellers handled distribution. The corpus includes literary texts alongside many more nonliterary ones. Over the course of these two centuries, English print addressed an ever-expanding range of topics, from politics and religion, to travel narratives and news from abroad, to poetry, to cookbooks and prayer books, as well as to natural philosophy and medicine, not to mention the occasional bawdy ballad. Books were written by clergymen and poets, hacks and philosophers, revolutionaries and visionaries, and kings and queens.

In short, EEBO provides a wide-ranging sample of early modern printed discourse. It is a general corpus that includes documents from many different genres. Unlike, say, a collection of digitized novels, EEBO is designed to provide detailed evidence for an extremely broad range of potential historical inquiries. This makes EEBO particularly well suited for a study, like this one, meant to demonstrate general approaches to corpus-based cultural analysis.

Plan for the Book: People, Words, Places

Although the chapters that follow will build on each other in some ways, the book's organization is modular, and readers are invited to take the chapters in any order. Each is meant to be readable as a stand-alone, independent piece. The first three chapters offer case studies that loosely track my three primary frames of analysis: people, words, and places. The final chapter offers a theoretical summation of the whole. Readers who are most curious about quantitative theory in general may want to begin with chapter 4—some reviewers of the manuscript suggested it might be more appropriate to place that chapter at the beginning—but my sense is that most people will appreciate the chance to consider an example or two in detail before diving in to generalities and abstractions, and so the chapters are organized in what I consider to be their order of difficulty.

Chapter 1, "Networks and the Study of Bibliographical Metadata," examines the conceptual form and structure of EEBO's metadata, focusing in particular on how such data organizes and describes relations among people. Every time a document is attributed to more than one person—to the printer, the bookseller, the author, &c—EEBO represents that title as a point of connection between them. Books function like links connecting nodes in a large network. Tracing patterns within this network reveals how the digital archive sorts itself into segments, or communities. To understand these communities, how they function and exist in relation to one another, I borrow ideas from graph theory and network science. EEBO displays many characteristics of "real-world networks" found in other areas of human life, where some people have many connections and serve as local hubs while others sit on the outskirts. Such communities are not mere mathematical fictions; they reflect actual conditions faced in the London book trade. People who appear near each other in EEBO's metadata mostly lived around the same time. Partnerships among printers and booksellers structure the network as a whole, dividing the corpus into large communities.

I will suggest that these groups offer a different way to think about historical periodization. Bursts of publishing activity create clusters in the network that, when distributed over time, look something like historical periods. The boundaries between such groups are not marked by events or specific years, however, but by "structural holes" that reflect gaps in the network, areas where connections are unusually sparse. Structural holes mark points of disruption in the book trade where one generation of stationers has begun to turn over to another. Across these groups, canonical authors like Erasmus and Shakespeare, whose work was reprinted and adapted by later generations, provide crucial bridges that tie the corpus together over time.

This case study is offered first because it is the most straightforward, conceptually and historically. Analyzing copublication metadata is a relatively common application of network methods, and the broad picture of the evolution and growth of the early English book trade that emerges from analysis is meant to feel very familiar. Gaps in the network align neatly with conventional divisions among early modern periods: the "Renaissance" is clearly visible, as are the Civil War, Interregnum, and Restoration periods, each of which have their own characteristically active authors and stationers. Everything fits. Nothing in this chapter is meant to be surprising, except perhaps for the fit itself. Scholars should find it jarring, if not quite surprising, to see how well the concepts of network science describe historical phenomena that have been so thoroughly examined in other ways. A network model of EEBO's metadata represents literary history as an aggregate of basic elements—simple bibliographical facts about who published what, when, and with whom. From that aggregate, the model can generate complex representations of literary history that are true in broad strokes and at more granular scales. The advantage of a mathematical, complex-systems approach to bibliographical metadata is that it makes such perspectives possible.

In chapter 2, "The Computation of Meaning," I extend this line of argument by turning attention from authors and publishers to the words on the pages. In exactly the same way that collaborators are linked in a copublication model, words are connected in a semantic model if they appear in the same documents. Just as EEBO's copublication records provide a surprisingly accurate representation of historical periodization, so too its lexical collocations provide a surprisingly accurate representation of early modern conceptuality. Although lexical data are far denser than their bibliographical counterparts, and therefore some statistical tests used to evaluate lexical relationships are different, the underlying mathematical structure is very similar. A network model of copublication produces something that looks like historical community; networks of word collocation produce something that looks like meaning.

My goal in this chapter is to develop a theory of meaning and textuality that explains why this is the case, why word-collocation models are so successful at parsing various kinds of semantic relatedness. To this end, I'll describe a fundamental continuity among very different ways of thinking about language and meaning, comparing Julia Kristeva's theory of intertextuality to distributional semantics as it developed in the fields of machine translation and information retrieval. Kristeva's adaptation of Mikhail Bakhtin's theory of "dialogism" proposed a spatial logic for meaning, such that all uses of a word and their various textual combinations could be described mathematically as a single, simultaneously existing structure. In the fields of machine translation and information retrieval, Margaret Masterman, H. P. Luhn, Gerard Salton, and others developed protocols for automatic language processing that rested on very similar principles. Words would function as minimal units, providing points of connection that bind together a vast matrix of a document collection's intertextual relations.

These scholars were working across radically different disciplinary contexts and, as far as I can tell, had no communication with each other. Yet, I'll argue they shared a key insight: they viewed words as part of an algebraic or geometric system. Every word entails latent connections with the others, and these connections make possible their meaningful recombination in human discourse, whether that recombination happens in a graph, a search query, or a poem. Every word in every text is a node connecting that text to a larger network of language, where the word appears in many variations that supervene over every particular use. Computational semantics embrace intertextuality's basic premises while grounding them in empirically observable units and thus lending that theory greater precision and analytical power.

To demonstrate that power, this chapter provides many examples of how, using a very simple set of statistical measurements, the EEBO corpus can be queried to expose various conceptual relations among words. I look at early modern uses of words involving color (*black*) and animals (*frogs*) as well as terms that cross discourses of anatomy (*bladder*), philosophy (*consciousness*), and literature (*heart*). I then show how words can be decomposed and recombined to reveal different shades of meaning and contexts of use, exploring representations of the Atlantic slave trade (*jamaica* x *slave*) and English gender ideologies (*woman*—[*wife* + *mother* + *daughter*]). I show how the semantic model can be manipulated to compare and contrast works of specific authors as well as to identify historical events or show conceptual change over time.

Computational linguists and others have debated whether semantic models capture "meaning" in the human sense, but I argue their debates miss a more important point. I conclude by suggesting that our very understanding of meaning itself should be shaken by the success of word-collocation models. These models couldn't work as well as they do unless scholars, as a community, had an incomplete understanding of how language operates. Kristeva's theory of intertextuality provides the closest account I know of to a theory of meaning that is sensitive to the semantic relationships these models capture.

Chapter 3, "Conceptual Topography," is a little different from the others. Whereas the first two chapters place greater emphasis on theoretical framing and stick to accepted applications of statistical measurements, this chapter places more emphasis on historical argumentation and gets a bit more creative with its metrics. I use a common measurement of geographical distribution in a very uncommon way. For any given variable, it's easy to show its "spread"; that is, its average position along coordinates of latitude and longitude and its average distance from that centroid. I apply this metric to EEBO's lexicon to show how words in the corpus have differing geographical associations, and I map those associations to identify what I call their *conceptual topography*.

Research for this chapter began as a data-curation project that identified toponyms in the corpus. Building from a small collection of early modern geographical textbooks, we found almost 15,000 unique word forms in the corpus that name over 9,000 unique geographical places. Among those places, EEBO records the coordinates of latitude and longitude of almost 2,500. Using this data, I track the evolution of geographical writing over the period, showing which places English writers referred to most frequently and how that changed over time. The basic method can be broken down to two steps: (1) identifying the places mentioned in each document and (2) identifying which words were used in books about those places.

Geographical text analysis offers a radically new way to study the history of geographical thought and, I argue, exposes limitations and inaccuracies in the received wisdom about early modern world geography. Literary historians tend to interpret the period's geography retrospectively as a prehistory of the British Empire. They focus overwhelmingly on exotic locales in America and Asia, and they emphasize English nationhood and its budding imperial ambitions. Consequently, they underestimate how Eurocentric Anglophone geography really was. Only at the very end of the seventeenth century does a coherent sense of English nationality and transatlantic community take shape. Literary historians also grossly underestimate the enduring importance of antiquity, especially biblical antiquity. A significant portion of all English-language geographical discourse was devoted to retelling and explaining Christian myth. England did not sit alone at the center of a global world. Rather, it was a geographically marginal actor in the economic and political systems of Europe, with manifold connections to its neighbors, and with a profound ideological commitment to scriptural tradition. The conceptual structure of this emerging world system, I argue, shaped virtually all aspects of the language, as different spatial modalities (nation-states, markets, global trade networks, print culture, domesticity, universalist divinity, and human embodiment) came to be differentiated across various regions of the conceptual topography of the early modern world.

However, I wouldn't want the practicalities of the method or the details of my contrarian historical argument to distract from the chapter's central claim, which is neither about the seventeenth century nor about any particular computational method. The chapter will offer a proposition about the relationship between language and actuality. Books about Bethlehem will use a lot of the same words as books about Nazareth; so too, books about Liverpool and Manchester. On its face, the proposition is meant to feel obvious. Yet, it suggests that geographical location is somehow embedded in language. Place is part of the conceptual structure that subsists among words. When I draw a conceptual topography of the early modern world, I'll show how, using nothing but the geocoordinates of places mentioned in books, I can sort the lexicon of EEBO into conceptual groups as coherent as some topic models. Just as the network model in chapter 1 organizes early modern discourse by the people who wrote and published together, the geographical model shows how the corpus can be sorted by space. Meaning and spatiality, I'll argue, are intimately connected over the same lexical and textual features.

The book's final chapter, "Principles of Literary Mathematics," offers a theoretical summation of the whole. My goal in this chapter is to pare cultural analytics down to the bone. I begin by describing distant reading's foundational premises, asking what reason we have for believing that observable variations in a corpus will have anything to do with the histories of the people whose lives are recorded in that corpus. By working through what I believe to be distant reading's basic assumptions, I'll offer a revision to the "distributional hypothesis" first proposed by Zellig Harris in the 1950s. Harris said that difference in meaning correlates with difference in distribution, an idea usually stated more simply in the phrase, "Similar words tend to appear in similar contexts." I will extend this idea by offering a slight alteration: "Similar words tend to appear in documents with similar metadata." Similar words will be written by similar authors, published by similar editors, posted online by similar social media users, sold in similar bookstores in similar cities during similar decades. The stuff of language and the actualities through which language disseminates are intimately and measurably connected.

After laying out this general theoretical framework, I then briefly survey the mathematical concepts most directly useful for describing variations in a corpus. This second half of the last chapter is meant both as a theoretical introspection into methods employed throughout the book and as a primer and guide for students in the field. As I define it, *literary mathematics is the practice of representing critical concepts using formal expressions that describe relations among literature's countable features.* Given any collection of literary objects, by which I refer to any kind of text, it's possible to identify a system of relations among them, to describe the distribution of difference across those systems, and to evaluate the significance of those differences. How are things structured? How are some things different from others? Which differences are most significant or surprising? These three broad categories of critical inquiry—form, difference, and significance—correspond loosely to three kinds of quantitative reasoning—discrete mathematics, linear algebra, and probability theory. In this chapter, I propose a general framework for corpus-based research. I propose a set of mathematical tests for describing how the formal structures of the corpus enmesh words, books, and people in a web of time.

In the book's conclusion, I return focus to my most central theoretical argument: *Similar words tend to appear in documents with similar metadata.* I offer this strangely worded proposition as an invitation to consider the fundamental principles of cultural analytics and to open new lines of inquiry between literary studies, digital humanities, the social sciences, and the information sciences. Quantitative approaches to textual studies can only proceed effectively if grounded on rigorously conceived principles. Those principles, once articulated, reveal how little we actually know about the deep structures of language and history. But they also suggest a path forward and open new vistas of historical and theoretical inquiry.

CHAPTER 1

NETWORKS AND THE STUDY OF BIBLIOGRAPHICAL METADATA

CONSIDER FOR A MOMENT THE CONVENTIONAL form of an early modern title page. What information does it communicate? Already by the sixteenth and seventeenth centuries, the title page had stabilized into the basic shape it continues to hold today. For example, we learn from its title page that *Hesperides* (fig. 1.1) includes the works "of Robert Herrick," which were "Printed for *John Williams,* and *Francis Eglesfield,* and are to be sold by *Tho: Hunt,* Book-seller in *Exon.* 1648."[1] Of course, title pages can be misleading, so scholars must always be on guard for omissions, mistakes, parodies, and lies. Yet, in common practice, we depend on them quite heavily. We take for granted that there was such a person as Robert Herrick whose poems were printed and sold in such a year as 1648. Facts like these are the basic, inescapable elements of literary history. Considered individually, any one of them might turn out to be wrong, but together, they are the taken-for-granted foundation of our work. Neither "early modern print" nor "seventeenth-century literature" (nor, for that

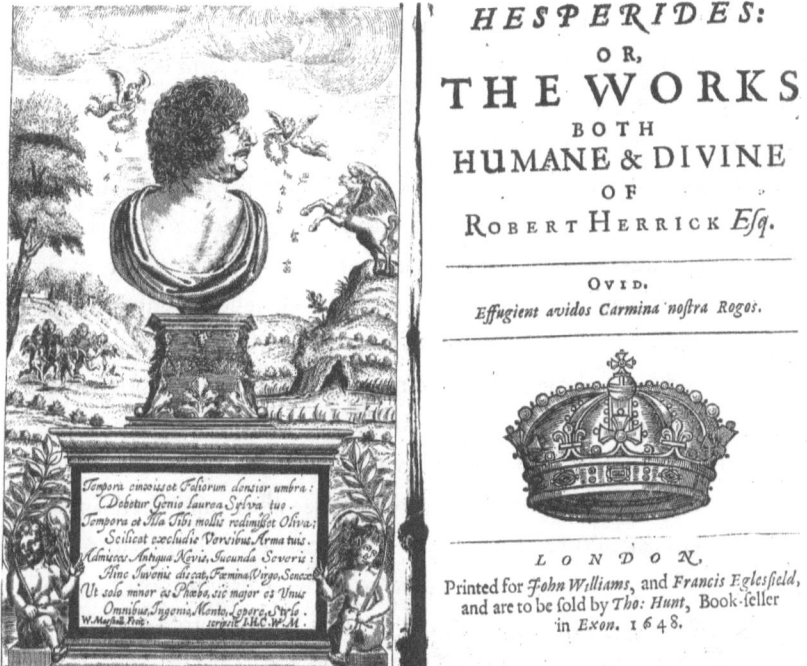

Figure 1.1. Early Modern Title Page. Frontispiece and title page to Robert Herrick's *Hesperides*. EEBO image courtesy of the Huntington Library.

matter, "literary studies") could exist without a general belief that title pages refer to real events in the histories of books. Every other practice of our discipline rests on this basic assumption.

When converted into library catalog records or listed in bibliographies, facts gleaned from title pages take a form that is even more regularized and indeed so familiar as to feel almost natural. But it isn't natural at all. Every title page and every list of works cited is a structured presentation of bibliographical metadata. Strangely, given the centrality of this data structure to our discipline, most students are never trained to study or analyze bibliographies. At least, I wasn't. I was trained to gather references, to evaluate and compare records, and to perform bibliographical descriptions of books. In graduate school, I was also trained to perform rhetorical analyses of title pages and frontispieces while reflecting critically on theoretical abstractions like "authorship" or "print culture." But I was never asked to look at a works cited page and describe what I saw. I was never invited to consider the basic facts of literary history as objects of literary knowledge.

In this chapter I'll describe a model for analyzing these bibliographical elements and demonstrate what literary history looks like when considered as an aggregate of them. That perspective is visualized in figure 1.2, which represents authors, printers, and booksellers as nodes in a vast network that extends over two hundred years. From this view, literary history resembles a large, tangled knot. Stationers who published many books occupy important positions in the network. They often collaborated with each other and worked with a wide variety of authors, most of whom are not visible in this figure because they published only once or twice. This structure also reflects the constraints of mortality. Printers and booksellers who collaborated together were in most cases contemporaries. This means the largest clusters in the network correspond loosely with moments in time. They reflect broadly diffused events in the history of English print, bursts in publishing activity when groups of stationers were particularly active. Yet, the network cannot proceed in a single straight line of chronology. Every moment in history bends toward its past. As we'll see, the network assumes a very particular shape, with high concentrations of activity around prolific printers and booksellers, and with gaps among them bridged by canonical authors and by stationers with unusual careers.

To understand how these networks represent the past requires delving briefly into the history of network science. In its early instantiations, "sociometry" was concerned mainly with group dynamics and social psychology; it focused on how individual behavior was affected or even determined by interpersonal relationships. As the study of networks made greater use of mathematical techniques for representing social interactions, its scope similarly expanded and became more abstract as scholars investigated the flow of information across the "weak ties" that constitute society. This shift in emphasis directed attention away from the analysis of already identified, bounded groups and toward more

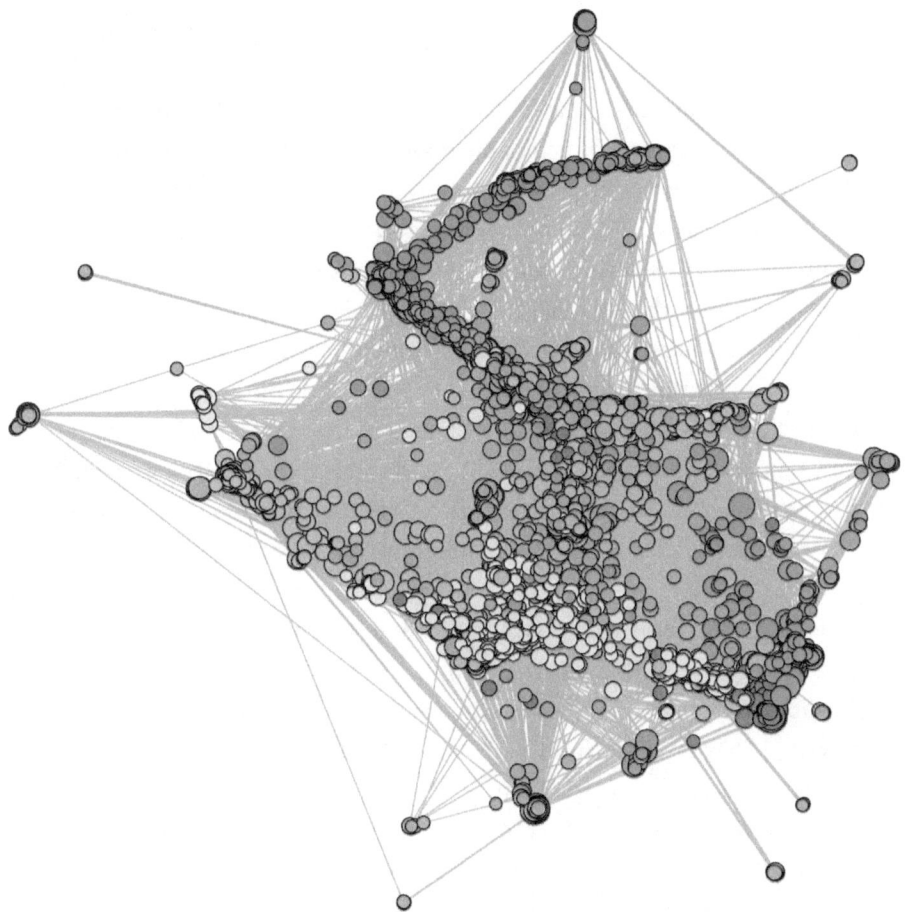

Figure 1.2. The EEBO Network. This graph shows the highest-degree nodes in EEBO's largest communities. Relationships in the network are loosely chronological, proceeding from the earliest publications of the fifteen and sixteenth centuries (*left*), through the early 1600s (*center left*). From there, the network splits and expands. At the center are nodes mostly active in the 1630s and 1640s (*center*), which push into two different directions: toward nodes from the Interregnum period (*top*) and toward those of the Restoration (*right* and *bottom*).

dispersed communities that, in many cases, were invisible or unknown to their individual members and, one might argue, in fact had no real existence outside of the analytical framework that identified them. In the 1990s, the study of networks was jolted by the work of physicists and other scientists who identified commonalities between the mathematical shapes of social networks and the structures of other phenomena—from the nervous systems of animals to ecologies, to corporate boards, to the internet, and to actors' movie careers. They found highly regularized structures across an unimaginably wide variety of social and physical systems. The study of networks is the study of such commonalities.

In what follows, I'll survey this structure in detail and examine how it situates EEBO's authors and stationers in historical relation to each other. But the purpose of the chapter is to invite scholars to reflect more generally on the possibilities for this "complex systems" approach to literary history. Every link in this network is based on nothing but the bare facts of EEBO's bibliography: the authors in the catalog and the stationers named in the imprints. Considered as a complex network extracted from corpus data, literary historicity is neither more nor less than an emergent effect of these simple interactions in aggregate.

Emergent Structures: Complex Systems and Network Modeling

Complex systems are built from simple blocks. The larger patterns observable in such systems are said to *emerge* when "well-formulated aggregate behavior arises from localized, individual behavior."[2] According to Albert-László Barabási, "Behind each complex system there is an intricate network that encodes the interactions between the system's components."[3] Examples of such systems abound. Network forms have been found in many different kinds of things. M. E. J. Newman's textbook covers everything from infrastructure (the internet, telephone and power grids, transportation and logistics, gas pipelines and rivers), to social networks (friendships, family structure, and professional affiliations), to biochemical networks (protein interactions, genetic transcription, neural systems), and larger ecological systems (food webs).[4] In 1999, geographer Manuel Castells used the same concept to describe multinational capitalism, claiming that we now live in a world defined by networks: "Networks constitute the new social morphology of our societies," he argued, and they affect all "processes of production, experience, power, and culture."[5] Surveying this new intellectual landscape that seemed to find networks everywhere, Duncan J. Watts remarked, "there appear[s] to be a common thread linking these systems together."[6] A network of networks, so to speak. And what binds these various systems together? Barabási explains:

> The exploding interest in network science during the first decade of the twenty-first century is rooted in the discovery that despite the obvious diversity of complex systems, the structure and the evolution of networks behind each system is driven by a common set of fundamental laws and principles. Therefore, notwithstanding the amazing differences in form, size, nature, age and scope of real networks, most networks are driven by common organizing principles. Once we disregard the nature of the components and the precise nature of the interactions between them, the networks obtained are more similar to than different from each other.[7]

Notice Barabási's emphasis on structure: He argues that, disregarding the details of the elements of these various systems, the formal relations among them will be more similar than different. These similarities suggest, to network theorists like him, that complex systems of very different kinds nonetheless share "common organizing principles" and perhaps are "driven by a common set of fundamental laws and principles."

The "complex systems" understanding of networks thus depends on an act of abstraction that allows researchers to compare radically different things—friends and foodways and neurons—by attending to their common structural features. That is to say, like all scientific models, networks operate by way of analogy.[8] This point bears emphasis. Humanists often contrast technical applications of network modeling from merely "metaphorical," qualitative uses of the term.[9] But networks are always metaphorical in that they are always working at the level of analogy by comparing relations among things. To say that oak trees are to acorns as sheep are to wool is to identify an equivalence between two very simple dyadic networks. Christopher D. Kilgore describes a network as a "*cognitive schema*" that provides an "abstract set of expectations used pragmatically to make sense of the world."[10] Like metaphors, network models abstract over the realities they purport to describe.[11] This abstraction serves an important purpose. As Caroline Levine has argued, "attention to the patterns governing networks will allow us to think in newly rigorous ways."[12] The network concept is "neutral enough" and "flexible enough," writes Kate Davison, to describe relationships of many kinds.[13]

This neutrality or flexibility comes as a cost—a cost that is paid deliberately. Critics sometimes complain that network models can't capture the richly complicated realities of social life.[14] Skeptics express concern about what's lost through abstraction. But that loss is precisely the point. What's "lost" in network science is what's deliberately stripped away. The "nature of the components and the precise nature of the interactions between them" (to return to Barabási's phrase) are actively disregarded in hopes of revealing a complex system's otherwise invisible organizing structure.

In this sense, twenty-first-century network science differs greatly from the field's original studies.[15] Early researchers were more likely to be concerned with small complicated systems than with large complex ones. Within psychology and sociology, network science's roots trace most directly to the study of group dynamics, which was concerned with the problem of how groups form, how beliefs come to be shared and exchanged among persons, and how individuals' attitudes are affected by their social environments. Jacob L. Moreno and Helen Jennings were among the earliest to quantify and visualize group behavior, a practice they called "sociometry." Writing in the 1930s, they devised the first sociograms to show how schoolchildren gather into cliques mediated by high-status individuals. Within the field of psychology, both Jacob and Zerka T. Moreno were early advocates for group therapy and role-playing, believing that the fundamental units of psychosocial being were "social atoms"—not individuals, but the relationships formed among them. In sociology, this line of inquiry was formalized and extended over the decades to follow by Kurt Lewin, who invented the term "group dynamics," and George Homans, whose goal was to uncover what he believed to be the fundamental elements of social behavior. Paul F. Lazarsfeld and Robert K. Merton studied "friendship as a social process" by evaluating how social status, racial attitudes, and religion affected the formation and maintenance of relationships.[16] Scholars contributed to this field of inquiry by studying families, workplaces, and, at the largest scale, tribes and small towns.[17] Under this framework, individuals participate in microsystems of exchange where they form emotional bonds while trading opinions and seeking their peers' approval. Small groups offer rewards and impose punishments that direct the beliefs and attitudes of the people bound up in them.

During the 1960s, mathematical models for group dynamics were still in their experimental infancy. Homans developed a technique for analyzing tabulated data that involved scanning tables visually and "shuffling" the columns by hand until patterns appeared.[18] A flurry of books were published in the following years that hoped to lend this work greater rigor; among them, Harrison White's *An Anatomy of Kinship: Mathematical Models for Structures of Cumulated Roles* (1963), Claude Flament's *Applications of Graph Theory to Group Structure* (1963), and Frank Harary, Robert Norman, and Dorwin Cartwright's *Structural Models: An Introduction to the Theory of Directed Graphs* (1965). Taken together, these books represent a major advance in the study of social systems. Although each has different emphases, taken together they explore similar techniques for analyzing sociometric data. They successfully reconciled three things: (1) sociometric visualizations like those devised by Jennings and Moreno; (2) graph theory, which was a new branch of mathematics; and (3) matrix algebra, which provided the foundations for data analysis. Even though they were data poor and the results they reported were not particularly impressive in and of themselves, these early attempts to apply network models to the social sciences showed how systems visualized intuitively with points and lines could be subject to rigorous statistical comparison.

Harrison White taught influential seminars during the years to follow, sparking what has come to be known as the "Harvard Breakthrough."[19] Many of his students went on to write important studies. Among these, Nancy Howell Lee's *The Search for an Abortionist* (1969) exposed how pregnant women before *Roe v. Wade* were forced to reach outside their immediate family to procure an abortion; and, similarly, Mark Granovetter described the "strength of weak ties" by tracing how people find employment. Most job seekers can't learn of open positions from their closest friends: news must travel through channels of acquaintances (among, for example, contacts from work or church) that stretch more widely across their communities.[20] Whereas the study of group dynamics was devoted to understanding social psychology—how people come to think and feel the way they do—the study of social networks was geared toward understanding how information moves through society, and thus how knowledge forms within communities and is transferred across them. In this shift from the study of "groups" to "communities," networks began to accrue their abstract, metaphorical character and mathematics became an increasingly useful analytical tool.

Interest in networks exploded during the late 1990s. Around the same time that postmodern geographers like Castells were describing the importance of networks to global capitalism, physicists like Watts and Barabási discovered that similar structures appeared in highly regularized forms across a wide array of social and physical systems. Unlike randomly generated networks, in which most nodes have roughly the same number of links, most real networks display a starkly skewed pattern: many nodes are loosely connected and occupy liminal positions on the outskirts of the network, while some key nodes operate as hubs connecting the whole. (Think of major international airports like those in Atlanta or Chicago, or major cities, like New York and London, that function as centers of global capital.) Watts refers to this as the "small-world phenomenon," by which he means that nodes in most networks, even very large ones, tend to be connected by relatively few steps: "a small fraction of very long-range, global edges . . . contract otherwise distant parts of the graph, whilst most edges remain local."[21] Barabási refers to the same phenomenon by arguing that many real-life networks are "scale-free"; they "lack . . . an internal scale, a consequence of the fact that nodes with widely different degrees coexist in the same network."[22] Real networks tend to exhibit homophily and propinquity at the local scale, where similar and geographically proximate nodes tend to cluster among each other while connecting to the whole through important hubs that provide global structure. These were powerful hypotheses that promised to describe a wide range of complex systems while proposing specific statistical tests that could be performed over them. In the decades since, these have been widely cited, expanded on, and debated.[23]

This line of research is only beginning to be registered in the fields of literary studies and book history. Until very recently, quantitative studies of bibliographic data were limited to econometric estimates about print runs and production costs.[24] However, in the last several years, a number of scholars have expressed optimism about network science as a framework for describing historical publication data.[25] This research is only sometimes quantitative. As Kate Davison notes, historians have long been concerned with social groups and with the ways print production and manuscript circulation facilitated forms of collectivity built on exchanges among individuals.[26] Book historians and literary scholars often use a language of "networks" when describing how written media produce groups of people, but such networks tend be loosely conceived.[27] Even scholars who do use digital tools to generate network visualizations tend to eschew statistical tests that might characterize their underlying structure.[28] This causes a problem. If we are to follow up on Caroline Levine's suggestion that "attend[ing] to the patterns governing networks will allow us to think in newly rigorous ways," we need a better and richer vocabulary for describing such patterns. That is, scholars need to embrace representations of networks that depend less on visualization and that enable more robust analysis and comparison.

The central discovery of network science is that many different kinds of complex systems exhibit common emergent structures. From this premise, we might ask: To what extent does bibliographical information obey the organizing principles of real networks? Does a model of the early modern book trade exhibit structures analogous to those of other systems? What does literary history look like when imagined under this abstract cognitive schema?

Toward a Network Topology of Historical Documents

In what follows, I will model EEBO's metadata as a copublication network among early modern printers, booksellers, and authors. By studying who published with whom, copublication networks describe something that might be called "collaboration."[29] But as we'll see, the relationships captured in our data often have little to do with the kind of real-life, shoulder-to-shoulder partnerships that the term "collaboration" invokes. It is important to remember that models of networks are not representations of the lives of real people. Instead, they are abstractions used to describe the underlying data; a network model of EEBO is neither more nor less than that.

Data for this study was collected while the EEBO-TCP was still in its "Phase I" release, and the total number documents included is 32,853. The first step in the data-gathering process was to regularize and supplement existing information, using a combination of algorithmic data generation and hand correction. The Text Creation Partnership inherited its bibliography from older library catalogs. Generally, the only persons explicitly identified are authors, although the "Author" field sometimes includes other contributors, like translators and engravers, as well as, rarely, dedicatees. Stationers are typically mentioned in each book's imprint, which can be easily retrieved and regularized.[30] After correction, the process found a total of 28,027 imprint attributions over the entire EEBO-TCP collection then available. These attributions were then combined with names extracted from the TCP's "Author" field. Excluding titles that were attributed to only one person or none, the total dataset includes 10,209 unique persons and 48,245 attributions for 15,961 documents.[31]

Notice that this network connects persons, not to each other directly, but to book titles. Each entry lists both the name of the document and its unique identifier in the corpus alongside the names of authors, printers, and booksellers as well as engravers, dedicatees, and other minor figures occasionally mentioned in the catalogs. A network constructed in this way joins two different kinds of nodes—books and people—and so is called a *bipartite network*. For example, consider two books. First, *The Tragœdy of Rollo Duke of Normandy* (1640). This second quarto of the play lists John Fletcher as its primary author along with Ben Jonson and Philip Massinger, who are listed as collaborating authors, and Leonard

Lichfield, the printer. George Chapman, who is believed by scholars also to have contributed, is not listed in EEBO's bibliography and is therefore excluded from the graph. Second, *The Workes of Beniamin Ionson* (1616). No other playwrights are named as collaborating authors in the entry for Jonson's *Workes*, but William Hole, the engraver responsible for its famous frontispiece, is, alongside both the printer William Stansby and bookseller Richard Meighen.

When converted into mathematical expression, the bibliography of these two EEBO documents takes the form of a bipartite graph that connects collaborating authors and publishers to the texts they produce (fig. 1.3). Although humanities scholars tend to experience network graphs only through visualization, it's important to understand their underlying numerical representation. A network constructed of bibliographical data is represented primarily as an *incidence matrix*, B, which is a large table with a row for each person and a column for each document. This matrix is made entirely of 1s and 0s, where 1 denotes a connection between the person and the book. In this small example, the incidence matrix has just 7 rows and 2 columns. When visualized graphically, bipartite networks conventionally are divided into two lines of nodes, like in the childhood game Red Rover, with connections drawn across them. However, typically when analyzing bipartite networks, a researcher will focus on one side or the other, so the bipartite graph must be projected onto a unipartite structure. Jonson, Hole, Meighen, and Stansby are all connected to each other via their shared participation in the *Workes*. Jonson, Fletcher, Lichfield, and Massinger are all connected via *Rollo*. To measure these relationships, you simply multiply the incidence matrix by the transpose of itself: $A = BB^T$. The resulting *adjacency matrix*, A, is 7 x 7 and shows which people are connected to each other. Conventionally, values along the diagonal of an adjacency matrix are set to zero so that no node connects to itself.

Important concepts for describing networks, which will feature in the analysis to follow, are *degree* and *betweenness*. Every node in a network is connected to others via a certain number of links—that number is its degree. Within A, the degree is simply the sum of each row. Ben Jonson

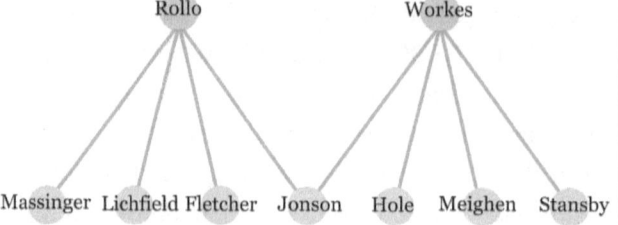

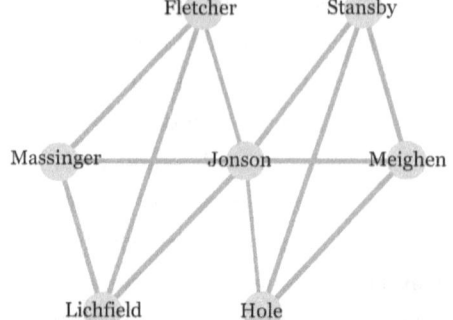

Figure 1.3. Network Projection. Bipartite networks (*above left*) can be projected onto a simpler form by multiplying its incidence matrix (*above right*) by the transpose of itself, a mathematical operation conventionally written BB^T. The resulting adjacency matrix, A (*below right*), identifies the links of the network's unipartite form (*below left*).

has a degree of 6 and all other nodes have a degree of 3. Betweenness is calculated somewhat more laboriously. It requires looking at each pair of nodes in the graph and identifying the shortest paths that connect one to the other. For example, the shortest path from John Fletcher to William Stansby involves taking two steps and passing through Jonson. The betweenness score for any node is the number of shortest paths that go through it. Because of how I selected these two books, Jonson scores very highly in betweenness; there are 9 shortest paths going in one direction or another that pass through him. The other nodes all have a betweenness of 0.

This small example also highlights an important issue that must be kept in mind when analyzing bibliographies, like EEBO's, that span centuries. The second quarto of *Rollo* was published in 1640, three years after Jonson's death. Nonetheless, that connection has the same weight and the same meaning as the publication of his *Workes*. This means that relationships modeled in a copublication network are fundamentally different from "social networks" in the colloquial sense of that phrase. People named together on common title pages may or may not have been friends, family, or collaborators in real life. In the case of posthumous publication, they may have lived hundreds or even thousands of years apart. The EEBO network includes many classical and foreign authors whose works were translated or adapted in England during the period. Both Virgil and Homer are author-nodes in the EEBO network, for example, and they have important statistical properties. To understand how the network is structured requires thinking about the difference between authors and stationers, both as real historical figures and as nodes in a graph.

Over the entire unipartite network, nodes with the highest degree tend to be monarchs and stationers who worked as printers to the crown (table 1.1). King Charles I and King Charles II took most frequent recourse to the press, often issuing proclamations and other notices to the public, both before and after the Civil War. In EEBO's metadata, they're listed as authors, and so they are the two most prolific and most powerfully connected authors in the model. The printers on whom they most often relied, John Bill and Thomas Newcomb, respectively, are therefore also

Table 1.1. Top Nodes in the EEBO Network. Nodes are sorted by degree (total number of links) and the ratio of betweenness (the number of paths passing through) by degree, rounded to the nearest integer

Degree		Betweenness / degree	
Bill, John	787	Erasmus, Desiderius	11,615
Charles II, King of England	648	Foxe, John	10,187
Newcombe, Thomas, II	544	Virgil	9,807
Barker, Christopher	445	Shakespeare, William	9,287
Bill, Charles	384	Raleigh, Walter, Sir	8,915
Newcomb, Thomas, I	369	Cicero, Marcus Tullius	8,343
Charles I, King of England	364	Lessius, Leonardus	8,314
Brome, Henry	302	Henry VIII, K. of England	8,206
Tooke, Benjamin, II	297	Davenport, John	7,962
Alldee, Edward	290	Bacon, Francis	7,894

among the most prolific contributors to the field. You'll notice that most nodes with the highest degree were active during the later seventeenth century. This is because of a general bias in the model toward those later periods, when the overall number of titles published annually had greatly increased. Indeed, although the network includes links from as far back as 1473, the median date is 180 years later, in 1653. This gives the network model (and, indeed, all of EEBO) a strong bias toward the Interregnum and Restoration periods. The only Renaissance figure among the top ten is Edward Alldee, a printer who was very active during his lifetime and who published many works by playwrights, including early quartos of Shakespeare.

This picture looks very different when nodes are rated by betweenness. We can look for people who are not among the most prolific but who function as bridges by connecting various parts of the whole. To find these people, we divide betweenness, the total number of shortest paths through a node, by degree, its total number of connections. Dividing by degree filters out those high-degree nodes like Charles II and exposes people who sit at important structural positions in the network by connecting otherwise disparate communities. They occupy a network's "structural holes."[32] From this perspective, the most important people in EEBO are all authors, some of whom were not in London or even alive at the time. The single most structurally important person in the entire corpus is Erasmus, whose works were frequently reprinted throughout the sixteenth and seventeenth centuries. He appears in the network very early on, when his *Familiarium Colloquiorum Formulae* (1519) was printed by Wynkyn de Worde, and at the very end, when Thomas Brown translated *Seven New Colloquies* (1699). Classical authors Virgil and Cicero occupy similar positions in the network. Major authors of the Renaissance like Sir Walter Raleigh, Francis Bacon, and William Shakespeare score highly because their works were often reprinted or adapted during the Restoration. Martyrologist John Foxe was fairly prolific during his lifetime, but he scores highly here because his work, too, was picked up by authors and publishers much later. Foxe is linked not only to contemporary printers like John Day and John

Charlewood but also to later controversialists like William Prynne and Peter Heylyn.

However, people like King Charles II and Erasmus are extreme outliers. Most people in the network are only loosely connected to the whole. Almost half of all nodes have just one or two connections, so even though the mean degree is more than 9, the median is just 3. Like wealth in a society, participation in the print marketplace was distributed unequally. A few highly prolific contributors have hundreds of connections, but the vast majority are only loosely connected and are barely known by historians. This kind of pattern is known as a "skew distribution" and is typical of many real-world networks—Barabási referred to such structures as "scale-free networks" (fig. 1.4). To see this structure requires looking at the *degree distribution*, which examines, not the degree of any individual node, but how many nodes can be found at different levels. Thousands

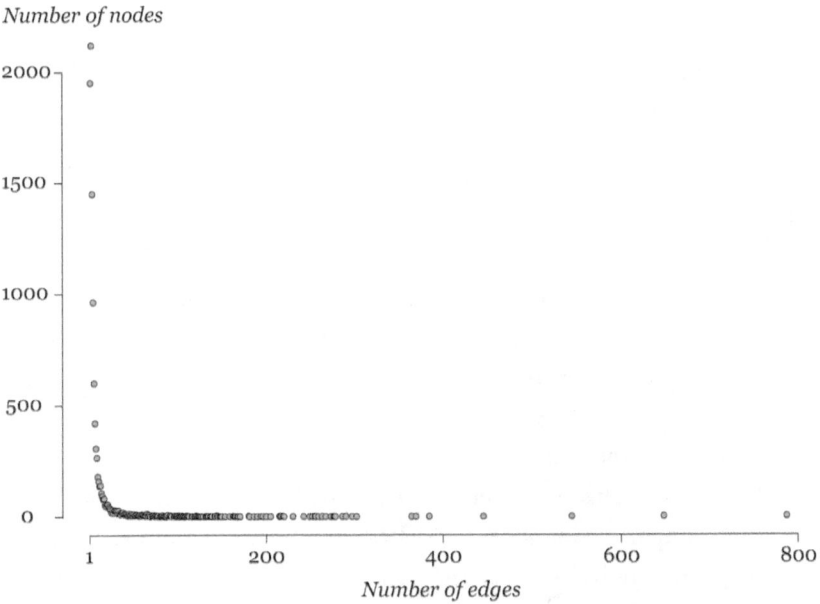

Figure 1.4. Degree Distribution of the EEBO Network. Thousands of people in the EEBO network have just 1 or 2 links (*upper left*), but a few highly active printers, booksellers, and authors have many hundreds of links (*lower right*).

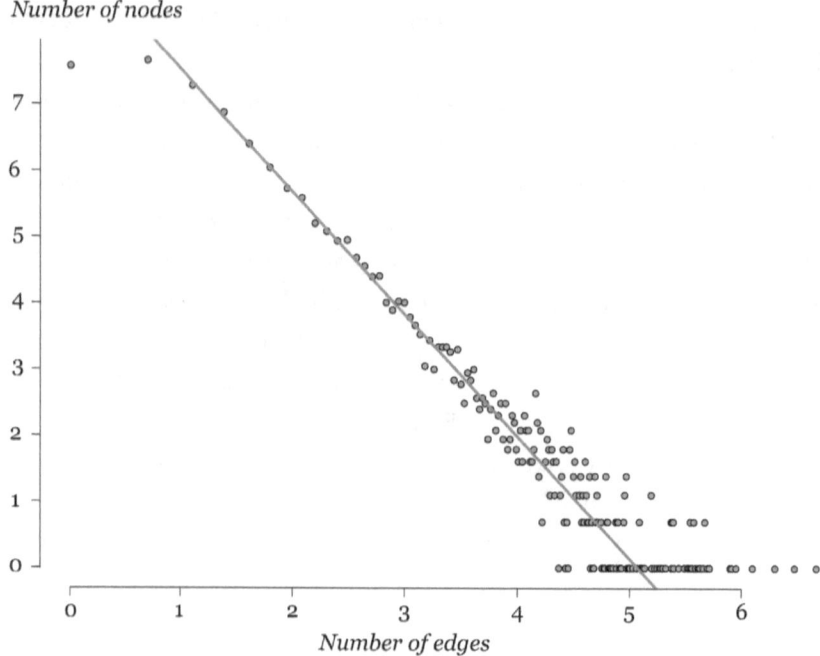

Figure 1.5. Log-Log Plot of the Degree Distribution of the EEBO Network. The degree distribution of the EEBO network, as in figure 1.4, can be visualized along a logarithmic scale. The downward slope of the line reflects how skewed the network is toward its most-connected nodes.

of people have just 1, 2, or 3 connections, but a few have many hundreds. Those outliers are called the graph's "long tail." Skew distributions like these are often represented on logarithmic scales (fig. 1.5). The extent of inequality in the network can be approximated by examining the downward slope of the log-log plot, called its *degree exponent*. Networks are said to be scale-free when their exponents fall below 3 and approach 2.[33] Across the entire EEBO collection, the degree distribution has a slope of 2.69, putting it directly in the center of that range.[34]

The early modern print marketplace thus exhibits many of the basic structural properties found in real-world networks from other domains. Like the wealth of individuals, the populations of cities, or clicks on the internet, the bibliography of EEBO is divided between a privileged center and a vast periphery of minor figures. In EEBO, this divide between the haves and have-nots corresponds closely to the different roles played by authors and printers (fig. 1.6). The early modern book trade welcomed thousands of unique authors (7,754 are named in the model), but control of the actual printing presses was tightly limited. The rules of the Stationers Company dictated that only a small number of printers could operate at any given time. To see a manuscript into print, would-be authors had limited options. For this reason, the bulk of the network is divided into two very different parts: a large number of loosely connected authors and a relatively small number of densely connected booksellers and printers.

However, that general statement does not account for all cases. Scale-free networks by definition cannot be described by measurements of their central tendencies. Most people sit on the "periphery" of any social network, but the statistical "outliers" are the most important contributors. From this perspective (fig. 1.7), a bias in the network toward printers still remains, but not nearly so strongly. Prolific and widely collaborating authors like John Dryden and Richard Baxter have more connections than all but the most active stationers. Even lesser-known figures like Joseph Hall score highly. (Hall published a few works of satirical poetry as a young man during the 1590s and early 1600s and, after being ordained, spent the rest of his life writing devotional works and contributing to

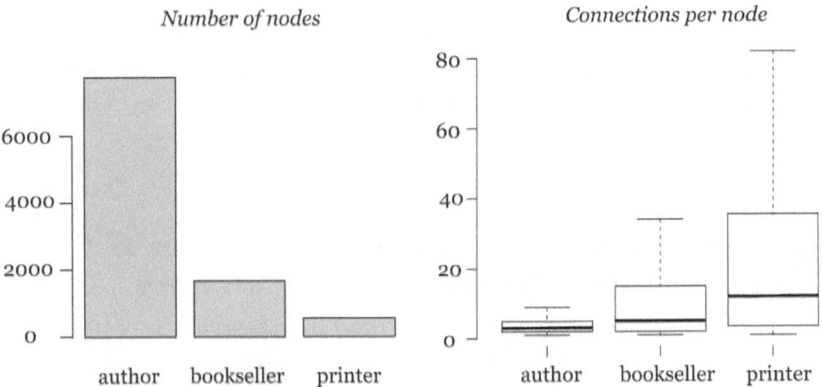

Figure 1.6. Nodes and Edges in the EEBO Network, by Role. There are many more authors in the network than other kinds of people, but booksellers and printers tend to have many more connections.

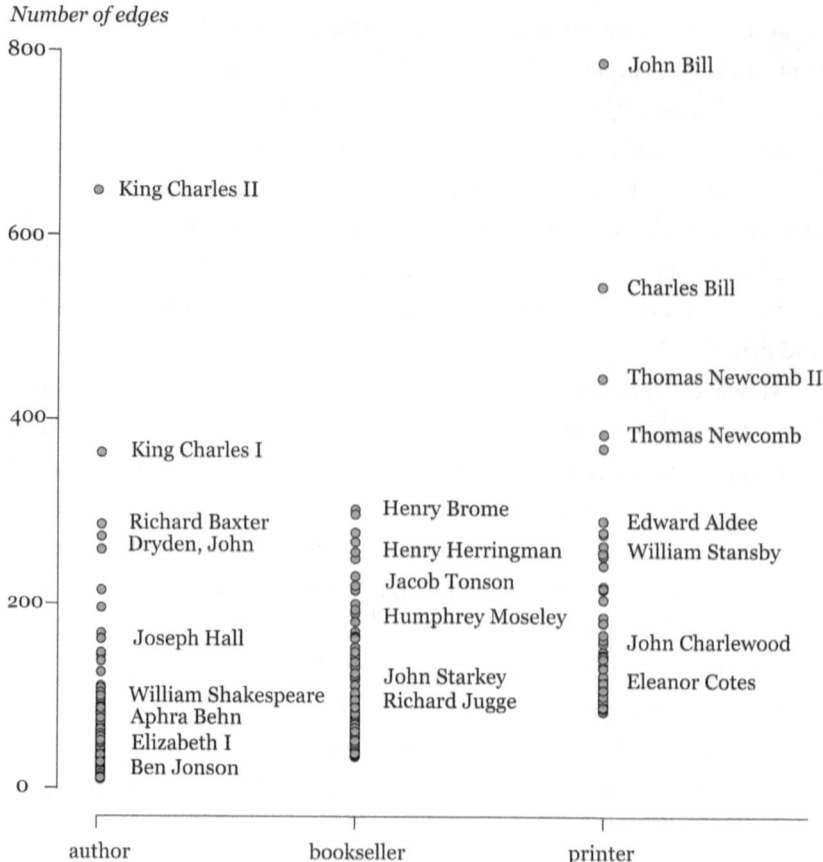

Figure 1.7. Highest Degree Outliers, by Role. The previous figure excluded outliers, but they are listed here with select nodes labeled. By far the most prolific authors were kings, who were often named on official proclamations, and the printers to the crown are therefore the most active printers.

the religious controversies surrounding the Civil War.) Restoration booksellers like Henry Herringman and Jacob Tonson have many connections, as would be expected, given the general increase in publishing over the period. However, despite the smaller numbers of titles, many sixteenth- and early seventeenth-century stationers are among the most connected nodes, such as Henry Bynneman, Richard Jugge, John Charlewood, Nathaniel Butter, Edward Alldee, and William Stansby. On the other hand, very few women score highly according to this metric. Elizabeth I and Aphra Behn are true outliers among women authors, though women printers and booksellers like Eleanor Cotes sometimes found success in the field.

Using Networks to Understand Periodization

One important feature of a copublication network is that its relationships, once encoded into the model, become permanent. If one author has chosen to collaborate with another, that fact exists eternally in the corpus and thus in the network. Franco Moretti noticed this aspect of networks, writing, "Here, nothing ever disappears. What is done, cannot be undone. . . . Making the past just as visible as the present: that is one major change introduced by the use of networks."[35] When taken as a whole, the network is a static reification of relationships that, in actual historical reality, were enacted piecemeal over time. However, it's not quite right to say that what is done cannot be undone. The temporal marker of each link is inherited from EEBO, which includes dates for each publication. Using these markers, we can systematically isolate subsets of the corpus for each year, thus showing how the network changes over time. It's not exactly that time is "turned into space," as Moretti puts it, but that time functions as a principle for reorganizing the network by providing structured instances of contemporaneity.

Figures 1.8, 1.9, and 1.10 show a few basic facts about how the network changes over time, in each case looking at a trailing ten-year window. Each point along these series represents a bird's-eye perspective on the book trade network, looking retrospectively over the previous ten years. The changes pictured here will be familiar to scholars of the period. Book trade activity increases steadily across the sixteenth and early seventeenth centuries as more titles are produced each year (fig. 1.8). From 1473 to 1639, the number of titles in the model increases linearly. On average, the network includes seven more titles each year than in the previous year. This trend continues until there is a large spike in activity in the year 1640. After that year, the network continues to expand at almost an identical rate (6.9 more titles on average each year, and so the slopes

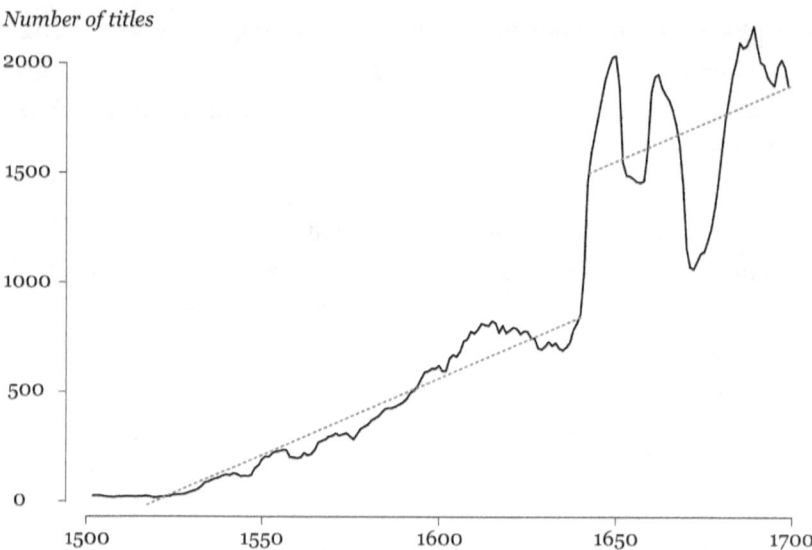

Figure 1.8. EEBO Network: Unique Titles Per Year. Values smoothed to a trailing ten-year window.

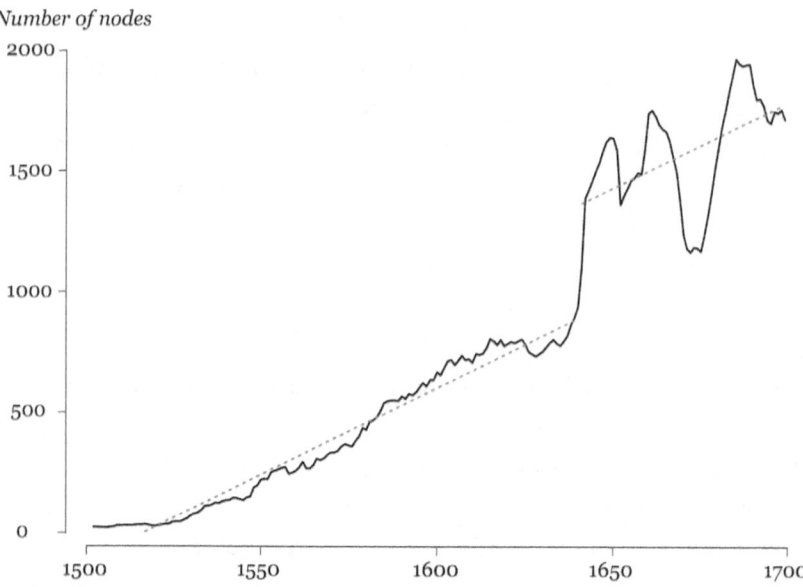

Figure 1.9. EEBO Network: Nodes Per Year. Values smoothed to a trailing ten-year window. The number of people in the network is closely connected to the number of unique titles.

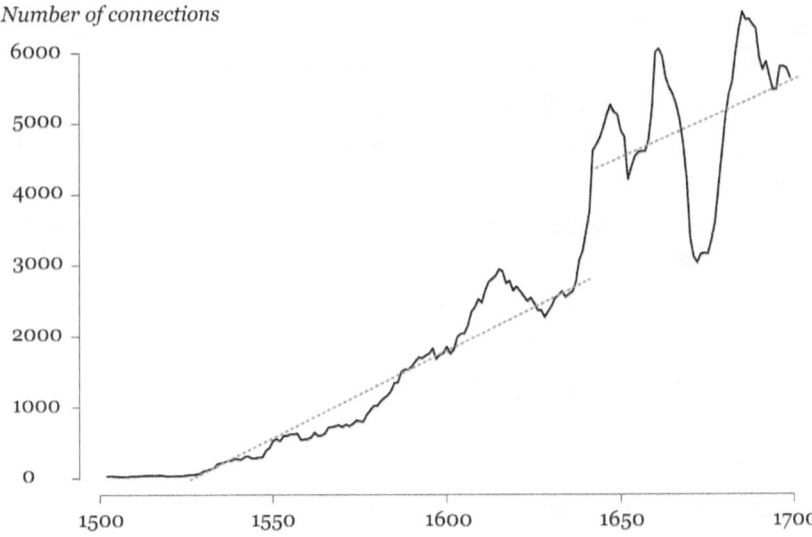

Figure 1.10. EEBO Network: Edges Per Year. Values smoothed to a trailing ten-year window. The number of links between nodes is closely connected to the total number of people in the network.

of the two trend lines are very similar), but from a much higher base and with greater volatility.

As the number of titles increases in the network, so too the nodes and edges (figs. 1.9 and 1.10). More activity overall corresponds to more people and more links among them. The number of new persons in the network increases almost exactly with the number of titles. Before 1640, the network includes 7.1 additional nodes each year; after, 7.2. Among these nodes, the number of connections also rises following a very similar pattern. Before 1640, the network gains 24.5 links per year; after, 21.8. Again, we see greater volatility in the later seventeenth century, as the size of the network and the richness of its interconnections become subject to greater fluctuation, marked especially by a huge dip in activity during the 1670s, under the reign of Charles II.

However, these overall statistics can be misleading, for a couple of reasons. First, because figures 1.8 through 1.10 all report raw numbers. Such graphs will always be most sensitive to variation where the values are the highest, so fluctuations during earlier years will be difficult to see. If we focused on the 1500s, we'd see plenty of sharp rises and falls, but that volatility is visually flattened when the *y*-axis is drawn to accommodate the post-1640 era. Second, because each value is treated separately. When visualized across separate graphs, the relations between them are difficult to scan with the eye. The number of people and the total number of connections might rise and fall together, but that general tendency masks subtle but important shifts in the social structure of the print marketplace.

Consider figure 1.11, which offers a slightly more complex look at the data. Rather than visualize the numbers of nodes and edges separately, we can track the average degree: How many connections does each person have, on average, and how does that average change over time? From the perspective of this metric, the sixteenth century remains a period of sustained growth. As the print marketplace expanded, more people were provided with more opportunities for collaboration. The number of connections grew even more quickly than the number of people, and the book trade became more interconnected as it grew more populous.

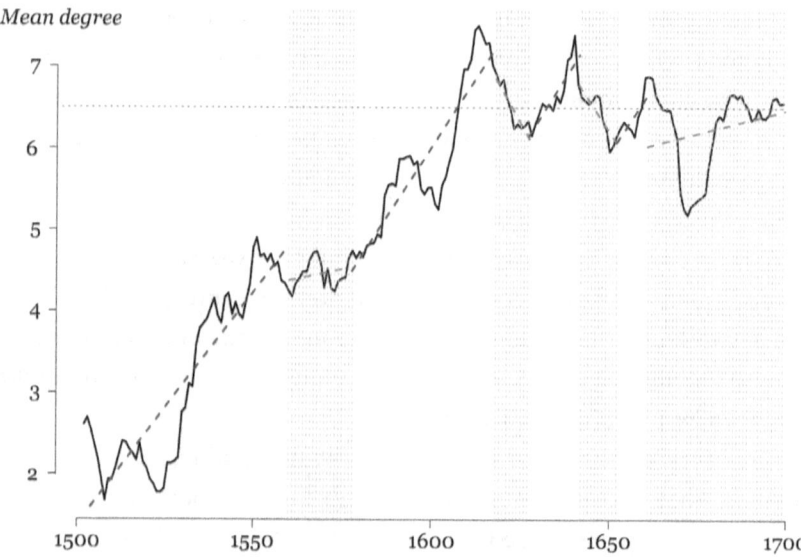

Figure 1.11. EEBO Network: Mean Degree by Year. Shaded regions represent years with eigenvector centralization greater than 0.995. Values are smoothed to a trailing ten-year window.

This trend continued until around 1610. From that peak of social activity, the network fluctuated while experiencing a general decline over the next several decades, until it stabilized around a mean degree of about 6.4. From its highest peak to its lowest trough, the mean degree declined from 7.5 in 1613 to 5.2 in 1672. Over that period, the average author, bookseller, and printer allowed their names to appear with others' 2 fewer times. That decline might not sound like much, but it represents a 31% dip in the general level of socially stipulated publishing activity. Just as nominally small declines in GDP can signal wrenching disruptions in an economy, declines in the average degree suggest a broad dampening of activity across the print marketplace, even as the network as a whole continued to expand. Fewer people felt safe or motivated to put their names together on imprints. More people joined the book trade, but they collaborated on fewer publications and made fewer connections.

Shaded regions of the graph represent years when publishing activity was most tightly centralized, when the most prolific authors, printers, and booksellers were collaborating more or less exclusively with one another. As might be guessed from my previous discussions, these were years when monarchs and their printers were most active, and these periods correspond closely to times when monarchs were most aggressively asserting control over the press. Between 1560 and 1578, the most authoritatively positioned node each year is Richard Jugge, longtime printer to Elizabeth I.[36] Over the next two decades the press was unusually centralized; growth in mean degree stalled. We see a similar pattern forty years later. Between 1618 and 1627, the most dominant node is Bonham Norton, who, after his cousin's death in 1612, had secured control over the King's Printing House in partnership with John Bill and Robert Barker.[37] In the 1640s, King Charles I flooded the press and appears as the most dominant node by almost any measure. After a brief period in the 1650s under Oliver Cromwell, King Charles II was restored to his father's position, both on the throne and in the public sphere.[38] These intervals all correspond to times when the average degree was either stagnant or declining. During years when monarchs hadn't been flooding the print marketplace with proclamations, the mean degree increases by 0.063 connections per node per year—that's a rate of one connection every sixteen years. During years when monarchs are most active and the graph is most tightly centralized, the mean degree is flat and actually declines. The slope of those years, when combined, is slightly negative.

These measurements correspond loosely to well-known events in the history of the London book trade and English state politics. The first period of stagnation follows directly on the heels of the establishment of the Stationers Company and Elizabeth I's accession; the second, during a time when King James I was battling Parliament over the power of taxation; the third, around the Licensing Order of 1643; and the last, after the Restoration. These political events all correspond with changes in the leadership of the Stationers Company and in particular with the appointments of new royal printers.[39]

From the perspective of this metric, the most interesting period might be the 1670s and 1680s, when the book trade underwent explosive growth (relative to its low point) despite the crown maintaining its dominant position. The new propaganda machine allowed for growth in the total system while maintaining a tightly centralized position for official publications. The political turmoil of this period was famously peaceful, at least insofar as the rejection of James II did not immediately embroil England in a second civil war. The Glorious Revolution came to be known as "bloodless," despite protests and violence that did actually occur and despite the lingering threat of Jacobite resistance. However, history's sense that the transition of 1688/89 was basically peaceful should not be dismissed as mere Whiggish mythmaking.[40] Understood in light of transitions in the book trade, the most striking feature of 1689 is its continuity. The king had changed, but the printers to the king remained the same. The elder Thomas Newcomb had been printer to Charles II; his son would continue as printer, not only to James II, but to King William and Queen Mary as well. Charles Bill inherited his share of the office in 1682 and, like the younger Newcomb, would serve uninterrupted through the entire reign of James II. Things largely carried on like normal. The revolution of 1688 proved to be momentous in terms of government and politics, but the book trade experienced much less disruption than it had during earlier crises. Previously, the print marketplace allowed for either broadly shared growth or concentrated authority. Under Charles II, it came to allow for both, laying the information infrastructure for a constitutional monarchy. In this context, the lapse of the Licensing Act after 1694 seems less like a mistake or an oversight than like the natural extension of a trend that had been developing continuously over the previous two decades.

Another striking feature of figure 1.11 is how neatly shifts in its data correspond to conventional divides among historical periods. The extended market growth from 1500 to 1610 looks an awful lot like a "renaissance" divided into two halves, and the intervals of tumult that follow correspond closely with the time line of political events commonly used to segment the seventeenth century into a series of befores and afters. To discover these divisions, I rely on two metrics: average degree, which examines the overall health and vitality of the network, and centralization, which examines how tightly connected the network's highest-degree nodes are. These metrics are sensitive to subtle variations in the data, and they closely track the book trade's most important functions, as both a platform for government propaganda and as a public sphere where authors traded opinions. Taken together, these metrics provide a robust vocabulary for describing how the print marketplace was changing along both of these vectors at any given moment. Visually obvious breaks in the data suggest points of division that correlate closely with conventionally accepted boundaries between periods, which in turn suggests that historically significant events had broadly dispersed consequences across a range of cultural domains.

This point is worth emphasizing because it runs counter to the notion, advocated by Ted Underwood and others, that the study of large-scale corpora will direct attention away from historical periods, as such. Underwood argues that computational methods are most effective when used to "map broad patterns and trace gradients of change."[41] Such studies, he claims, will focus less on moments of rupture and discontinuity in favor of describing "continuous, gradual change" over the *longue durée*.[42] Of course, the figures here all trace gradients of change over a long span, but they also suggest points of reference that mark important discontinuities in the data. There is nothing about quantification, in and of itself, that dissolves the boundaries between historical periods. Nor are those divisions arbitrary, as is sometimes asserted.[43] Narratives of rupture that separate the Renaissance from the Restoration are not mere analytical fictions. The London print marketplace was demonstrably different from one period to the next. Those differences did not come about through gradual processes, but through jarring shifts that punctuated the book trade and left gaping structural holes in their wake.[44]

These structural gaps are best seen when looking at the network overall. Taken in its entirety, EEBO's metadata covers hundreds of years. This interval is far greater than the lifespan of a human being, let alone the typical length of a stationer's or author's career. Of course, being alive and present isn't always necessary for publication. Authors' works were often published posthumously. As I mentioned, Erasmus first appears in the network in 1519 and keeps popping up all the way until the end in 1699. Similarly, printers sometimes owned special patents and would appear on imprints even when they had no direct hand in the book's production, and sometimes their names, like authors', were added posthumously. But these situations are unusual. Most people appear in the network only briefly and only during their lifetimes. Authors, printers, and booksellers who collaborated on new books were usually contemporaries. To be near each other in the topology of the corpus, they usually needed to be near each other spatiotemporally. It was the hand-press era, remember; customers and authors alike could walk from shop to shop and mingle with one another in the streets. Inheritances, intermarriages, and apprenticeships among stationers blurred the lines between business and family. For this reason, the structure of relationships in the network model is powerfully influenced by the rhythms of life and death, as each generation gives way to the next. Figure 1.12 exposes this temporal progression, showing connections only among the network's most prolific printers, whose activities are passed down from one generation to the next over a winding path that traverses centuries. Mortality marks the lineaments of time.

When the network is considered as a whole, these lineaments aren't simple boundaries that separate one cultural moment from the next. The pasts and their futures overlap and connect. However, links across periods are sparser than links within them. Structural holes mark the absences where interconnections are unusually thin. Consider the image with which I began this chapter (see fig. 1.2), now compared to the data presented in table 1.2. The visualization depicted the entire EEBO network as a single entity, after running a simple community-detection

Figure 1.12.   The EEBO Network, Printers Only. When the network is reduced to include only printers, the chronological shape of the data appears more clearly. Time flows in EEBO, not along a simple timeline, but following a circuitous route among printers. In this subset, the network has a diameter of 21, meaning that it takes 21 steps to get from the two nodes who are farthest away. By contrast, the full network, with thousands more nodes, has a diameter of only 12, because canonical authors like Erasmus and Shakespeare provide so many bridges from one era to the next.

Table 1.2. Highest Degree Nodes in the EEBO Network, by Community and by Role. Nodes sort loosely, but imperfectly, by chronology.

	Early 1500s
Authors	Erasmus (97), Arthur Golding (77), Abraham Fleming (63), John Calvin (54), John Stow (51), Thomas Paynell (49), Cicero (46), Seneca (44)
Stationers	Henry Bynneman (144), John Day (134), George Bishop (119), Thomas Berthelet (115), Thomas Marsh (100), William Seres (92), Henry Denham (91)
	Late 1500s / Early 1600s
Authors	Joseph Hall (168), John Taylor (147), Robert Greene (110), Thomas Dekker (106), Nicholas Breton (102), Anthony Munday (92), Thomas Heywood (90)
Stationers	Edward Alldee (290), Felix Kingston (290), Nathaniel Butter (277), Bernard Alsop (267), George Eld (263), Thomas Creede (263), William Stansby (255)
	Before and During the Civil War
Authors	William Prynne (162), Francis Bacon (110), Richard Sibbes (102), Thomas Goodwin (101), Stephen Marshall (87), James Shirley (86), Peter Heylyn (71)
Stationers	Thomas Cotes (205), Richard Cotes (162), Andrew Crooke (153), Edward Griffin (142), William Marshall (128), John Rothwell (120), George Miller (100)
	Restoration Public Sphere
Authors	Richard Baxter (286), Roger L'Estrange (126), Edward Stillingfleet (111), John Tillotson (104), John Owen (100), Gilbert Burnet (99), Robert Boyle (96)
Stationers	Henry Brome (302), Thomas Parkhurst (220), Walter Kettilby (215), Thomas Bassett (200), Richard Royston (190), Brabazon Aylmer (181)
	Interregnum
Authors	Thomas Fairfax (109), George Keith (88), John Goodwin (71), George Fox (65), Edward Burrough (64), William Penn (64), Oliver Cromwell (61)
Stationers	John Macocke (276), Giles Calvert (230), Edward Husband (217), Nathaniel Brooke (136), John Field (131), Mathew Simmons (123), Henry Cripps (111)

	Monarchs, Royal Printers, &c.
Authors	Charles II (648), Charles I (364), William III (273), James II (215), Mary II (196), Scotland Privy Council (59), Louis XIV (34), George Savile, Halifax (27)
Stationers	John Bill (787), Thomas Newcomb I (544), Christopher Barker (445), Charles Bill (384), Thomas Newcomb II (369), Henry Hills I (278), Henry Hills II (275)

	Restoration Poetry
Authors	John Dryden (259), William Shakespeare (144), Aphra Behn (138), John Fletcher (109), Nahum Tate (109), Virgil (101), Thomas D'Urfey (97), John Davies (95)
Stationers	Henry Herringman (256), Richard Bentley (249), Jacob Tonson (217), Humphrey Moseley (194), Randolph Taylor (165), Richard Baldwin (163)

algorithm over the data to expose the network's largest cliques. From this perspective, nodes that appear near each other in the network tend to be historically approximate. People who collaborated on many books tended to live around the same time. One community is almost exclusively composed of people who lived during the sixteenth century. This community features Erasmus along with major printers of the period, like John Day and Henry Bynneman. Where its members link to outsiders, they mostly connect to nodes in the next group, which primarily consists of people active during the later sixteenth and early seventeenth centuries. This clique includes most of the period's playwrights, from early figures like Anthony Munday and Robert Greene to Thomas Dekker and Thomas Heywood. Ben Jonson is in this group, though not prolific enough to be among the top nodes. Shakespeare, we'll see, is placed elsewhere, for reasons I'll explain.

At the center of the network, nodes of different groups intermingle more freely. Whereas the human mind imagines time as a linear progression, network models tend to describe a core-periphery structure. In EEBO, the middle seventeenth century sits at that core and communities stretch in various directions. One community represents nodes mostly active before and during the English Civil War. William Prynne exemplifies this group. From there, the graph splits. One community contains people like Thomas Fairfax who were most active during the war and the Interregnum. Another large group is dominated by major figures of the Restoration public sphere, such as Richard Baxter, Roger L'Estrange, Edward Stillingfleet, and John Tillotson, while a much smaller and more compact clique is made almost entirely of monarchs, their direct associates, and printers to the crown. Lastly, are all the poets and playwrights of the Restoration, such as John Dryden and Aphra Behn. In this group, also, are William Shakespeare and John Fletcher as well as several other authors from the Renaissance. Because their works were often adapted by the new generation of poets, the community-detection algorithm placed them among later seventeenth-century authors and stationers, rather than among their more direct historical contemporaries. From this network-level perspective, Shakespeare looks much like any other prolific Restoration poet. (To see why, compare his position in the network with Ben Jonson's, as pictured in figures 1.13 and 1.14.) If you go back and look at figure 1.2, this group appears along the top, with many links to the past that effectively tie the entire network into the shape of a large and tangled knot, in striking contrast to the wandering line of the printers-only subset.

Historical periods are better understood not as intervals of time but as overlapping and interconnecting bursts of publishing activity (fig. 1.15). The communities found in the network sort more or less neatly into periods, but at any given point in time (after about 1550 or so) multiple communities are represented in the network simultaneously. As one period is winding down, others will have already begun. For example, in the 1580s people like George Bishop were still closely connected to stationers whose careers had crested. Bishop was a printer who collaborated with Christopher Barker on famous books like the Holinshed's *Chronicles* and Haklyut's *Voyages*, and he was married to the daughter of John Cawood. Both Barker and Cawood were most active in the network during earlier decades.[45]

On the other side but at the same time, John Charlewood was a peripheral figure who long had a reputation (among later bibliographers) as

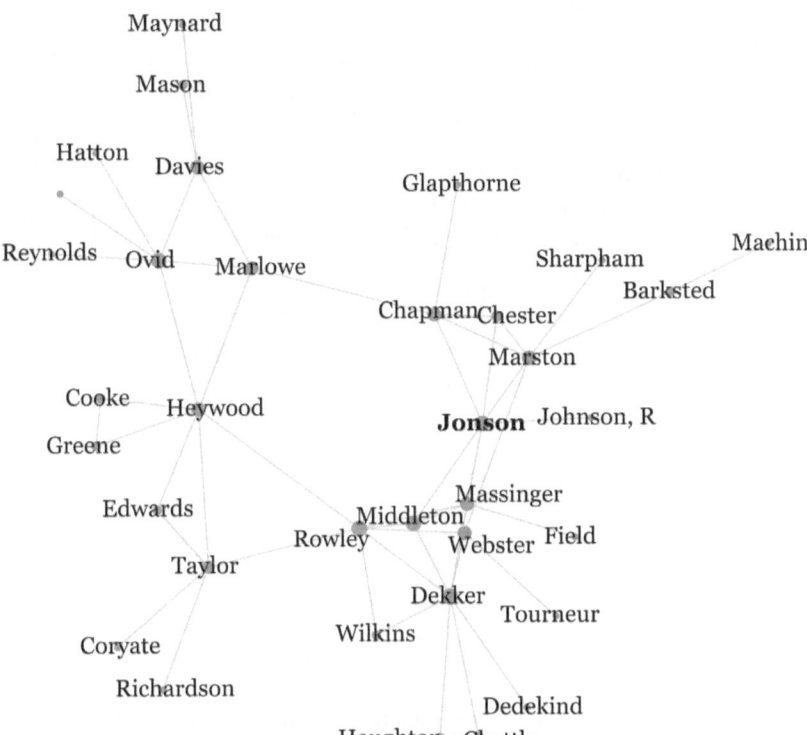

Figure 1.13. Ben Jonson's Neighborhood (Authors Only). Nodes are included if they meet three conditions: (1) if they are authors, (2) if they are within two steps of Jonson, and (3) if they are grouped in the same community.

something of a pirate, due to being involved in the unauthorized posthumous publication of Sir Philip Sidney's *Astrophil and Stella* (1591).[46] But he also published many other poets, including Anthony Munday and Robert Greene, as well as works by Thomas Nashe and translations of Tasso. Indeed, Charlewood is a leading figure in the group that includes most Renaissance poets and is, in some ways, that community's most exemplary figure. Charlewood's contributions are both early and substantive. Insofar as "Renaissance poetry" involved the social practice of bringing manuscript verse and play scripts to readers through print, Charlewood was an innovative figure who established protocols that would be imitated for generations.

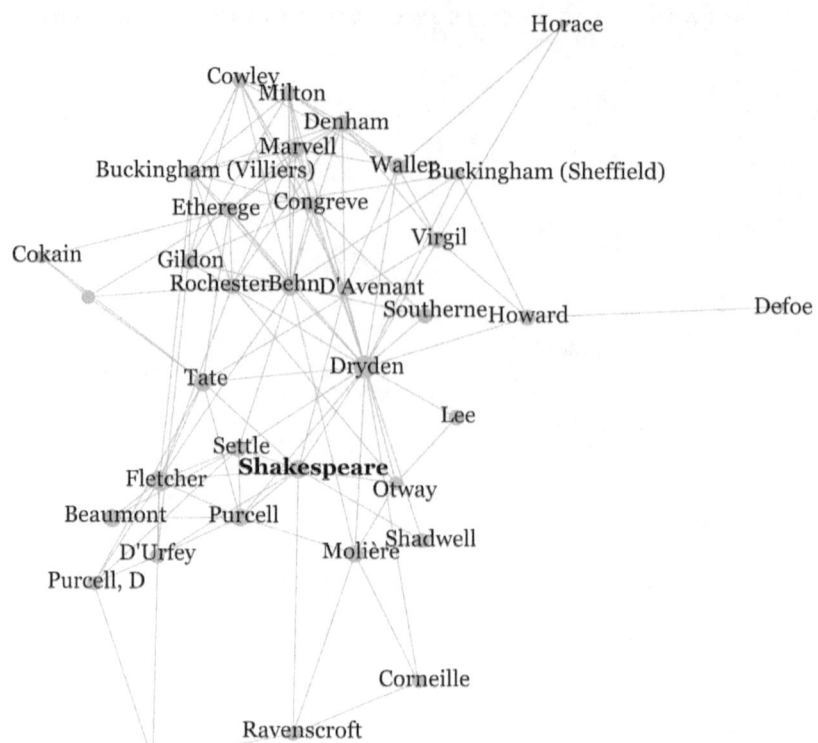

Figure 1.14. William Shakespeare's Neighborhood (Authors Only).

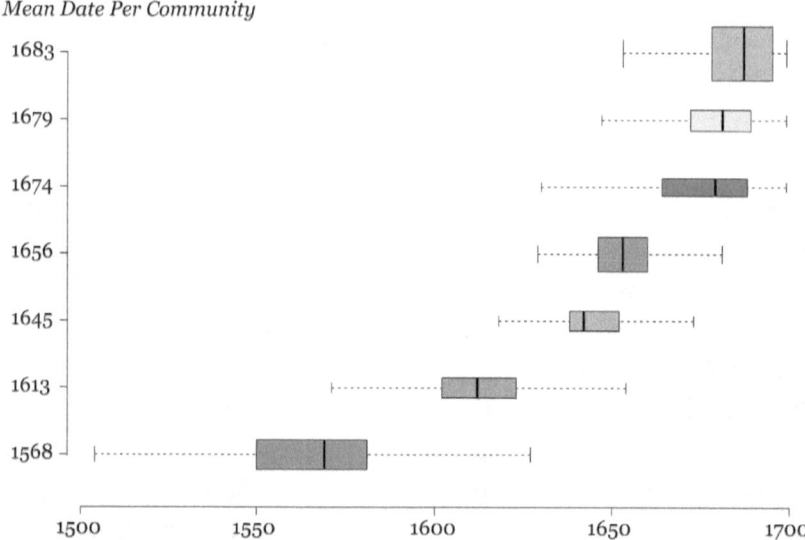

Figure 1.15. Chronological Distribution of Nodes, by Community. This boxplot displays the range of publication dates that make up the edges of each community. The height of each box represents the number of nodes in that community.

A stationer who occupies a very similar position in the network, but at a different point, is Humphrey Moseley, the Royalist bookseller who was most active during the Civil War and Interregnum periods but who is grouped by the algorithm, not with his direct contemporaries, but with later people like John Dryden and Henry Herringman. Like Charlewood, Moseley published early and often. His checklist includes Milton's *Poems* (1645) and Sir John Suckling's *Fragmenta Aurea* (1646). Moseley was so involved in preserving and remediating literature of the earlier decades that David Scott Kastan has credited him with the "invention of English literature."[47] During the 1650s, Moseley established numerous partnerships with authors, printers, and other booksellers who would remain active after his death in 1661. Especially after the theaters reopened, these partners continually turned back to Moseley's predecessors in the early century for source materials and inspiration. Just as Charlewood provides a bridge between the earliest Renaissance playwrights and those of the seventeenth century, so too Moseley bridges a gap between the Restoration and its literary past.

Consequently, the network in its entirety sorts into a strange serpentine shape. Practices of republication and adaptation create links between the Restoration poets and their predecessors of an earlier generation, but those links exist across yawning gaps that separate one period from the next. What Dryden might have called a divide between the "last Age" and the "present Age" appears in the network as a structural hole that separates nodes of one community from those of another. It is sometimes said that canonical authors have "stood the test of time," but here we can see them bending time—or perhaps, bending not time itself, but cultural time as experienced under the conditions of textuality.

Conclusion: "We already knew that!"

My sense is that readers who specialize in British literature are likely to find most of the results presented here to be broadly familiar. Once you understand how bimodal networks are structured and projected onto unimodal form, many aspects of the network could be anticipated: the local prominence of successful printers and booksellers, the bridging effect of canonical authors, and even perhaps the sorting into period-like clusters. By itself, though, this very familiarity is strange. It's weird that the results all feel so... *expected*. The emergent patterns that recur across the network are determined by nothing except aggregated statistics of the simplest bibliographical facts, and yet they closely mirror received notions about the changes in English politics and culture over hundreds of years. It is extraordinary to note that EEBO's bibliographical metadata fits so neatly under the descriptive framework of network science. There's certainly nothing in literary theory to suggest that mathematical models championed by network scientists could capture anything true about the history of literature. But they do.

More importantly, they say something true about how literary history relates to other kinds of cultural phenomena. By stripping away prior qualitative knowledge and treating each element as a simple part of a larger complex system, network models expose the underlying structures of bibliographical data to reveal deep commonalities between our object of study (the literary past) and the kinds of social and physical systems studied in other disciplines. Literary history, it turns out, enjoys no immunity against the fundamental laws of social life. If that's true—and I believe I have shown it to be—then these commonalities open a wide horizon of potential inquiry. Research in the humanities has barely begun to scratch the surface of network theory. If we have good reason to believe that textual networks behave like networks in general, we have good reason to believe that theoretical advancements from across the disciplines can be applied to textual data successfully. We have built a new bridge—a link, an edge—between our knowledge and the larger world.

CHAPTER 2

THE COMPUTATION OF MEANING

IN THE TWENTIETH CENTURY, AN EXTRAORDINARY discovery was made in the information sciences. Namely, that documents can be identified and classified using simple statistical measurements of the words they contain. This insight is known primarily for the technical accomplishments it made possible. Since the 1980s, computers have been able to search efficiently through millions of documents, to extract their keywords, and to group them automatically under subject headings. As the technology has continued to advance, computers can now perform increasingly complex tasks, like translating across languages, answering questions, suggesting edits, paraphrasing documents, and even writing new text on the fly. These systems work so well, in fact, that they've prompted growing debate over the question of whether computers can now actually understand language. "The main controversy," according to computational linguists Magnus Sahlgren and Fredrik Carlsson, is "whether a language model that has been trained to perform some language game actually has any *real* understanding of language, or if it is confined to purely structural knowledge."[1] Skeptics argue that meaning and intention are mental and social acts that computers can't possibly replicate, no matter how elaborately they've been programmed.[2] And, indeed, if meaning is defined narrowly as the communication of an intent from one mind to another, computers continue to fall short. They don't have brains, and brains are hard to simulate. Anyone who asks Siri an off-the-wall question will immediately encounter the limits of the machine. Meaning and intention, when understood as cognitive and intersubjective phenomena, continue to pose many well-known challenges for researchers of artificial intelligence.

However, there's a mirror-opposite challenge, less well known, that engineers have posed to us. True, computers can't keep up their half of a conversation, but the language games they can perform are remarkable. How could Google Search work unless its programmers had a robust and sophisticated theory to describe how meaning is distributed through discourse? What do they know that we don't? Not about computers, but about language and textuality? This question requires an answer. Philosopher Juan Luis Gastaldi argues that "we need to consider their success as something more than a purely technical feat" and examine what textual computing tells us about "the nature of language itself."[3] Semantic models that represent the meanings of words aren't just fancy gizmos. They reveal a fundamental commensurability between the mathematical structures of computationally recorded discourse and the meaningful structures of language as used and intended by persons. Skeptics complain that this commensurability should not be mistaken for full equivalence. Computers don't really understand meaning the way people do, the argument goes, so we should reject the hype and focus on all the ways computers seem to fail. But that reflexive backlash, though tempting and self-flattering, misses a more important point: our colleagues in the information sciences are onto something. In the past several decades, their theory of language and meaning has become a dominant paradigm, though known only to specialist researchers. As literary scholars and intellectual historians, we should be curious about their work, and we should look for points of connection that bring their ideas into conversation with our own.

Such, at least, is the goal of this chapter. I'll chart a path through two very different fields of inquiry to identify what I believe to be an important commonality across them. First, I'll look at the notion of "intertextuality" in literary theory, especially as that idea was first articulated by Julia Kristeva when introducing the work of Mikhail Bakhtin to French intellectual circles in the 1960s. Kristeva was a visionary critic who understood language as a vast network of interconnected semiotic action. All texts carry within themselves something else, something more, some invisible web of connection that binds words and texts to each other. In the information sciences, research on this topic began in a very different way by seeking means to very practical ends: to teach computers how to parse, understand, and manipulate human discourse as a first step toward developing software that could translate between languages or search automatically though library catalogs. The core methods evolved from the 1940s through the 1990s, supported through research by information scientists like Warren Weaver and Claude Shannon, by linguists like Zellig Harris and John Firth, by philosophers like Yehoshua Bar-Hillel and Margaret Masterman, and by computer scientists like H. P. Luhn, Gerard Salton, Karen Spärck Jones, and Susan Dumais. Over the decades, they developed a technique that goes under various names: *distributional semantics*, *latent semantic analysis*, *vector-space semantic modeling*, or, most simply, *vector semantics*. I will argue that their methods share many important assumptions with the theory of intertextuality and that these very different scholars shared a common structuralist vision.

This vision of language can be glimpsed in figure 2.1, which offers a broad lexical survey of the EEBO corpus. The basic notion that informs this figure is *vector representation*, which defines a word as a sequence of numbers that record how often it appears near other words. Much like how social-network graphs track relations among people, semantic models track relations among words. Across their various connections, words can be shown to cluster into concepts or topics, but those concepts never form discrete entities. Meanings in a semantic model have little in

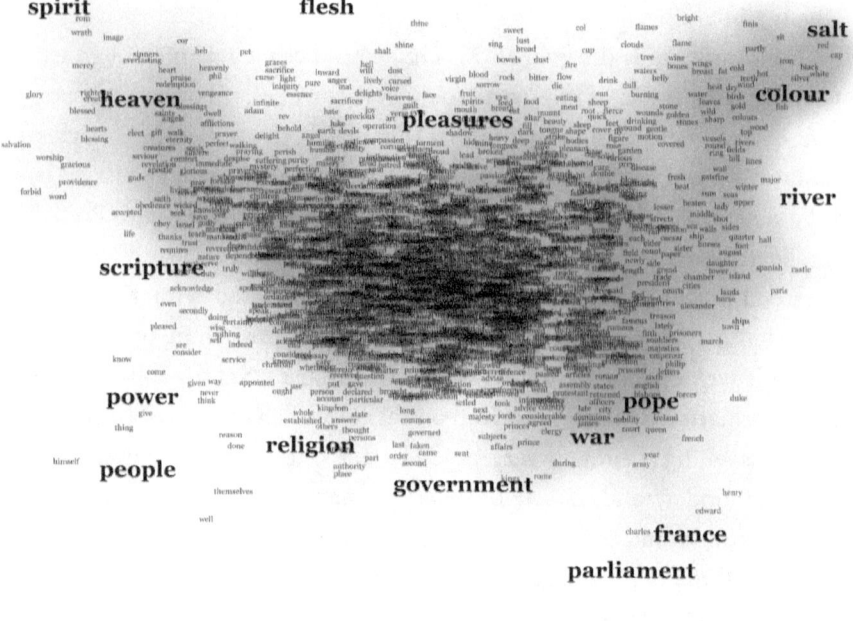

Figure 2.1. EEBO's Semantic Space. Two thousand keywords from the EEBO corpus, positioned and grouped based on collocation data, with select words highlighted for reference.

common with dictionary definitions. Words aren't defined by statements that paraphrase them. Instead, vector-space models embed words in an intertextual space of discourse where the meaning of any individual term emerges through its interactions with others. According to Gastaldi, in such systems, meaning is "less related to the cognitive capacities of individuals than to an internal dimension of the organization of language itself." Such models, he writes, "envisage language as a collective playground, as a reservoir where the significant distinctions resulting from a collective construction of signs are deposited."[4] To this end, after discussing the relevant theories, I'll turn to a survey of the EEBO corpus itself, and I'll demonstrate how computational methods can be used to explore this depository of historical signs. I'll show how semantic models approximate the meanings of words, how they decompose concepts, and how they can be used to analyze individual texts, compare authors, or describe change over time.

Language processing, I'll argue, puts into practice and brings to life a set of ideas only hazily grasped in literary criticism and theory. Kristeva sensed that Saussurian linguistics rested on shaky psychological grounds. Bakhtin's notion of dialogism violated conventional notions of meaning. He envisioned writing, not as a switchboard that shuffles thoughts among minds, but as a living system where the meaning of any text is produced by the various relations it proposes to others. To be sensitive to those relations meant attending to the alternate senses of every word, even when those senses didn't seem to apply in context. For Kristeva, this meant critiquing what she called the "unicity of the subject" and with it the tripartite connection between signifier, signified, and referent. As we'll see, computer scientists had a head start on all these ideas, simply for the reason that their work necessarily began where literary theory often ends. Computers can't intuit contextual relevance, so *of course* all senses of a word are potentially relevant. Computers lack access to the minds of writers and readers, so *of course* whatever meanings they measure will emerge through the system of language. The constraints and limitations of computing forced researchers in that field to adopt a theory of meaning that shared a great deal of common ground with certain strands of structuralist and poststructuralist thought, despite the fact that there was little or no conversation between these fields. The purpose of this chapter is to chart that common ground.

Kristeva's Bakhtin: Intertextuality

At the age of twenty-four and having recently immigrated from Bulgaria in 1965, Kristeva was quickly welcomed into the intellectual scene of Paris, where she joined a group of writers who contributed to the avant-garde journal *Tel Quel*, which was edited by Peter Stollers, whom she married shortly thereafter. Kristeva attended seminars at École Pratique des Hautes Études and soon gained notoriety for her knowledge of Russian critic Mikhail Bakhtin, whose work she helped introduce into French theory. Kristeva became a leading voice for a new science of language: "semiotics," sometimes spelled Σημειωτική. For Kristeva, semiotics would be a broad interdisciplinary endeavor with a wide explanatory reach.[5] But it started with criticism. Bakhtin provided her with a useful starting place.[6] His theories of the carnivalesque and the dialogic emphasized how literature, and especially the novel, brought various discourses into a single aesthetic experience. Kristeva called the phenomenon "intertextuality."[7]

Kristeva's early discussion of Bakhtin is worth returning to and describing in detail, because her concept of intertextuality is the closest literary theorists come to the model of language that informs distributional semantics.[8] The key notion Kristeva adapted from Bakhtin's work involves what he calls the "internal dialogism of the word."[9] Linguists and philosophers focus their attention on the relationship between signifiers, signified concepts, and referents. To understand how language works is to understand how arbitrary distinctions among signifiers are used to match concepts to real things. For Bakhtin, this semiotic triangle failed to account for the social dynamics of language—what he called its "dialogic orientation." Every time someone uses a word, they do so in dialogue with the latent possibilities of other speakers and writers, who might use different words and who respond in expected and unexpected ways:

> Indeed, any concrete discourse (utterance) finds the object at which it was directed already as it were overlain with qualifications, open to dispute, charged with value, already enveloped in an obscuring mist—or, on the contrary, by the "light" of alien words that have already been spoken about it. It is entangled, shot through with shared thoughts, points of view, alien value judgments and accents. The word, directed toward its object, enters a dialogically agitated and tension-filled environment of alien words, value judgments and accents, weaves in and out of complex interrelationships, merges with some, recoils from others, intersects with yet a third group: and all this may crucially shape discourse, may leave traces in all its semantic layers, may complicate its expression and influence its entire stylistic profile.[10]

Any time a speaker or writer tries to describe anything, they do so against a historical background and within a rhetorical context that necessarily directs their speech.[11] "The dialogic orientation of discourse," Bakhtin explains, "is the natural orientation of any living discourse."[12] Whenever we try to say what we mean, we do so in the context of others' expectations. Our words are always somehow alien to ourselves.

Referentiality is thus both enabled and compromised by its social foundation. Bakhtin explains: "The linguistic significance of a given utterance is understood against the background of language, while its actual meaning is understood against the background of other concrete utterances on the same theme."[13] Bakhtin represents words like points in a multilayered space. It's not so much that words *have meanings*— "linguistic significance" is a misleading concept, according to Bakhtin. Rather, "actual meaning" happens because words carry with them latent echoes of all their past uses. This historical and rhetorical tension exists among words within every language. Bakhtin called it "the primordial dialogism of discourse."[14]

The biggest difference between Kristeva's "intertextuality" and Bakhtin's "dialogism" is that, by substituting the notion of the "text" where he says "utterance," Kristeva specifies and regularizes the spatial metaphor at the heart of Bakhtin's theory. In Kristeva's telling, words are defined by their "status," their position within language conceived as a multidimensional space: "The word's status is thus defined *horizontally* (the word in the text belongs to both writing subject and addressee) as well as *vertically* (the word in the text is oriented towards an anterior or synchronic literary corpus)."[15] Whereas Bakhtin described the social context of discourse as somehow impinging on words, Kristeva effectively flips his spatial logic inside out. Words become links that mediate among texts:

> The word as minimal textual unit thus turns out to occupy the status of *mediator*, linking structural models of cultural (historical) environment, as well as that of *regulator*, controlling mutations from diachrony to synchrony, i.e., to literary structure. The word is spatialized: through the very notion of status, it functions in three

dimensions (subject-addressee-context) as a set of *dialogical*, semic elements or as a set of *ambivalent* elements. Consequently the task of literary semiotics is to discover other formalisms corresponding to different modalities of word-joining (sequences) within the dialogical space of texts.[16]

Within language, all words serve this basic structural purpose. They connect texts to each other. They mediate and regulate discourse by positioning speakers and addressees within cultural and linguistic contexts. What we think of as *meaning* is better understood as a continual process of position-taking.[17] Words produce the conditions for literature, and even for subjectivity, within their own dialogical space: "The addressee," Kristeva explains, "is included within a book's discursive universe only as discourse itself. He thus fuses with this other discourse, this other book, in relation to which the writer has written his own text." In Kristeva's telling, by emphasizing the fundamentally rhetorical character of language, Bakhtin upends rhetoric as such. Rather than words being traded among persons to create common understanding, the semantic relations produced among words build the very foundation of personhood. "The notion of *intertextuality* replaces that of intersubjectivity," Kristeva argues, and "any text is constructed as a mosaic of quotations; any text is the absorption and transformation of another."[18]

Words are ambiguous because they occur in different texts. Texts are ambiguous because they join the same words in different ways. A vertical axis; a horizontal axis. At its core, the concept of intertextuality is elegant and coherent, even simple (in the best sense of that word). However, the whole thing immediately became a lot more complicated, because this vision of language had wide-ranging implications and meant different things to different people, and so it inspired very different kinds of theoretical speculation. First, intertextuality provided a justification for the critical practice of close reading, especially for the explication of irony and ambiguity.[19] If words and texts are ambiguous in this way, a good critic should be as attuned as possible to the matrix of lexical relations within which every text is suspended. For Roland Barthes and, later, Michael Riffaterre, this meant embracing reader-response theory and grounding literary meaning in the experience of reading (and especially of re-reading) a text.[20] "The reader is the space," Barthes declared, "on which all the quotations that make up a writing are inscribed."[21] For Gérard Genette, this idea was far too abstract. He was a narratologist and primarily interested in genre and form, so when he picked up the idea in *Palimpsests*, he watered intertextuality down to mere quotation and literary allusion while multiplying the terminology to include transtextuality, paratextuality, metatextuality, and hypo- and hypertextuality.[22]

But back in the 1960s, Kristeva was younger, more audacious, and her ambitions were altogether more totalizing. For her, the death of the author meant something like the death of science: a profound reconsideration of all knowledge based on the discovery of a new general law of human society—a law that recognizes that everything we do and know, we do and know through language. At the same time, the reverse was also true. Everything that happens in language depends on the inner workings of our untrustworthy minds. For this reason, Kristeva turned to Freudian and Lacanian psychology. To understand how texts produce meaning seemed to require understanding how minds draw meanings from texts, but minds are not simple, unitary things. Selves are constantly produced, destroyed, and reproduced through mental and biological imperatives that Freud called "drives." The subjectivity experienced through reading and writing was therefore in every way entangled with Freudian implications. Taken together, Bakhtin's critique of language and Freud's critique of consciousness demanded a new account of . . . well . . . *everything*. Kristeva envisioned a comprehensive science of semiotics that would provide a new foundation for social theory by drawing simultaneously from linguistics and psychology.

In the decades that followed, Kristeva's revision of Bakhtin was largely subsumed by other concerns, by theorists (including Kristeva) who wanted to challenge ideologies of science, capital, and sex, and by critics concerned narrowly with literariness and poetic language. Against these concerns, both large and small, intertextuality was more exciting for what it seemed to disrupt than for anything in and of itself. Yet, in her creative re-reading of Bakhtin's dialogism, Kristeva articulated something very close to a model of textuality that would, through very different routes, transform the information sciences. She writes:

> By establishing the status of the word as *minimal unit* of the text, Bakhtin deals with structure at its deepest level, beyond the sentence and rhetorical figures. The notion of *status* has added to the image of the text as a corpus of atoms that of a text made up of relationships, within which words function as quantum units. If there is a model for poetic language, it no longer involves lines or surfaces, but rather, *space* and *infinity*—concepts amenable to formalization through set theory and the new mathematics.[23]

Again, it's worth pointing out how simple and elegant this idea is. Taking words as the minimal unit of analysis means that a text can now be understood in two ways: as a sequence ("a corpus of atoms") and, when aggregated with others, as part of a network ("relationships"). Where she says that "words function as quantum units," she means that every word becomes a point of connection that binds together every text using that word. You can analyze any word by comparing its uses across texts, and you can analyze any text by comparing its peculiar sequence against others that join similar words in different ways. Importantly, this way of looking at language implies new possibilities for mathematical formalization. A word becomes, in this model, a subset of the language that necessarily reaches across texts and contains within itself all prior uses. Every text represents a selection from those subsets, containing within itself their manifold connections. By thinking about language in this way, Kristeva argues, "Bakhtin deals with structure at its deepest level."

However, she never developed an empirical program for studying language in this way, because she was convinced early on that the answers had to lie in psychology. So, while Kristeva sometimes expressed her ideas mathematically, she could do so only "metaphorically." Her book Σημειωτική includes equations meant to represent functions that select and redistribute word meanings within poetic language. For example, she offers an existence theorem from set theory, "for all sets

$x_1, \ldots, x_n, \langle x_1, \ldots, x_n \rangle \in A \bullet \equiv \bullet \, \varphi(x_1, \ldots, x_n)$" to demonstrate "the impossibility of establishing a contradiction in the space of poetic language."[24] Unfortunately, the elements of these sets were not observable, and indeed they weren't even notionally discrete, so the formulas could never be anything more than abstract re-statements of Kristeva's otherwise qualitative speculations. Alan Sokal would later dismiss her work as "fashionable nonsense." He was right in some ways. Her equations didn't really make sense (she largely stopped using them as her career matured), and it's certainly true that Freudian psychology is understandable only on its own strange terms, but he was wrong to dismiss her work. In her discussion of Bakhtin, Kristeva came remarkably close to figuring out how to describe meaning mathematically, and computer scientists would eventually land on a model very similar to hers.

Her mistake was a very simple one, in fact. If, as Bakhtin argued, words are the minimal, quantum units of discourse, and if they enable meaning by creating relationships across texts, a mathematical theory needs to take every instance of each word as *its* quantum unit. The basic elements in such a system cannot be the minds of readers or authors. They can't even be the words themselves, considered in their totality. As we'll see, the quantum unit of discourse is every *instance* of each word as it appears in each text. The difference between a word and its instances might seem subtle, even trivial, but it suggests and requires an entirely different mathematical apparatus. And in the end, that's what Kristeva lacked: a mathematics appropriate to her intuitions. Instead of borrowing from formal logic, she needed an analytical method as sensitive as her own reading mind to the ambiguities of natural discourse.

The Origins of Computational Semantics

In the field of computational linguistics, the study of meaning has a long tradition going back to the middle of the twentieth century. Many operations of natural-language processing depend on training computers to discriminate among the ambiguities of natural language. I'll focus on two: machine translation and information retrieval. Machine translation requires parsing the meanings of words in context to ensure they're properly matched when translated into the target language. Information retrieval parses words to ensure users get the most valid results to a search query. The challenge for researchers involves learning how to train computers to make sense of words in ways that approximate as closely as possible what people are probably thinking when writing, reading, and searching. Computer models approximate the meanings of words by creating structured frames for analysis then measuring the distribution of each word across that frame. Within any given language, words with similar meanings almost always share similar patterns of collocation. They tend to appear in the same documents or the same paragraphs or near the same keywords, depending on how the model is built. When used for the analysis of words or concepts, these models expose their many possible connotations. They do so, I'll argue, by representing a corpus as an intertextual network of lexical correlation.

However, when these methods were first being imagined, the concept of "meaning" presented a real problem. Meanings are unobservable. It's often not even clear, when linguists or literary critics talk about the meaning of an utterance or a poem, that they're referring to anything that actually exists outside their own minds. So how could meanings possibly be studied scientifically? In *Methods in Structural Linguistics* (1951), Zellig Harris proposed a systematic disregard for meaning altogether. In meaning's place, Harris advocated for statistical measurements of linguistic distribution: words like *Albuquerque* and *applesauce* will appear in different contexts, and that measurable difference, Harris argued, was a more appropriate object of study than subjective judgments about what words seem to denote. Harris was therefore among the leaders of a midcentury effort to secure linguistics on mathematically and scientifically sound principles. George Zipf's *The Psycho-Biology of Language* (1935) and Claude Shannon's and Warren Weaver's *Mathematical Theory of Communication* (1949) sparked enthusiasm for statistical approaches to language, suggesting that trustworthy mathematical models of human communication and culture were not just possible, but within close reach. This belief gained further momentum in the immediate wake of World War II, especially for American and British code breakers, whose success proved that human language could be subject to machine-based analysis and manipulation.

Among the American cryptographers was Weaver, director of the Rockefeller Foundation Natural Sciences Division, who proposed in 1949 a set of computational techniques for translating among natural languages. The futuristic promise of machine translation captured the imagination of scholars like Harris, and, over the next ten or fifteen years, machine translation became a major research field that swallowed up millions of dollars in federal grant funding. At the University of Pennsylvania, Harris's group tried to bring his linguistic theories to bear on the project, and similar efforts were underway by Anthony Oettinger at Harvard, Erwin Reifler at the University of Washington, Margaret Masterman in Cambridge, and Yehoshua Bar-Hillel, Victor Yngve, and Noam Chomsky at MIT. Many believed early on that Fully Automatic High Quality Translation, or FAHQT, as it was sometimes abbreviated, was a reasonable goal. Soon, machines would not only translate scientific papers (the immediate aim) but also political communication and literature, even poems. Automatic translation would promote international communication and cooperation and would thus help usher in a new, peaceful world order.[25] This vision was not realized, however. A report by the Automatic Language Processing Advisory Committee (ALPAC) in 1966 recommended that the funding stream be cut, and in 1968 Chomsky declared the entire project a misguided failure.

With the benefit of hindsight, machine translation looks much more successful now than it did in the late 1960s. Modern, internet-based translation engines work far better than most people then believed possible, and these engines, much like the field of computational linguistics in general, trace their roots back to postwar efforts. More to our purposes, though, is that this research focused squarely on problems of meaning. Scholars who hoped to make automatic translation a reality faced an obvious obstacle. Many words have more than one meaning, so translating among languages would involve, first and foremost, teaching machines to disambiguate words. As Margaret Masterman wrote in 1960, "The basic problem in Machine Translation is that of multiple meaning, or *polysemy*."[26]

One way to describe the origins and development of computational semantics is to trace it back to a tension in Zellig Harris's linguistic philosophy. When he proposed a structuralist disregard for meaning, Harris suggested a method for breaking language down to primitive simples and evaluating patterns across them. Like any "regularities in selected aspects of human behavior," he wrote, language could be studied by "associating discrete elements with particular features or portions of continuous events, and then stating the interrelations among these elements."[27] To study language, Harris argued, linguists should break the continuous field of talk into small parts and then describe the relations that pertain among those parts. This approach suggested two very different lines of inquiry, both of which Harris pursued. On the one hand, his theory suggested that sentences could be broken down into semantic "kernels"—simple, conceptual primitives—which were transformed by deep structural processes into human statements.[28] Harris's student, Noam Chomsky, extended this line of inquiry into a complex but theoretically finite set of transformational rules through which a theoretically infinite number of statements might be made.[29] This grammatical, rule-based method investigated language through very small, hypothetical sentences to examine how they are or aren't meaningful.[30]

The other side of Harris's research agenda—and the work for which he is now most well-known—involved statistical measurements of corpora. In 1954, Harris formulated what has since come to be known as the "distributional hypothesis." Rather than rely on subjective judgments or dictionary definitions, linguists should model the meanings of words with statistics, because "difference of meaning correlates with difference of distribution." He explains,

> If we consider *oculist* and *eye doctor* we find that, as our corpus of actually occurring utterances grows, these two occur in almost the same environments.... In contrast, there are many sentence environ-

ments in which *oculist* occurs but *lawyer* does not; e.g., *I've had my eyes examined by the same oculist for twenty years*, or *Oculists often have their prescription blanks printed for them by opticians*. It is not a question of whether the above sentence with *lawyer* substituted is true or not; it might be true in some situation. It is rather a question of the relative frequency of such environments with *oculist* and with *lawyer*.[31]

This passage reflects a subtle shift in Harris's thinking. In *Structural Linguistics*, he had proposed that linguists attend to distributional structure as a theoretical principle. Here the emphasis is slightly different. He says that distribution "correlates" to meaning. *Oculist* and *eye doctor* mean pretty much the same thing, and they appear in sentences with pretty much the same words. Rather than turn away from meaning, Harris here offers a statistical proxy for it. His theory was picked up and expanded on by J. R. Firth, whose 1962 comment, "You shall know a word by the company it keeps," has become a truism of computational semantics.[32]

The apparent simplicity of the distributional hypothesis fanned enthusiasm for machine translation, as Warren Weaver and Erwin Reifler had proposed techniques that shared these assumptions for disambiguating polysemous words. Rather than map each word directly onto an interlingual dictionary, Weaver proposed that documents should first be subject to an additional stage of processing. To know which meaning of a word was being used at any given time, you'd need to look at the other words that appear in its immediate context. Weaver explains:

> If one examines the words in a book, one at a time as through an opaque mask with a hole in it one word wide, then it is obviously impossible to determine, one at a time, the meaning of the words.... But if one lengthens the slit in the opaque mask, until one can see not only the central word in question but also say N words on either side, then if N is large enough one can unambiguously decide the meaning of the central word.[33]

Of course, a computer can't tell the difference between "table" and "table." It's just looking at the word as if, in Weaver's evocative image, "through an opaque mask." Through this tiny little hole, the word exists by itself and seems to carry within itself all the latent possibilities that Bakhtin described. But if you expand that context window just a bit, you'll quickly be able to tell the difference between "plates on the table with the dishes" from "columns of the table contain data fields." Furnishings and spreadsheets contribute two senses to the word "table," and those conceptual differences might be measured (or, at least, approximated) using collocation data. The informing idea here is that different words will tend to appear in different contexts, and therefore one can guess at a word's meaning by attending to the words that appear near it. What began as a specific practical solution to a challenge in scientific communication was immediately recognized for having the potential to transform the study of semantics. Theory and engineering seemed to align.

However, statistical approaches to word meaning faced at least three major obstacles. The first was theoretical. Yehoshua Bar-Hillel objected on principle, claiming that many statements depend for their legibility on contextual knowledge that only conscious minds can hold. Giving the example of a child playing with a toy box while in a playpen, Bar-Hillel suggested that a sentence like *The box was in the pen* could never be translated by machine.[34] No statistical profile of the word *pen* could help a machine differentiate between possibly relevant meanings. The second problem involved a lack of data. To be reliable, every word would need to be included many times in all of its variations, and no such corpus existed.[35] Third, the limits of computer memory kept the datasets small. Machines were still operating on punch cards, and researchers often resorted to simulating decision-tree algorithms by hand.[36] These problems were all insurmountable at the time, and so it wasn't until the late 1980s and 1990s that corpus-driven research became popular in linguistics.[37]

One way proposed to get around these problems involved developing semantic dictionaries that organized words under larger headings, much like a thesaurus. Margaret Masterman of Cambridge was a leading proponent of this technique. A philosopher and former student of Ludwig Wittgenstein, Masterman founded the Cambridge Language Research Unit (CLRU), which was an important center for the study

THE COMPUTATION OF MEANING

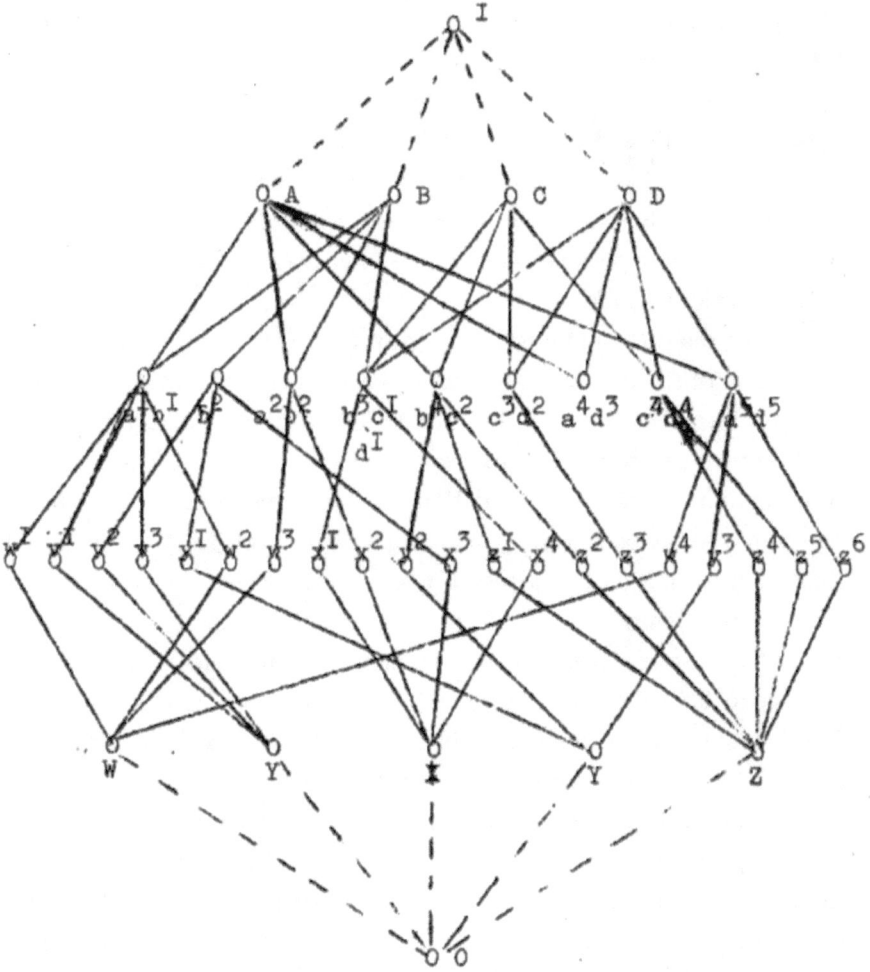

Figure 2.2. The Lattice-Shaped Semantic Network. From Margaret Masterman, "What Is a Thesaurus?"

of computational semantics through the 1980s. Along with Karen Spärck Jones, Masterman developed the first computer-based thesaurus, drawn from *Roget's*, for modeling word meaning. Words, Masterman believed, distributed meaning through a corpus in a lattice-shaped network (fig. 2.2).[38] On the bottom of the lattice was the language as a whole, from which words were selected to make statements. Words used in a sentence (W, Y, X, Y, and Z) corresponded up the network to their various locations in the thesaurus, where co-occurring words were themselves organized into larger groups, which she called *archeheads* (*A*, *B*, *C*, and *D*), and which together formed an abstract conceptual superstructure that divided the language into headings, much like a subject index in a library catalog. With researchers at the CLRU, Masterman designed algorithms for reading over the lines of the thesaurus's semantic network to paraphrase English sentences and convert them into Latin, and vice versa.[39]

During the 1970s and 1980s, after the promise of machine translation had seemed to falter and while corpus-based linguistics was relatively inactive, research continued in information retrieval, where the practical problems were both more urgent and easier to solve. The central problem of information retrieval (IR) is to identify documents—whether books in a library, scientific papers, legal records, or, later, websites—that are most relevant to a search query. Much like machine translation, information retrieval confronts the problem of ambiguity.[40] When entered as part of a search query, polysemous terms undermined what IR researchers called the "precision" of returned results (because the query would return many irrelevant documents) while also limiting the system's "recall" (because relevant documents that used slightly different vocabulary would be missed). The challenge was to group documents into categories that would correspond meaningfully to what users had in mind when entering a query. It was in information retrieval that the distributional hypothesis matured into a full-fledged theory of semantic space. Two scholars often credited with this development are Hans Peter Luhn and Gerard Salton.

Information retrieval, too, traces its origins to the postwar period. Luhn worked at the IBM Research Center in the 1950s, where he developed business intelligence systems that sorted through large catalogs of documents. Conventional indexing methods used controlled vocabularies for subject headings. Luhn argued that such vocabularies suffered from two major disadvantages. On the one hand, they were prone to become obsolete as catalogers changed ideas about was and wasn't important in their collections. On the other hand, users often struggled to navigate catalogs because controlled vocabularies required them to guess among possibly relevant terms. Traditional cataloging techniques were for these reasons insufficiently sensitive to variations among human recorders and users. Luhn proposed instead to categorize documents using single keyword tags, which he called "elements":

> The elements enumerated by recorders to identify a topic will necessarily vary as no two recorders will view a topic in identical fashion. Similarly, no two inquirers, when referring to the same subject will state their query in identical fashion. It is therefore important that a system recognizes that these variations arise and that they cannot be controlled. It must then become the function of the system to overcome these variations to a reasonable degree.[41]

What Bakhtin described as the primordial dialogism of the word, Luhn encounters as a fairly straightforward, obvious, and unavoidable technical problem. People simply don't use the same words for the same concepts. You can't rely on a controlled vocabulary for your search engines because people don't write or think that way. That's just not how language works. Luhn's solution to this problem was novel. By breaking vocabularies down to their component elements, then allowing for those various elements' recombination, the system could identify similarities and differences across differently cataloged items.

The terms themselves can be compared mathematically using a vector-space model. By treating search terms as points in space, the system could return all documents that sit within their shared proximity.

> If we consider a concept as being a field in a multi-dimensional array, we may then visualize a topic as being located in that space which is common to all the concept fields stated. It may further be visualized that related topics are located more or less adjacent to each other depending on the degree of similarity and this is so because they agree in some of the identifying terms and therefore share some of the concept fields.[42]

We see here the earliest statement of a set of principles that would come to inform computational semantics (fig. 2.3). First, that human concepts can be represented in high-dimensional vector spaces, and second, that

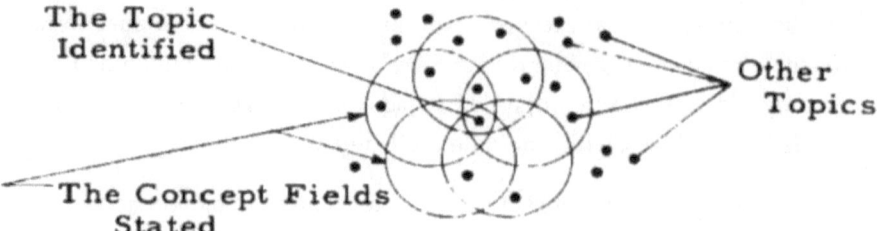

Figure 2.3. Concepts and Topics as a Multidimensional Array. In 1953, H. P. Luhn imagined representing an index of subject headings for library catalogs in the form of a multidimensional array of keywords. From "A New Method of Recording and Searching Information."

similarity of meaning could be approximated by measuring the geometric distance between concepts within that space. To realize this vision, Luhn proposed using a Keyword-in-Context (KWIC) technique for sorting titles, creating de facto subject categories based on any word.[43] From these terms, the system Luhn designed would deal with polysemy by building a "dictionary of notions" that, much like Masterman's thesaurus, grouped related keywords under common, fixed headings.[44]

The basic idea of automatic indexing, then, was to replace the work of human catalogers with an algorithmic process using keywords to identify groups of similar documents, then building the index from there. Gerard Salton, professor of computer science at Cornell University, extended this line of inquiry by designing a framework for removing the work of human catalogers altogether. As early as 1963 he suggested associating documents by creating an "incidence matrix" of their shared keywords.[45] In 1975, Salton, with Andrew Wong and Chungshu Yang, proposed "A Vector Space Model for Automatic Indexing," in which they put forward a mathematical technique for organizing documents into thematic clusters. Their basic premise was to define the multidimensional space of the document collection in terms of word counts. If you imagine a collection of documents indexed by the frequencies of just three terms, those word frequencies can be plotted in a three-dimensional Cartesian frame (fig. 2.4). Documents that use similar words will appear near each other in this space and so can be grouped into automatically generated clusters. In practice, such frequencies are measured over hundreds, even

THE COMPUTATION OF MEANING 79

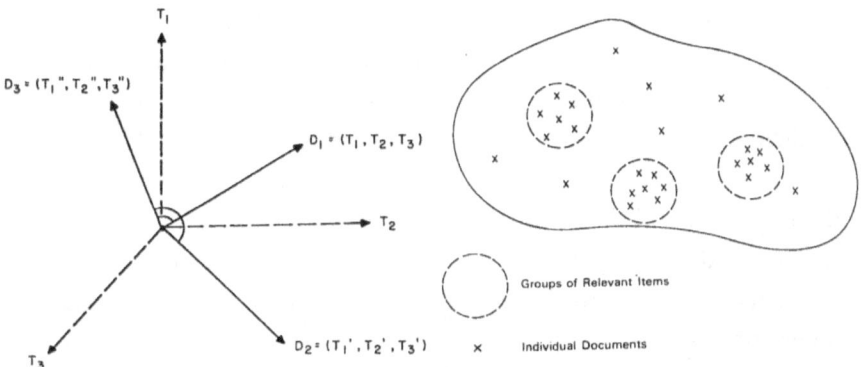

Figure 2.4. Vector Representation of Document Space. By treating the frequency of each keyword as a spatial dimension (*left*), a vector-space model compares documents by analyzing their proximity within that space. Considered abstractly and reduced to two dimensions (*right*), such models can be shown to group documents into clusters that reflect their shared vocabulary. From Salton et al., "A Vector Space Model for Automatic Indexing."

thousands of dimensions, so you could never visualize them directly on the page. Nonetheless, the basic geometry of meaning continues to apply, so it's still possible to calculate similarities among the trajectories each word follows through the corpus. To create a profile of any given word's various uses requires two basic steps: first, finding the words that tend to appear in similar contexts, then second, comparing those words to each other and thereby sorting them into conceptual groups.

The key insight here is to move away from hierarchically defined structures of meaning. Rather than organize titles into predefined subjects or categories, like a thesaurus, Salton proposed using word co-occurrence (here, at the document level) to project search results into an imaginary field. Salton's original goal was to automatically generate subject headings, but it was quickly realized that this technique allowed for much greater flexibility. Whatever the search query, it was now possible to rank documents based on their location in space. Any time you search a catalog and the results are sorted by "relevance," odds are you're using a system built on this principle.

Vector-space models use spaces like these to record word meaning. With the availability of large corpora and increased computing power in the 1990s, it became possible to create profiles of all words, measuring how often they appear in each other's contexts. Consequently, words themselves, not just documents, could be projected into what Hinrich Schütze called "sublexical space," or "Word Space."[46] Zellig Harris long ago proposed that word distribution correlates to meaning; the challenge then was to discriminate among words' putatively discrete definitions. Using dictionaries or thesauri made sense because it was presumed that words had fixed meanings that could be made to fit more or less neatly under subheadings. Words were polysemous, but not excessively so. Vector space models dispense with this assumption. According to Schütze, "Vector similarity is the only information present in Word Space: semantically related words are close, unrelated words are distant" (fig. 2.5). In his 2006 study, Magnus Sahlgren extended this idea to what he called the "geometric metaphor of meaning": "Meanings are locations in a semantic space, and semantic similarity is proximity between the locations."[47] Word-sense disambiguation works by finding clusters in a word's semantic space, then measuring how closely any individual use of the word sits near each cluster.

The study of computational semantics reached a tipping point in the early 1990s, when desktop computing suddenly made it easy for

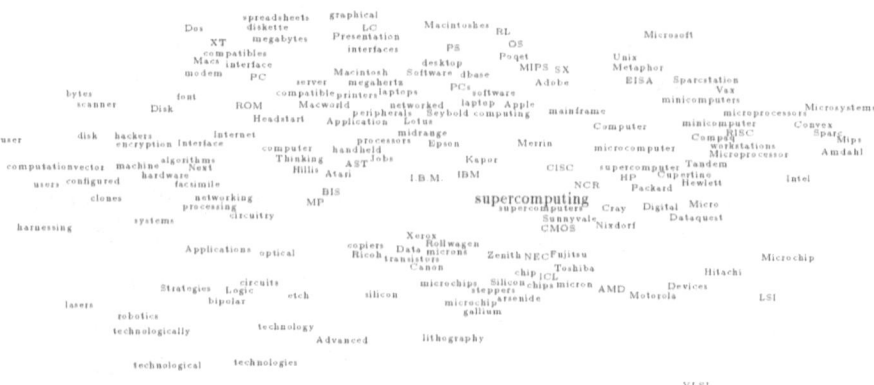

Figure 2.5. Word Space: The Semantic Field of *Supercomputing* in Sublexical Space. When projected onto a two-dimensional frame, Word Space looks like what we now call a word cloud. However, unlike a word cloud, position in the graph reflects each word's underlying semantic profile. From Hinrich Schütze, "Dimensions of Meaning."

researchers working individually or in small teams to experiment with corpora that were large enough to produce robust semantic data. Like Schütze, others experimented with techniques for projecting corpora into vector space. Susan T. Dumais and Thomas K. Landauer were leading figures in developing a technique called "latent semantic indexing" (when dealing with bibliographic records) or "latent semantic analysis" (when dealing with words alone).[48] The term *latent* referred to their use of linear algebra to reduce the dimensions of their data's underlying matrices. Rather than thousands of dimensions for each document or each keyword, they could project their data onto the latent axes that were responsible for the most lexical variation. This dimensionality reduction improved performance of the model, especially when working with documents and bibliographical records.

Since the 1990s, and especially since 2010 or so, the mathematical procedures for semantic analysis have exploded in both variety and sophistication.[49] Machine-learning algorithms use sampling methods to "predict" or "learn" the shape of the underlying semantic space. Rather than systematically count each word then statistically manipulate those counts afterward, they sample little bits of the data one at a time and perform statistical transformations as they go. Latent semantic indexing has since been replaced as state-of-the-art by "topic modeling," latent semantic analysis, by "word embeddings."[50] Such sampling methods are absolutely crucial for very large datasets, such as studies of social media, where the number of documents being analyzed can quickly reach into the millions or billions. Even with smaller corpora, however, machine-learning approaches have been shown to improve performance of many tasks—such as guessing synonyms, performing analogies, searching records, or translating languages—inspiring some scholars to proclaim, "Don't count, predict!"[51]

The sheer quantity and variety of research published in the fields of computational linguistics and natural language processing can be daunting to outsiders, but these techniques all share the same basic premise that was intuited in the 1970s; they transform word-collocation measurements into a multidimensional space. What matters for humanists is that these models replace dictionary definitions with a direct representation of each word's "status," to return to Kristeva's phrase, within the intertextual space of the corpus. In Word Space, definitions and categories are replaced with similarities and proximities, opening a critical vocabulary for describing ambiguities of minutely fine gradation that stretch in countless directions. Insofar as intertextuality and vector semantics provide theories of meaning, they provide theories of ambiguity, pushing strongly against the impulse to draw clear boundaries that isolate words into discrete concepts.

For software engineers, the goal is to design systems that accurately guess what people mean to say; that is, to reduce language to the level of human communication where words are more commercially valuable (as in, for example, filtering programs that target online advertisements). However, in order to achieve this, research in information retrieval and machine translation needed to develop a way of modeling ambiguity that was itself unambiguous. The result was a mathematical theory of finite space that measures lexical relationships across thousands of dimensions, where meaning as such is both completely depersonalized and radically indeterminate.

Vector-space models build meaning from the corpus up. Every use of a word is recorded and embedded in a semantic profile that reflects its distribution over the corpus as a whole. Just as Kristeva described words as both "atoms" and "relationships," a vector-space model takes every instance of each word—every act of lexical expression performed by EEBO—as a link that binds its texts together. Every instance of a word is a countable thing, an atom, or what corpus linguists call a "token." Tokens can be counted because they are individual but not unique; every token has a particular spelling, or "type," that it shares with all other instances of the same word. Considering words as both tokens and types allows us to see them, not just as things unto themselves, but also as connecting threads that weave through a corpus. The result is a vast and thickly connected network where each link represents a *semantic simple*, a decision, made by some speaker or writer, that a particular word makes sense when written in a particular document. Each such decision is, in its own small way, purposeful and meaningful, and vector-space models provide a robust framework for aggregating those decisions and generalizing about them. Vector-space models are built to be sensitive to every historical use of a term—at least, to every use of a term as represented in a corpus—and are premised on the assumption that the best way to know about language is to compile and compare as many examples as possible. The resulting model disregards the meaning of any individual statement in order to describe the deep structure of meaningfulness implied in uses that can be observed across many statements.

Defining EEBO as a Vector-Space Model

In "Distributional Structure," Harris imagined breaking a corpus into sentences, but most studies follow Schütze in using a simpler "context window" method, which measures bare proximity, using a range of a certain number of characters or words, regardless of grammar. Essentially, this method involves building a concordance, then counting the context words that appear under each heading, and then placing those values into a large table, sometimes called a *term-term matrix* or a *context-word matrix*. In these models, each word is represented as a large sequence of numbers showing its occurrence across the corpus. The model defines a relationship between two sets of word types—high-frequency keywords, K, that are chosen for analysis prior to the concordancing process, and lower frequency words, W, that are observed to appear near those keywords when the concordance is assembled. Formally, we define every context word, w_i, as length-n vector,

$$w_i = \{k_1, k_2, \ldots, k_n\},$$

where each value, k_i, represents the number of times the context word appears in range of that keyword. When represented in tabular form, each of these words becomes a row and each keyword becomes a column. The corpus as a whole is represented as an $m \times n$ matrix, V, where n is the number of keywords and m is the number of context words in the total vocabulary.

Any sequence of numbers like w_i can be interpreted geometrically as a vector pointing away from the origin, as in figure 2.4. Two words are *semantically similar* insofar as they share similar patterns over the model, where similarity is defined as the cosine of the angle between any two vectors, w_1 and w_2:

$$\cos(w_1, w_2) = \frac{w_1 \cdot w_2}{|w_1||w_2|}$$

Essentially, taking the cosine between two vectors creates a ratio that shows how much overlap they share. The numerator (*top*) of this formula is the dot product, and the denominator (*bottom*) is the product of the unit vectors. I'll say more about this calculation in chapter 4. What matters here is that the product of the unit vectors (*bottom*) represents the maximum possible overlap any two vectors might share, and the dot product (*top*) represents how much overlap they actually share. Thus, the dot product is always less than or equal to the product of the unit vectors. If the two words share high frequency values among the same keywords, the cosine between them will approach 1, the maximum possible score that can happen only when the vectors are identical (that is, when you measure any vector against itself). If two words tend to be used in very different contexts and very different kinds of sentences, they'll share fewer keyword collocations, and the similarity will be lower, approaching zero. Taking the cosine of the angle between two words doesn't give you their meanings; it measures similarities among the statements that contain them.

In the analyses that follow, I will focus only on a subset of EEBO that includes titles published between 1640 and 1699. I exclude earlier documents because orthographic variation across the sixteenth and early seventeenth centuries complicates analysis. I want to keep things as simple as possible by minimizing such external factors so that I can focus on the mathematical and theoretical concepts. Within these 18,351 documents, I compiled a list of 2,002 keywords, excluding about 300 stop-words made up of prepositions, pronouns, and various oddities caused by the transcription process. I built a concordance for each keyword using a context window of five words, then placed the resulting frequency counts into a large matrix, where $m = 32,245$ (for each collocate term, excluding extremely rare words) and $n = 2,002$ (for each keyword). Each row thus represents a word in the corpus as a vector of 2,002 values, showing its frequency of co-occurrence with each keyword. Measured over the 18,351 documents selected from EEBO, the total number of collocations is about 1.42 billion. To ensure this model captures the most significant interactions among the data, V is subject to a further step of processing in which each frequency value is normalized using a process called *positive pointwise mutual information* (PPMI). This statistical test measures each value in the matrix against its expected value, taking into account both the total frequency of the keyword and each collocate context word. Some words, like *god* and *man*, appear very frequently across the corpus, while others, like *intercession* and *reconciliation*, appear much less frequently. A keyword might appear, in raw terms, much more frequently near *god* while nonetheless being more important to the meaning of *intercession*. Normalization techniques like PPMI have the effect of accounting for and smoothing out these differences, measuring frequency values against each word's expected baseline, rather than in absolute terms.

For example, consider the word *foot*. Between the years 1640 and 1699, the term was used often enough to be among the keywords for the corpus, appearing 83,701 times overall. To get a sense of where these values come from, consider some of these snippets of discourse, all captured in the model:

> ... of the Breast is two Geometricall **foot** and two Inches. Swathing a cause ...

> ... the people both horse and **foot** which marched under the Catholique banner ...

> ... Camp consisted of 20000 **Foot** and 9000 Horse, all of them Germans, except ...

> ... pair of stairs of six **foot** square, to serve for every of the same stories and ...

> ... to go bare-**foot**; to wear stockings of Goats-leather; and to keep ones self very ...

... issued forth for the Horse and **Foot** to march towards Sterling, in order to ...

... to tread upon him, and trample him under **foot**, to crucifie him, to bury him ...

... sawed Timber, of about five inches square, and four **foot** high above the Rails ...

Across these snippets we see instances of *foot* that suggest the word was used primarily when describing either (a) measurements of length and breadth, (b) military engagements that involved infantry, or (c) the foot of a human body.

The context words that appear most frequently near *foot* include *horse* (16,465), *two* (7,929), *thousand* (6,170), *long* (5,903), *set* (5,731), *three* (4,947), *hundred* (4,152), *high* (4,065), and *inches* (4,028). When measuring semantic similarity, we normalize those counts using PPMI then query the model to ask which words tend to co-occur with the same keywords in similar proportions. The terms most semantically similar to *foot* include *foot* (1.000), *paces* (0.764), *horse* (0.697), *yards* (0.690), *breadth* (0.690), *mile* (0.689), *broad* (0.688), and *inches* (0.677). Relations of semantic similarity can then be compared and visualized. Figure 2.6 shows the forty words with collocation profiles most similar to *foot*, grouped using hierarchical clustering and projected onto a two-dimensional plane.

In the seventeenth century, *foot* was invoked most distinctively in two contexts (fig. 2.6). First, it served in military discourse as a synecdoche for infantry, and so it scores highly similar to words like *regiments, battalions, dragoons,* and *squadrons*, while the cluster of number words near the top suggest the sizes of these companies. Second, *foot* was used as a unit of measurement for *length* and *breadth*, where it corresponded closely to *yards, inches, miles,* and *furlongs*. We might think of the word as referring primarily to the part of the human body, but except insofar as *foot* invoked certain kinds of movement (*paces*), such uses were not among the most distinctive associations of the term. Dividing *foot*'s uses in this way provides a straightforward example of word-sense disambiguation. The

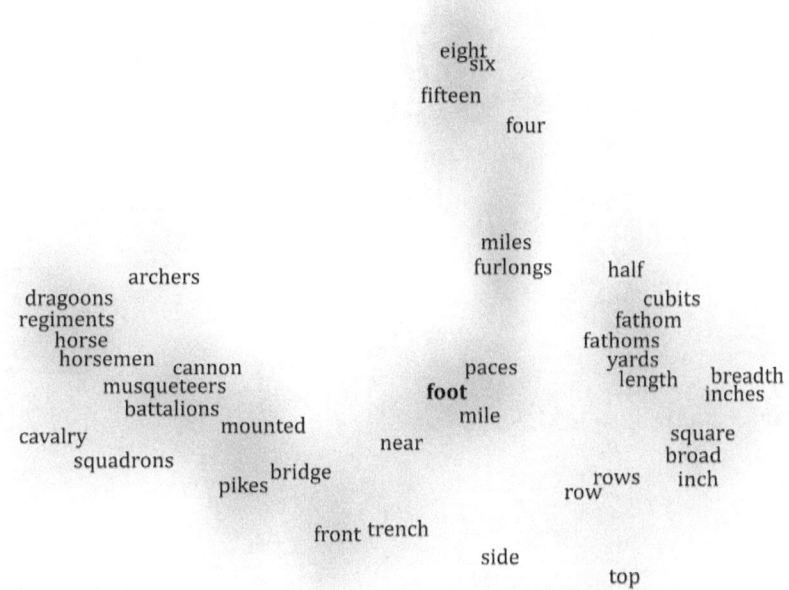

Figure 2.6. Semantic Field of *foot* in the EEBO Corpus. The forty terms most semantically similar to *foot* are plotted using principal-component analysis and grouped using hierarchical clustering.

term had different meanings, and those meanings can be teased apart through a fairly simple statistical extrapolation.

If we imagine a search engine trained on seventeenth-century data, the task would be to guess which sense of *foot* a user was interested in and to return documents that correspond to that meaning. The system must differentiate between the word in general and its intended use in any particular context. The simplest and most common technique is called *vector composition*.[52] If a user were to enter the search query "square foot," the system could break it apart into two words and multiply together their corresponding word vectors into one composite

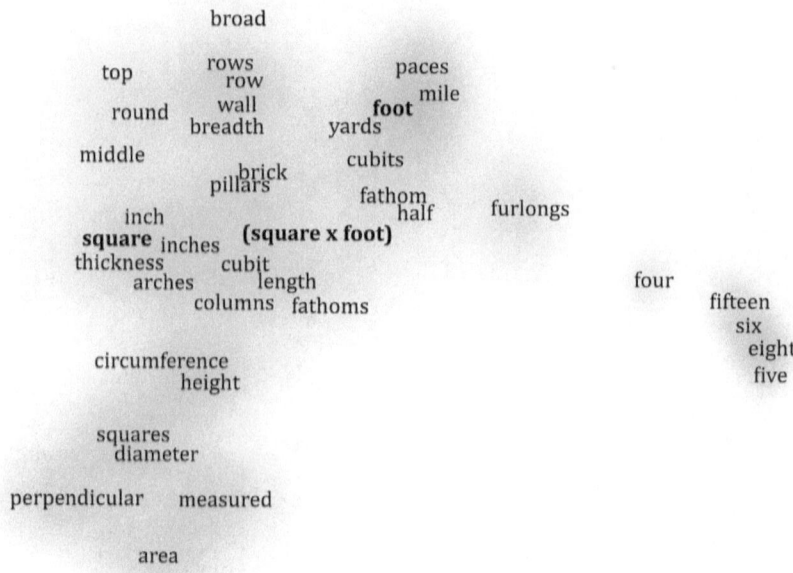

Figure 2.7. Semantic Field of the Composite Vector, *square × foot*." Vectors are here composed by taking element-wise multiplication. The effect of multiplying two vectors together is analogous to taking the intersection between them, exposing their overlap, and eliminating extraneous fields of reference.

sequence (fig. 2.7). The effect is the same as if you took the mathematical intersection between the two sets of collocates. The angle of this aggregate vector's trajectory through Word Space cuts through the middle of each of its components, exposing the semantic area they share while stripping away less-relevant terms and sometimes teasing out new connotations. The composite vector *square × foot* veers far away from *foot*'s military associations, focusing on terms of measurement, mathematics, and architecture.

Semantic similarity provides a distance function for the model, endowing its lexicon with the properties of a continuous metric space. Dominic Widdows explains, "Continuous methods enable us to model not only atoms of meaning such as words, but the space or void in between

THE COMPUTATION OF MEANING

these words. Whole passages of text are mapped to points of their own in this void, without changing the underlying shape of the space around them."[53] Thus, we can find meaning, not just in individual words, but between and among words as they're variously combined. Vector-space models use matrix operations to make these distinctions in extremely fine gradations. This process has the practical effect of decomposing the concept and exposing its various parts, but it does so while responding to the unthinkably various shades of difference that structure sublexical space. Words become, not merely "double," as Bakhtin suggested, but massively heterogeneous.

EEBO's Semantic Spaces
In what follows, I offer a brief guided tour through EEBO's semantic spaces by presenting a few select results from the model (figs. 2.8, 2.9, 2.10, 2.11). These keywords exemplify different kinds of semantic relatedness captured by vector-space models and show how such a model can be taken in subsets or otherwise manipulated to reveal contextually meaningful associations. What's remarkable, and what continues to astonish me (even if it no longer surprises me), is how well this kind of analysis works. Vector-space models capture word-use patterns in extremely fine detail—detail that is invariably lost when analyses are condensed down to mere "findings" in a research article. Instead, I'll offer a broad survey with lots of examples of gradually increasing complexity. My goal is simply to share with you what language looks like when subjected to this kind of rigorous formalization.

EEBO's Lexicon: A Few Keywords
Simple concepts tend to group together, not only with each other, but also with their larger categorical words. The term *black*, for example, correlates closely with other common colors, like *white*, *red*, *green*, and *yellow*, but it's also similar to *colour* in general. As you can see, vector-space models capture a very general kind of semantic relatedness. You don't just find synonyms. Instead, you find anything that tends to be talked about using the same words, which in practice often means in the same

Figure 2.8. Semantic Field of *black*.

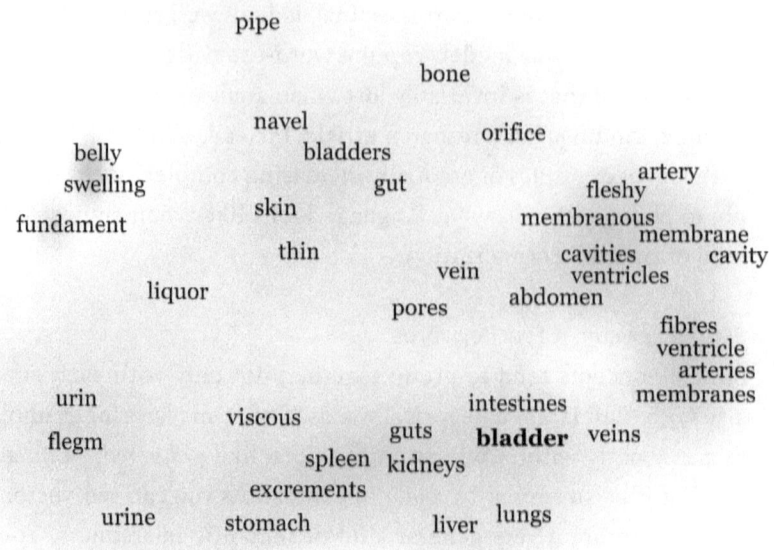

Figure 2.9. Semantic Field of *bladder*.

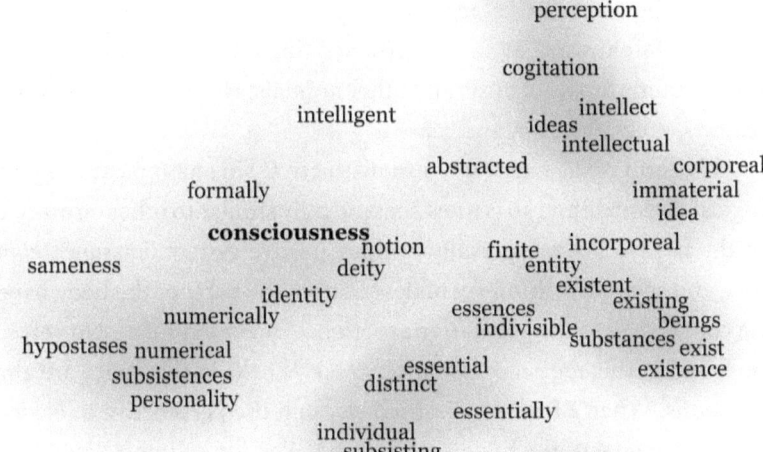

Figure 2.10. Semantic Field of *consciousness*.

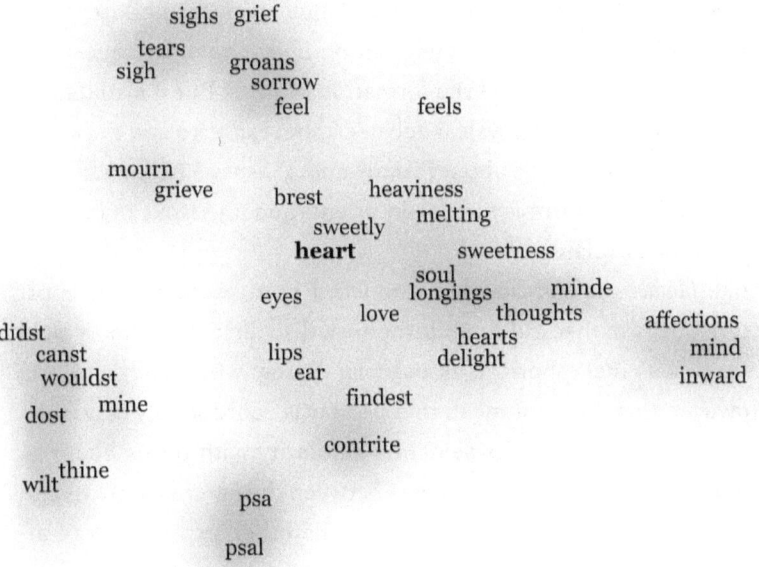

Figure 2.11. Semantic Field of *heart*.

sentences. In this case, we can ask, "What were early modern authors writing about when they mentioned colors?" Or, to put the same question a different way, "What is EEBO looking at?" The answer is surprisingly straightforward: birds and other animals. Notice context words like *feathers*, *wings*, *tail*, *hair*, and *claws*.

The term *bladder* appears most distinctively in anatomical and physiological discourse and so is most semantically similar to other terms related to the human body, especially in the digestive system (*intestines*, *kidneys*, *guts*, and *spleen*). At this level of description, the parts of the body have little connection to the subjective experience of embodiment. No verbs can be found in this region of semantic space. Words in this space are almost all nouns. When EEBO is glimpsed through the perspective of *bladder*, it reveals a model of the human body as a collection of interrelated organs. Those organs are defined, not by actions they perform, but by their inert suspension within a physiological system. The rich and highly specialized language of anatomical description thoroughly occupies the space.

Like the human body, the conscious mind was subject to rigorous description using a large and peculiar vocabulary. The term *consciousness* provides a point of entry into the complex language of the philosophy of the mind. Such discourse often centered on epistemological questions about *sensation*, *perception*, and the formation of *ideas*. But it also tended toward more general metaphysical debates about *existence* and *essence* as well as very basic questions about *identity* and *sameness*. Though associated with a *deity*, the term is secular in orientation and lacks many specifically sacred correlates.

Unlike *bladder* or *consciousness*, the word *heart* was not used most characteristically in medical or philosophical discourse. Its primary field of reference was metaphorical, associating closely with *mind*, *soul*, and *love*. However, this does not mean that *heart* was conceptually disassociated from the body; notice its semantic similarity with terms like *eyes*, *lips*, and *ear*. Its semantic field mediates between the *inward affections* and *thoughts* of the *mind*, on one side, and, on the other, expressions of affect that reveal *sorrow* to others through *sighs* and *tears*. The specifically intersubjective character of *heart* is suggested by its association with the pronouns *mine* and *thine* as well as with modal verbs that mediate among subject and predicate, and so also between self and other: *didst, canst, dost,* and *wilt.* Unlike *consciousness*, which was construed in more strictly epistemological and metaphysical terms, *heart* situates the self and the self's body in a social field of others.

EEBO's Lexicon: Semantic Decomposition

Vector-space models make it possible, not only to compare words but also to combine and recombine them in ways that expose their various parts. Concepts can be manipulated using simple arithmetic.

- Addition: Adding two vectors describes their union. It reveals the sum total of what the concepts have in common.
- Subtraction: Subtracting one vector from another describes the complement of two sets. It reveals what's left of a concept's many associations when the collocates of some related term are abstracted away.
- Multiplication: Multiplying two vectors identifies their intersection. It reveals what any two concepts have in common.

Consider another fairly simple example (fig. 2.12). Unlike anatomy and epistemology, zoology occupied a comparatively diffuse semantic region, more like the conceptual neighborhood of *heart*. We already know from the example of *black* that animals of different kinds were described using a common vocabulary, especially involving color. For this reason, the vectors of word collocations that make up animal concepts tend to be similar to each other, even across animals we might want to separate into different species or animal kingdoms. Seventeenth-century printed books did not accumulate a particularly distinctive vocabulary for categorizing animals, which tended to be grouped, not taxonomically, but contextually. For example, the term *frogs* was most distinctively used like *vermin* of various kinds, such as *flies, rats, snakes, locusts,* and other *insects*, but it was also similar to farm and woodland animals as well as birds.

To see what's distinctive about frogs, when compared to descriptions of other animals in EEBO, one need only subtract some other animal term from *frogs*. We can ask, "What does *frogs* minus *cats* equal?"

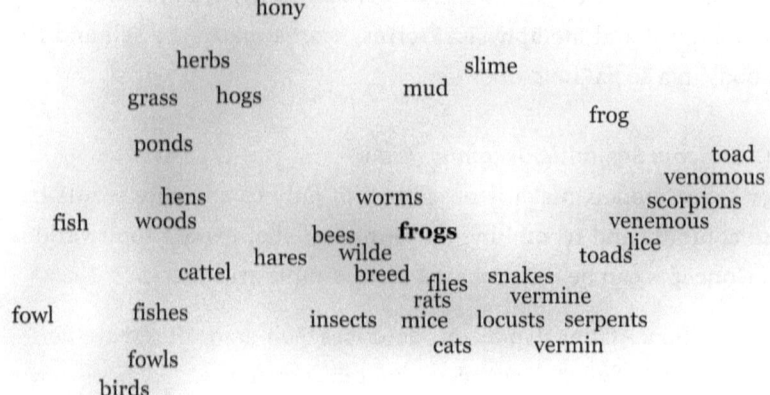
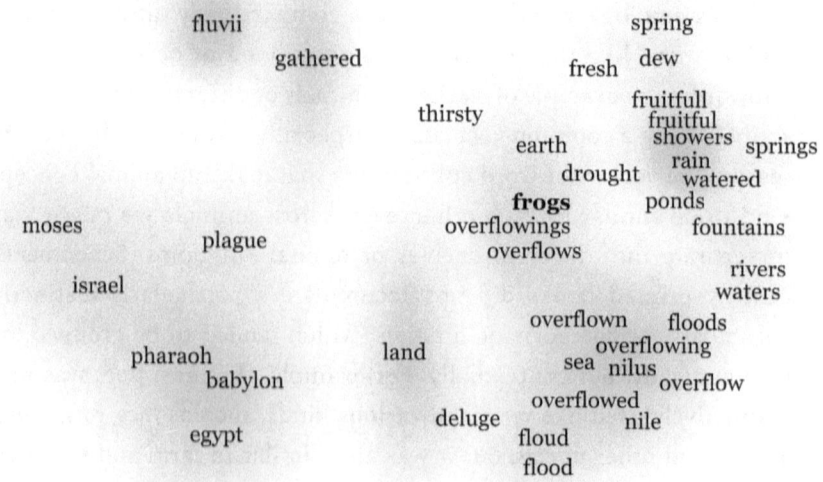

Figure 2.12. Semantic Field of *frogs* and *frogs – cats*.

It's a strange question, I admit. (But remember, digital humanists promised you we'd use computers to ask questions that couldn't be asked before. Well . . . *here you go!*) Subtracting *cats* from *frogs* is like saying, "Start with *frogs*, then take away any associations that are *cats*-like." This will take away all the color words, as well as all terms related to physical description like *skin, claws,* and so on. All those word collocations that made *frogs* similar to *cats* are eliminated. This composition abstracts away all discourse of animality to identify some aspect of *frogs*, as a concept, that exceeds animality. What would be left? The resulting vector focuses much more distinctly on the contexts within which frogs were construed. What you're left with isn't a depiction of frogs as one kind of vermin among others. Instead, you're left with water. What remains are words related to the places where frogs might be found. Notice terms like *rivers, ponds,* and *springs* as well as biblical figures featured in the plagues of the Old Testament. To think of animals without animality is to think ecologically.

Now allow me to turn to more serious examples (fig. 2.13). Semantic decomposition is an extraordinarily powerful tool for understanding how historical concepts relate to one another. Consider *jamaica*. Descriptions of places in the Americas are not very common throughout the EEBO corpus, so the semantic neighborhood of *jamaica* does not include a large lexicon peculiar to Jamaica as such. Instead, *jamaica* is most semantically similar to other terms that name geographically similar places, including other islands in the East and West Indies, such as *malacca, cuba, hispaniola,* and *sumatra*. Terms of geography, navigation, and colonial exploitation populate the space. References to the slave trade can be glimpsed in *jamaica*'s similarity to *guinea* and *plantations.*

What of *slave*? The *Oxford English Dictionary* lists as its first meaning of *slave*: "One who is the property of, and entirely subject to, another person, whether by capture, purchase, or birth; a servant completely divested of freedom and personal rights," while relegating other, less serious applications of the term to secondary meanings. The semantic field surrounding *slave* in EEBO (fig. 2.14) suggests how dangerous it is for scholars to trust sources like the *OED*. Those secondary meanings were

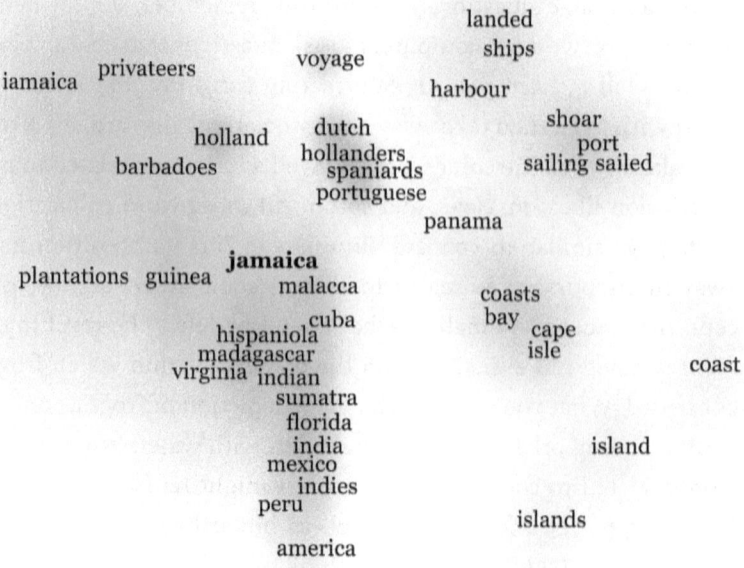

Figure 2.13. Semantic Field of *jamaica*.

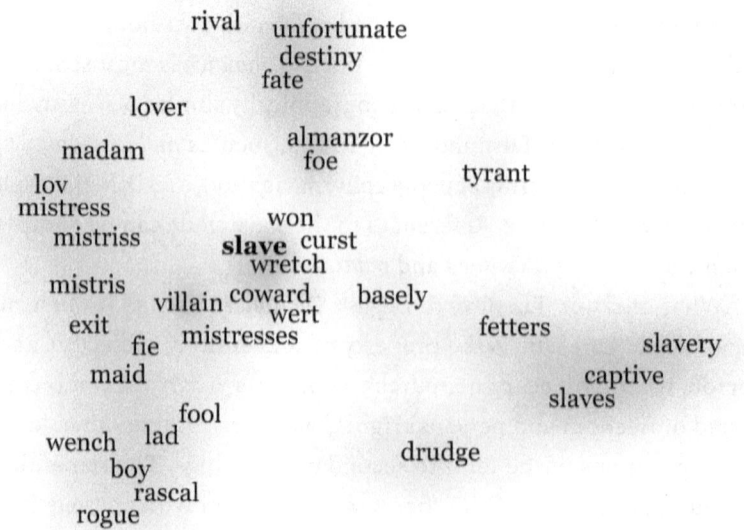

Figure 2.14. Semantic Field of *slave*.

in fact very common ones across the later seventeenth century, when *slave* was used most distinctively on stage as a term of abuse or flirtation. The terms most semantically similar to *slave* are epithets like *coward*, *wretch*, and *villain*, but it also appears near words like *mistress* and *madam*. The term *lov* is a variant of *love* that appears when the term is contracted (as in *lov'd*), suggesting that much of *slave*'s surrounding semantic field is driven by poetry. The term *almanzor* is the name of a character in John Dryden's heroic drama, *The Conquest of Granada* (1672), further suggesting that the lexicon of slavery in the seventeenth century was primarily literary, not political. At bottom, *slave* was a literary concept that provided a conceptually weak but highly stylized moral frame for describing power relations among men as well as between such men and similarly stylized women. The concept remained almost entirely disconnected from the Atlantic slave trade and colonialism.

Almost, but not completely. Although the most prominent conceptual associations with *jamaica* are geographical, and those with *slave* involve banter among fictional men and women, these concepts overlap inside a highly specialized region in EEBO's semantic whole: terms related to money and commodity exchange (fig. 2.15). However, even here, one finds strangely little evidence for descriptions of slavery as a social institution. Notice in particular that terms in this space suggest little or no reference to life among enslaved persons, neither their experiences nor their bodies. There is no awareness of race, nation, or gender. Everything we might associate with personhood is stripped away. Instead, discussion entirely centers on the abstractions of money and the exchange of goods and commodities. When EEBO is talking about Jamaica and about slaves, EEBO is talking in the language of money.

These results underscore the near-total disregard English writers and readers had for the emerging institution of Atlantic slavery as anything other than a specialized instance of capital exchange. Although it's possible to take individual publications out of context to show that the slave trade forced some early modern writers to grapple with questions of race—as, for example, scholars use Aphra Behn's highly idiosyncratic *Oroonoko*—in truth, few people in England noticed. This disregard should not be surprising, exactly, but nonetheless I find it quite jarring.

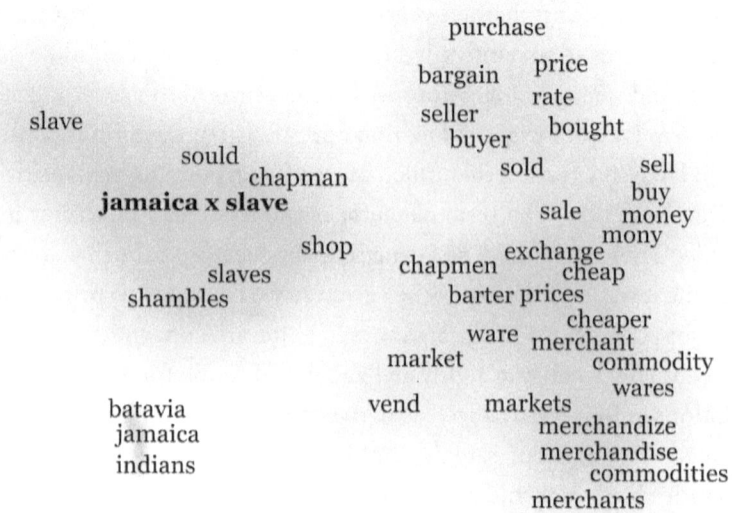

Figure 2.15. Semantic Field of *jamaica × slave*.

Gender concepts appear in the corpus with particular clarity. After removing all associations with the most common terms for male social roles, *husband*, *father*, and *son*, what remains of *man* is a highly abstract representation of personhood (fig. 2.16). Latin terms cluster nearby, inherited from specialized textbooks in anatomy and law. But the bulk of this space is occupied by terms related to the *mind*, the *senses*, and *rational judgment* and *understanding*. What's left of *man*, when abstracted from all sociality, is an entity that judges and thinks—genderless *man* decides what it deems *reasonable*, *impossible*, *difficult*, *ridiculous*, *ignorant*, *vulgar*, or *profitable*.

This semantic field differs very sharply from the field surrounding a similar decomposition of *woman*. After removing all associations with the most common terms for female social roles, *wife*, *mother*, and *daughter*, what remains of *woman* bears little resemblance to any concept of personhood (fig. 2.17). Like the decomposition of *man*, this decomposed vector also appears near Latin terms of anatomy, but whereas abstracted

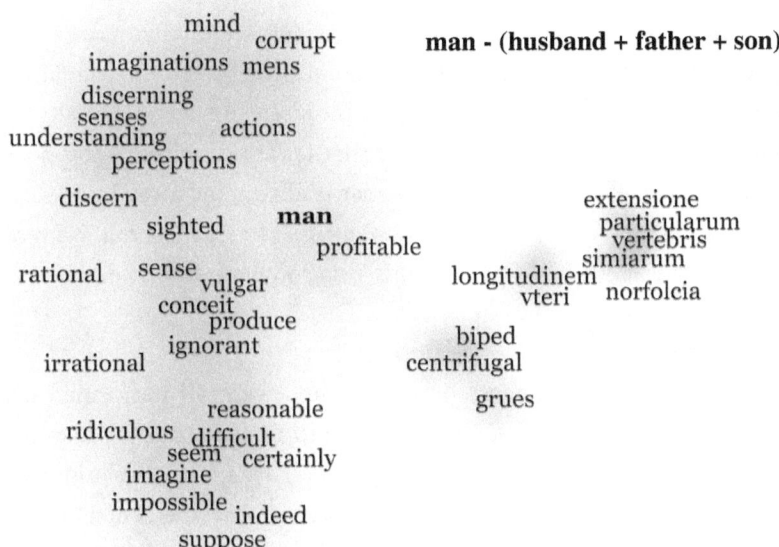

Figure 2.16. Semantic Field of man – (husband + father + son).

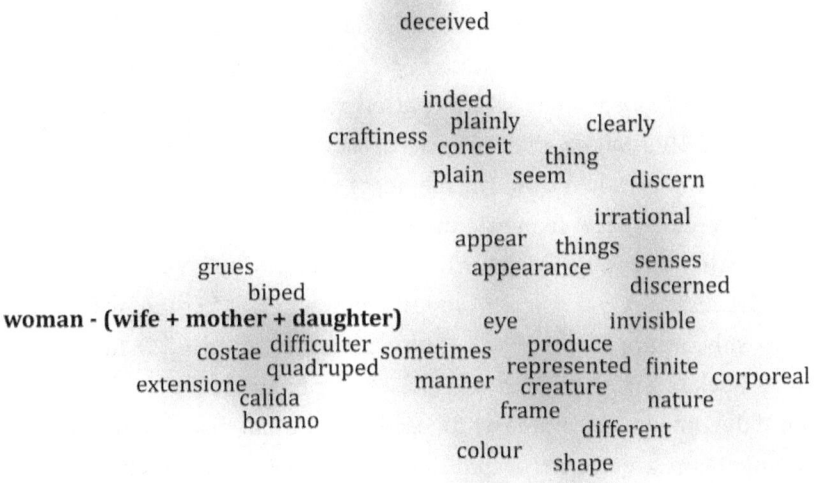

FIGURE 2.17. Semantic Field of woman – (wife + mother + daughter).

man was semantically similar to *mind* and *action*, what remains of *woman* is most like *thing* and *things*, defined on one side by their *appearance* in *colour* and *shape* and, on the other, by their *conceit* and *craftiness*. Tellingly, the term *woman* no longer even appears in the vicinity of the decomposed vector. What's left of *woman* after gender is abstracted away looks nothing like a person. All that's left is a *creature* in *nature*; a *thing* that is *irrational* and *corporeal*. In EEBO, *man* is *discerning*; *woman*, *discerned*.

EEBO's Lexicon: Conceptual Nonstationarity

The semantic measurements described here were all performed over the entirety of the EEBO-TCP corpus, 1640 to 1699. But it's also possible to take subsets of the corpus and to analyze lexical relationships that exist only within parts of the whole. Remember, the central insight of vector semantics is the distributional hypothesis, which holds that similar words tend to appear in similar contexts. This suggests that the local contexts of individual terms—the five-token windows used in the model—will themselves differ from one place to another in the corpus. Concepts don't exist in a single place. They will appear more frequently in some places than others, and they will also appear in differing relations to each other. The word *lord* will appear frequently in both sermons and parliamentary debates, but it will have very different collocates in each context. I use the phrase *conceptual nonstationarity* to describe the tendency of concepts to exhibit variation across large, heterogenous corpora like EEBO. Such variation exists across many possible axes of difference that can be taken from the metadata.

The vector-space semantic model can be used to support readings by situating a text against multiple subcorpora. Consider John Locke's *Two Treatises of Government* (A48901). Such analysis begins by identifying a subcorpora made of the 100 documents from EEBO most similar to Locke's *Treatises*. Because Locke's vocabulary is highly distinctive, these documents are similarly focused on political discussion: included among them are works by politicians, theorists, and polemicists like Robert Filmer, Algernon Sidney, Thomas Hobbes, Matthew Tindal, and others. These associations suggest in broad outline a picture that should be immediately familiar: when he published the *Treatises* Locke joined a dense body of political debate while intervening in particular around a set of unusually focused key concepts.

To understand the nature of that intervention, measures of semantic similarity can be triangulated between Locke's *Treatises*, the subcorpus of contemporary political discussion, and the larger corpus that stands as a proxy for the period as a whole. The details of these calculations don't really matter in this context—these measurements all just riff on semantic similarity and term frequency.[54] In each case, the key step is to measure the vector for a word as represented in the subcorpus, then compare it to uses of the same word over either a different subcorpus or over the collection as a whole. This tells you how distinctively any concept operates within a given domain, and it allows for highly detailed examinations of individual cases through comparison and contrast. In exactly the same way that *frogs - cats* returns what's peculiar about *frogs*, comparing Locke to his contemporaries allows you to specify how the *Treatises* contribute to EEBO's total semantic space.

Paraphrasing over table 2.1, we can say that the *Treatises* discuss how *power* and *authority* operate in a *government* among *men*, and that Locke addresses this topic by focusing in particular on the *natural* or *original* grounds of *authority*, as inherited from *Adam* or acquired through *property*. Locke joins a field of political discussion that, itself, had long debated sovereignty and legislative power, as they are tested in states of nature and states of war. Against this general discourse of natural law, Locke's *Treatises* stand out for their sustained attention to the domestic family as a unit of analysis, especially on the relationships among *children* and fathers.

Over EEBO as a whole, the term *children* is closely associated with education, domestic care, concerns over legitimacy, and echoes of biblical myth (fig. 2.18). Not so in Locke's *Treatises*. There, *children* is further from *moloch* and much closer to *grotius*; they are *begotten* by *parents* who confront the question of what might *reasonably* and naturally be limited, delegated, divided, and *owed* among them. Locke's children are entities in thought experiments about the distribution of power and property in

Table 2.1. Contextualizing Locke's *Two Treatises* Using a Vector-Space Model. Calculations were performed using the same keyword-in-context model already described, measured over each document (or group of documents) separately.

Documents most similar to Locke's *Two Treatises*	Similarity
A. Sidney, *Discourses concerning government* (A60214)	0.76
R. Filmer, *The free-holders grand inquest* (A41303)	0.73
R. Filmer, *Observations concerning ... forms of government* (A41307)	0.73
H. Parker, *A discourse ... concerning the right of subiects* (A56187)	0.71
T. Goddard, *Plato's demon, or, The state-physician unmaskt* (A42895)	0.71

Keywords in Locke's *Two Treatises*	
Most persistently conventional	power, government, right, authority, men
Most persistently deviant (from EEBO)	heir, adams, natural, property, original
Most persistently deviant (from peer corpus)	state, children, adam, father, adams

the commonwealth. Indeed, this semantic reconfiguration of *children* is an important hinge on which his argument turns.

We can also "zoom out" to focus on an author's works over their entire career. There are forty-five documents in EEBO where Behn's name appears as first author. Within that subcorpus, many of the most distinctively used words reflect abbreviations of the names of characters from her plays: *gall*, *tim*, and *pat*. This is a common and harmless artifact of semantic analyses when applied to drama. The other terms, though—*devil*, *soft*, *vows*, and *maid*—point fairly directly to her abiding concern with femininity and sexual ethics. Figure 2.19 shows how the terms *vows* and *devil* are distributed in the semantic space of Behn's works: *vows* sits at the center of amatory entanglements, while *devil* indicates, not a concern with supernatural beings, but a language of masculine banter, common in her plays, that invokes an altogether different perspective on the sexual politics of oath-making and swearing. From the perspective of

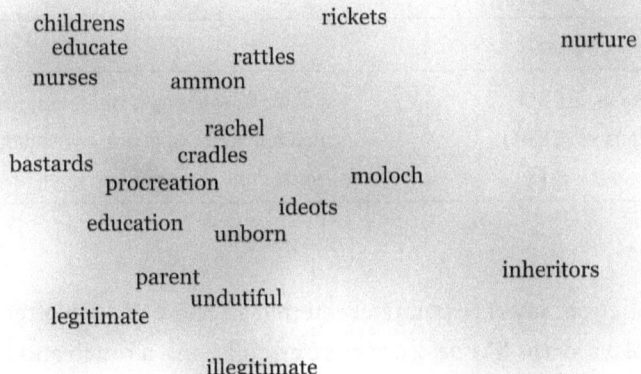
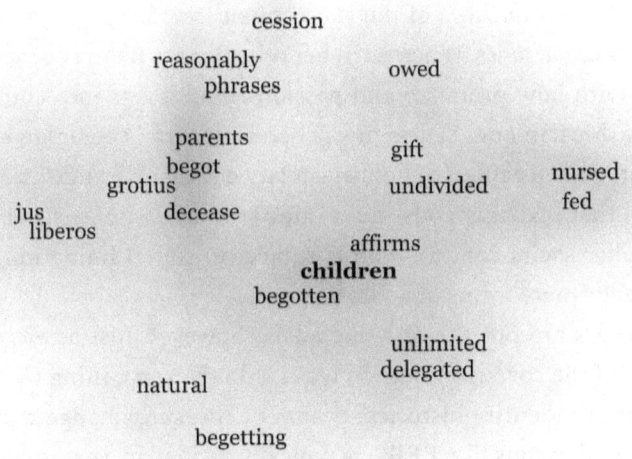

Figure 2.18. Terms Most Similar to *children*. Semantic similarity is computed over all of EEBO (*top*) and when limited to Locke's *Two Treatises* (*bottom*).

Table 2.2. Semantic Deviance in Aphra Behn's Fiction. Keywords were extracted by identifying the most persistently deviant word vectors in Behn's works collectively and in *Love Letters between a Nobleman and His Sister* (1684) particularly. Both subcorpora are compared to EEBO as a whole then against each other.

Keywords in Aphra Behn's works	
All works vs. EEBO	gall, devil, soft, vows, maid, tim, pat
Love Letters vs. EEBO	madam, business, lovers, gay, maid, charming
Letters vs. all works	times, thousand, soul, sex, read, love, even

Behn's fiction, *vows* are putatively eternal affective ties too often undone; in her plays, oaths like *devil* are mere ejaculations, a rough and ready language of homosocial exchange that structures male relationships fragmented by sexual rivalry. In *Love Letters between a Nobleman and His Sister* (A27301), Behn's interests revolve more centrally on the conditions of romantic address and critical judgment. When triangulated against Behn's works and all of EEBO, terms in *Love Letters* that stand out reflect an overriding concern with time and repetition, as, through the epistolary mode, abstract anchors of the subject (*soul, sex, love*) are *read* and pored over a *thousand times*. Whereas in her other works Behn is concerned primarily with how promises and passions bind lovers into compromised relationships, in *Love Letters* this general concern is complemented with another: we see echoes of how epistolary exchange brings into focus the illusion that sexuality constitutes one's true self, who exists in time outside of her social context, who is subject to self-examination, and who transcends mere forms of address.

Authors are not the only metadata, however. Just as we can select subsets of the corpus by author, we can do the same thing with publication date to identify historical events or measure change over time. A book-based corpus like EEBO is typically divided by year, so we can create sixty unique arrays measuring word collocation for every year, 1640 to 1699. We can then compare how each word is used each year against the whole, to find in what years any term is used in unusual ways.

Consider the words *oates* and *management*, as pictured in figures 2.20 through 2.22. The word *oates* was a fairly common alternate spelling for

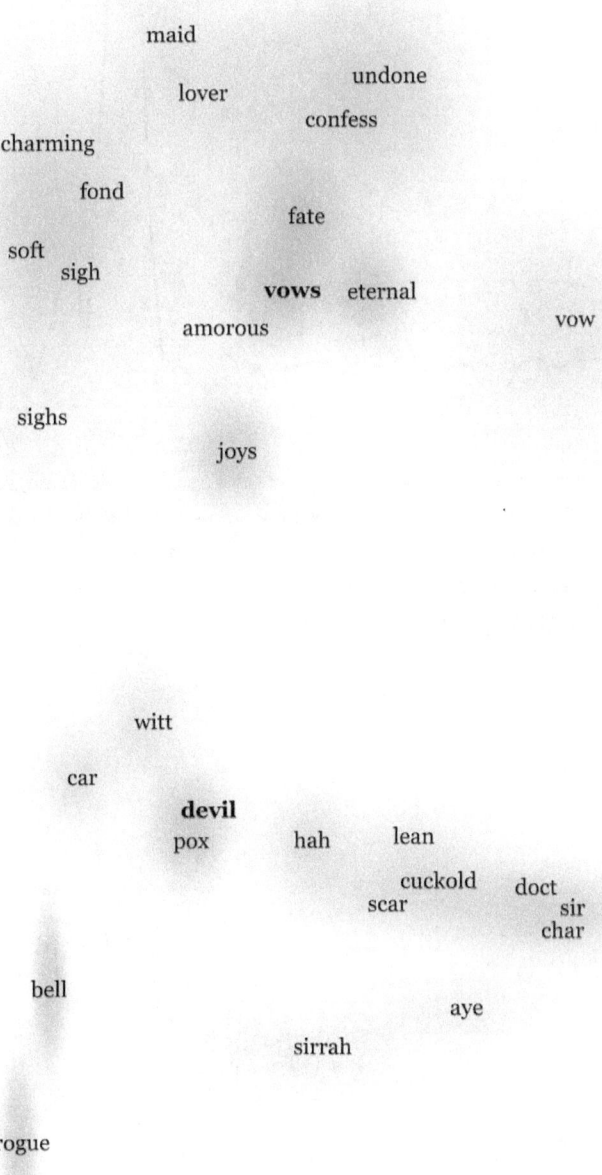

Figure 2.19. Semantic Similarity in Behn's Works. Terms most similar to *vows* (*top*) and *devil* (*bottom*) in a subcorpus of Aphra Behn's novels and plays.

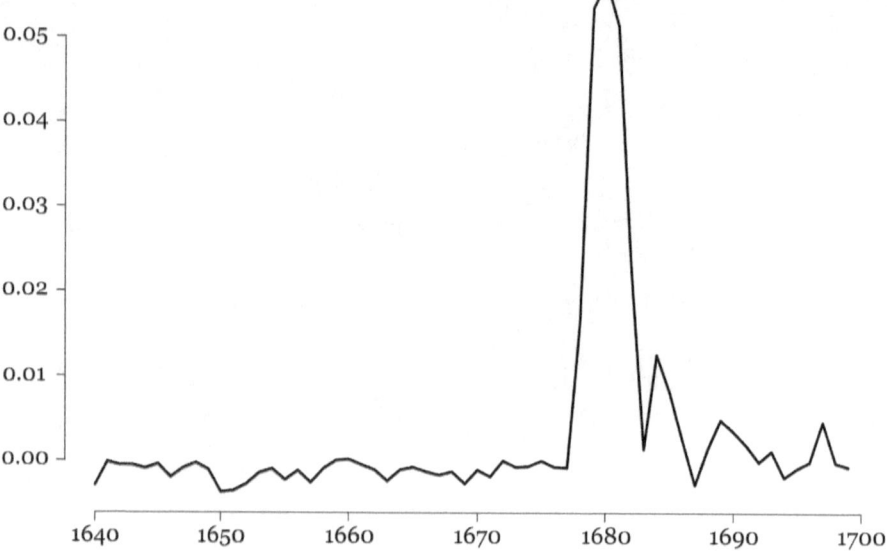

Figure 2.20. Topicality of *oates*, 1640 to 1699. Topicality is a single metric showing years when a word is used with below-average deviance (years when the word means something closest to its total meaning) and above-average frequency (measured in this case as the proportion of titles published that year that use the word). Titus Oates was a central figure in the Popish Plot, a major political scandal in England from 1679 through 1681.

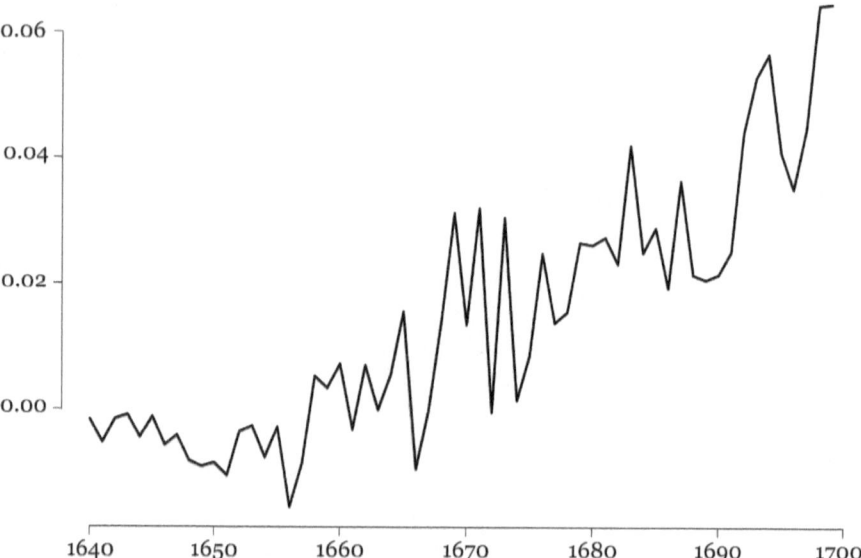

Figure 2.21. Topicality of *management*, 1640 to 1699. This graph shows an example of a gradual transition that accrues meaning over time. Whereas terms like *oates* are closely connected to specific events, terms like *management* shift through a more diffuse process.

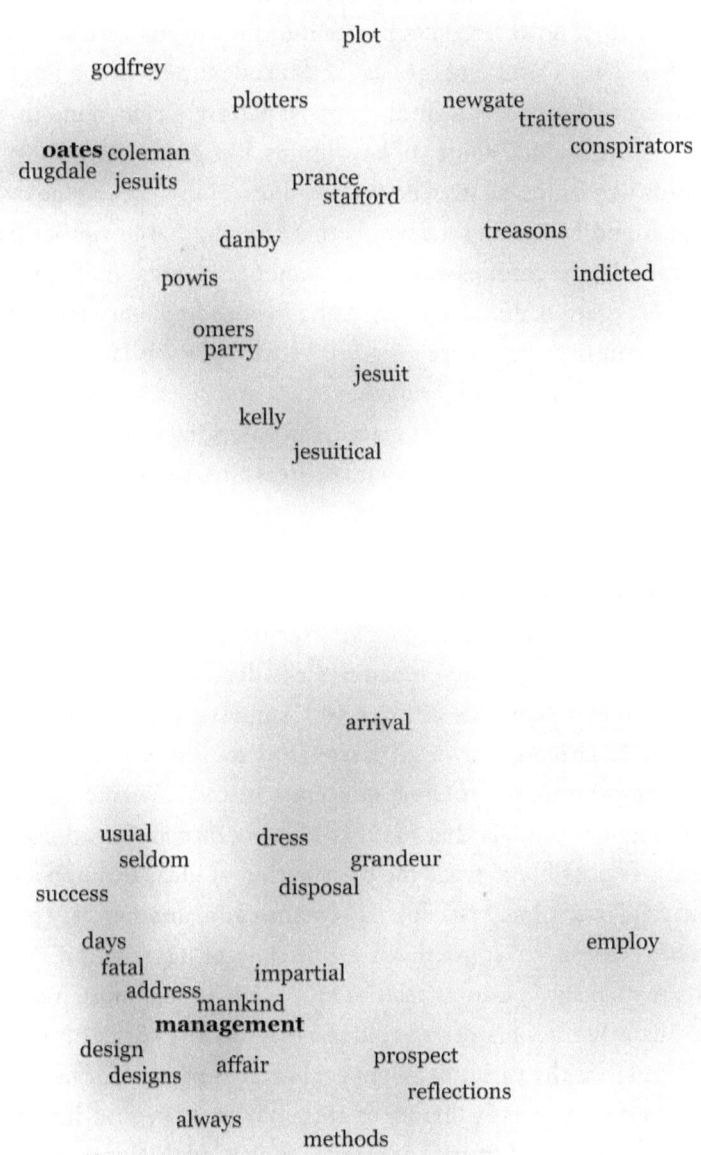

Figure 2.22. Temporal Similarities among Words. Similarity measurements over a matrix of the distribution of topicality over time to *oates* (*top*) and *management* (*bottom*). These words exhibit above-average frequency and below-average semantic deviance during the same years.

oats, without the "e," and so it's used sporadically for the first few decades. In 1679, however, *oates* bursts into the corpus with a new meaning when Titus Oates emerges as the central witness in the Popish Plot. Other terms that follow a similar topical pattern all surround this event; among these include names of key figures, like *godfrey* and *danby* as well as words like *jesuits*, *plotters*, and *conspirators*. Similarly, change over time can be found by looking for words that rise and fall in similar patterns. For example, the term *management* is among the most modern concepts of the Restoration, gradually increasing in both frequency and coherence over the century's last three decades. Terms with similar topical arcs include *impartial*, *reflections*, *methods*, *success*, and *designs*—all words related to the exercise of critical judgment in an emerging public sphere. Of the concepts inherited by readers and writers in London at the year 1700, these are the new ones.

Conclusion: The Model Works Because the Theory behind It Is True

Finding events and tracing change over time are just two possible extended applications. Once meanings are decomposed, they can be recomposed along any axis of interest. Combined with metadata, vector-space models become powerful explanatory tools that could be applied to almost any question of interest in literary history. When combined with social-network models that identify clusters of people and documents, it becomes possible to trace the distribution of ideas through a complex social field over time.[55] Geospatial semantics are another very promising area of research.[56] Geography is a principle of aggregation that transforms textual space into terrestrial space. Historians more interested in specifically literary histories could use this model to discover genres and to characterize the variation of concepts across literary forms. Critics focused on syntax and the history of grammar could begin with a different matrix structure that targets grammatical features.[57] Nor does the theory depend on any particular notion of historical periodization. Although the examples provided in this chapter all treat the later seventeenth century as the primary frame, corpora could be devised around any category of critical interest. The only requirement is that analysis begins with a large, heterogenous corpus that adequately represents the various uses of most words. (This is the reason, by the way, that most demonstrations of "distant reading" fail to produce compelling results. If your corpus is limited to a few hundred poems, plays, or novels, you can't capture the semantic complexity of each term, no matter how creative your analysis.)

I offered so many examples here because doing so is really the only way to communicate the broad field of application for computational semantics within intellectual history. Whether you're interested in the history of legal thought, Aphra Behn's fictions, the Popish Plot, or the animality of frogs, the model performs well. Anywhere you look, it successfully captures how the source documents describe their world, both in broad strokes across the corpus and in fine detail when applied to a particular word or document. Put another way: *the model works because the theory behind it is true.*

And what is that theory? The demonstrations are all offered in service of my larger argument that a fundamental continuity exists among very different ways of thinking about language, from Julia Kristeva's theory of intertextuality to computational semantics as it developed in the fields of machine translation and information retrieval. Kristeva provides the basic theoretical foundation. Her adaptation of Mikhail Bakhtin's notion of "the primordial dialogism of discourse" proposed a spatial logic for meaning, such that all uses of a word and their various textual combinations could be described mathematically as a single, simultaneously existing structure. In the fields of machine translation and information retrieval, Margaret Masterman, H. P. Luhn, Gerard Salton, and others developed protocols for automatic language processing that rested on very similar principles. Word instances would function as minimal units, providing points of connection that bind together a vast matrix of intertextual relations. The key insight these scholars shared was to view words as part of an algebraic system. Every word entails latent connections with the others, and these connections make possible their meaningful recombination in human discourse. Every word in every text is a node connecting that text to a larger network of language, where the word appears in many variations that supervene over every particular use. Computational semantics embrace intertextuality's basic ideas while grounding them in empirically observable units and thus lending that theory greater precision and analytical power.

Semantic similarity is measured as proximity within the multidimensional space of a corpus. This measurement provides a robustly theorized proxy for what is less precisely called "meaning." Every combination of words is a reconfiguration of vectors measured over the entire corpus. This mathematical procedure concretizes Bakhtin's theory of dialogism. Every word is double: both an instance in a sequence and a vector over a corpus, both a token and a type. Every word exists vertically as the aggregate of all its uses; every text operates horizontally by combining these aggregates in unique ways. Rather than a collection of tokens or a sequence of characters, a text is an ordered recombination of each word's otherwise-existing intertextual connections. Because these connections are both highly complex and relatively easy to generalize over, they provide accurate and detailed descriptions of the corpus and thereby capture meaningful relations across the archive, even though semantic similarity has little in common with the subjective experience—the feeling—of understanding someone else's discourse.

One major ambition of this book, and of this chapter in particular, is to show how we might reconcile theories of the text and styles of knowledge that developed across radically different disciplinary domains. If we step back and contrast Julia Kristeva with Gerard Salton, it's hard to think of two more different scholars. In the mid-1960s, when Kristeva was attending Barthes's seminar in Paris, Salton was helping found the first department of computer science at Cornell. Their careers would only diverge further. Yet, both were concerned with understanding the structure of discourse "at its deepest level" (Kristeva's phrase) and both, in pursuit of that concern, landed on strikingly similar models of language. Indeed, when considered from a sufficient level of abstraction, the two are achingly close.

It's perhaps interesting, then, to speculate about how and why the gap that separated them remained insuperable, even at a conceptual level. Why could these ideas never link up? Part of the reason might have been that Kristeva's proposed science of semiotics remained stubbornly on the outside of linguistics as such. In an early essay, she wrote:

> The theory of meaning now stands at a crossroad: either it will remain an attempt at formalizing meaning-systems by increasing sophistication of the logico-mathematical tools which enable it to formulate models on the basis of a conception (already rather dated) of meaning as the act of a transcendental ego, cut off from its body, its unconscious and also its history; or else it will attune itself to the theory of the speaking subject as a divided subject (conscious/unconscious) and go on to attempt to specify the types of operation characteristic of the two sides of this split, thereby exposing them to those forces extraneous to the logic of the systematic.[58]

Kristeva believed that linguistics had up to that point contributed very little to a theory of meaning. The sign-concept-referent triad was held together by fictionalized subjects who could effortlessly match signs to concepts, but only when they were considered without any human specificity as "transcendental egos." Kristeva imagined a science of language that would reach in a different direction by analyzing "forces extraneous" to the system, breaking up the unicity of the speaking subject and reconceiving meaning through the paradigm of psychoanalysis. For her, the study of language had to move in one direction or another.

In retrospect, we can see that in the 1960s the study of language was poised at a very different crossroad, one that Kristeva was in no position to recognize. The practical task of developing computer systems to infer meaning from a corpus required articulating a theory of language that was resolutely empirical and expressed through the formal language of mathematics. Decades later, in an essay titled "Dimensions of Meaning," computer scientist Hinrich Schütze wrote:

> Representations and processes tend to go hand in hand; the way knowledge is represented largely fixes appropriate processes and vice versa. The novel approach to semantic representation presented here, an approach made possible by the availability of supercomputers to

linguistic research, may thus lead to theories of semantics that look very different from today's.[59]

Schütze had no way of knowing that a theory of meaning very appropriate to his methods already existed and had, in fact, long circulated outside linguistics among scholars of literature and culture. The Sokal Hoax happened just a few years later, and the gap that separated these lines of inquiry only widened.

The result was one of the greatest missed opportunities in the history of literary studies. Whether this miscommunication negatively affected the information sciences, I won't presume to say. But it has left the humanities—including but not limited to the digital humanities—decades behind the curve. Over the last forty years, the most exciting and important advancements in our understanding of language have come, not from departments of literature or linguistics, but from across campus in colleges of engineering and computing. Literature professors missed the boat entirely.

Yet, Schütze's comment about "representations" and "processes" suggests a more optimistic and hopeful take. How we think and talk about knowledge is profoundly affected by what we can do with that knowledge, and vice versa. In her reading of Bakhtin, Kristeva had a representation but no corresponding process, so she had no way of putting her theory to work empirically except through her training and practice as a psychoanalyst. The only procedures available to literary scholars were criticism and close reading. Crude tools, those, for minds unable to escape themselves. Now, new kinds of evidence have thrust computational procedures to the forefront of scholars' attention. One challenge we now face, and which this chapter has hoped to address, is to develop an adequate vocabulary for representing the knowledge gained through computational processes. Maybe I'm wrong to see this story as a tale of missed opportunity. Perhaps that feeling of belatedness is really the ache of opportunity newly open?

CHAPTER 3
CONCEPTUAL TOPOGRAPHY

PEOPLE DESCRIBE PLACES. They talk and write about their homes, their cities, their nations, their worlds. When they do, they fill those places with meaning and memory. Michel de Certeau wrote that places are "fragmentary and inward-turning histories."[1] They're palimpsests of stories through which we move and in which we live every moment. In writing, places are layered with sediments of the past, but they're also alive with language. What geographers call the sense of place has a rich and exquisite lexicon. Think of all the words that have been written to describe the skylines of New York or Hong Kong, the coasts of the Mediterranean, the towns of ancient Judea, or the islands of the Pacific. Our ideas spread over the Earth and surround us like invisible, noiseless clouds. Our world is a world of words.

To say that places have meanings is for this reason also to say, in a rather roundabout way, that space structures meaning, that words have a spatial component. Think of anything you can think of, from video games to apple trees, from railroads to coral reefs to human rights. Our ideas about what things are can't be disentangled from our implicit assumptions about where they are, whether or not they're tied to a single location. Just as the sense of place is expressed through words, so too the senses of words are informed by the places of their expression and their reference, by the spaces in which the stories of their being unfold. Words are proper to the places of their expression. *Language dwells.*

In the discipline of geography, the sense of place is often contrasted with a narrower concept of location.[2] Location is taken to be mathematical and therefore scientific. A sense of place is subjective and bound up in language and so should be studied humanistically. Perhaps more than any other discipline, geography straddles the qualitative and quantitative divide in its very self-conception. "What the map cuts up," Certeau argued, "the story cuts across."[3] Places are marked with pins on a map, but as bearers of history they're impossible to pin down. The essence of geographical thinking is to reason across this apparent contradiction.

In the twenty-first century, we've developed new ways to think through this contradiction. With computers, quantitative methods intrude more deeply into all aspects of humanistic inquiry. A technique called *textual geography* or *geospatial semantics* provides a quantitative framework for studying the language of place.[4] Its basic method is disarmingly simple: just count the words used to describe different places. With a bit of creativity and a few statistical tricks, we can now precisely measure the vocabulary of geographical description. The nebulous fields of meaning associated with places can be charted and analyzed like any aspect of physical geography.

Meaning is distributed unevenly across geographical space. Places will have distinct *semantic profiles*: the hills of Napa Valley will be described using a different lexicon from the hills of Appalachia. Words segregate—they'll have distinct *semantic footprints*. The word *cactus* will be used to describe many of the same places where lizards are also mentioned but where few people remark upon oysters or jet skis. Together, these principles suggest that places exert a kind of conceptual gravity on language. Because the meanings of words can't be disentangled from the

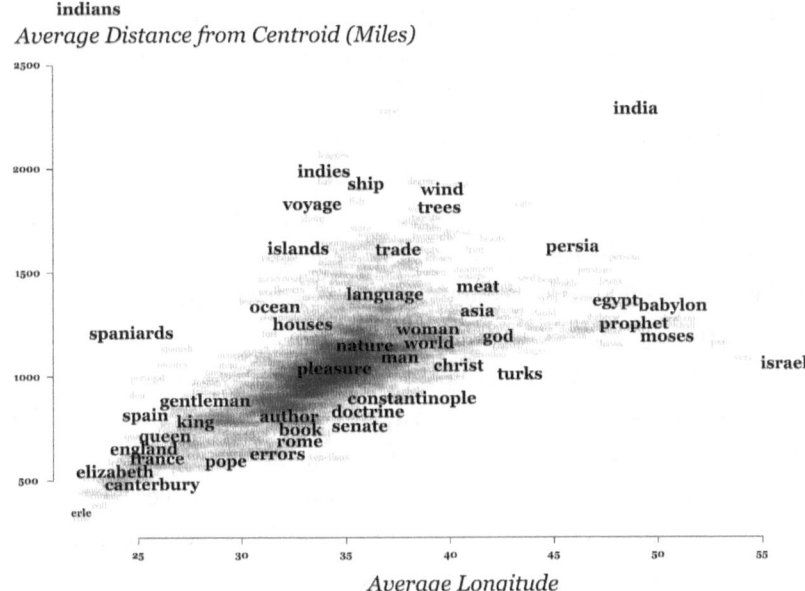

Figure 3.1. Geographical Spread of 2,000 Keywords in EEBO. Terms are plotted based on the geographical locations mentioned in books that use each word. The x-axis represents the average longitudinal position (west to east) of mentioned places. The y-axis represents the average distance of those places from that centroid.

spaces of lived experience, geography has an invisible conceptual structure and concepts have an invisible physical geography.

Figure 3.1 offers a first glance at EEBO's conceptual topography. The words of the corpus sort spatially. Some associate closely with England; they sit far to the west and tend to cluster in local spaces. By contrast, terms associated with biblical antiquity stretch EEBO far to the east, where the myths of ancient Israel and Egypt provided constant points of reference. Between these poles and above them, a discourse of the emerging world system of Europe, as well as of global exploration and trade, structures the rest.

This isn't a map in the conventional sense. What does conceptual topography measure? We might call it the "lexical production of space" by way of analogy to what Henri Lefebvre called the "social production of space."[5] Rather than conceive space as a fixed and empty field occupied by human society, Lefebvre argued that space is, in and of itself, produced through social relations, especially labor relations. The space of a city, a nation, or a trade network comes into being through the activity that manifests and stipulates it. Spaces are both physical realities and representational concepts that designate regions, demarcate boundaries, and govern the movements of people and goods. Lefebvre advanced this argument in the context of work by scholars like Fernand Braudel and Immanuel Wallerstein, who traced the evolution and expansion of a "world-economy" emanating from Europe, with the sixteenth and seventeenth centuries as a crucial period of transition.[6] Lefebvre emphasized the spatial components of this process, arguing that different labor relations in the world system produced different spatial configurations, from the alleys of medieval towns to the vast network of trade in commodities.[7]

The social production of this world system left a heavy imprint on the cultural record. In this chapter, I'll report results from a study of geographical place names in the EEBO corpus. When I analyze the collection, I'll focus on one key data point—something so simple it's almost scandalous—that is, how often the name of any place appears in the same book as any other word. For example, the word *gentleman* was most often associated with places in England and western Europe, while *prophet* tended to appear in books about Israel and Egypt. As figure 3.1 suggests, we can calculate these geographical biases quite precisely. Aggregated across thousands of places and thousands of words, we can draw in outline the contours of early modern geographical thought and so map its conceptual topography.

Early print, I'll argue, communicates an idea of the world, which isn't so much a single idea as a network of interrelated concepts that unfold over multiple layers. Often, these spaces look like the world Wallerstein, Braudel, and Lefebvre describe. They include nation-states, the built environments of towns and cities, domestic homes, and the global trade in commodities. Other spaces are somewhat harder for economic historians to account for: the spaces of the body, of the heavens, or of antiquity. Ultimately, I offer a parable of the ideological work needed to create what Jean-Luc Nancy called the "sense of the world."[8] In early modern print, that sense was fundamentally geographical—to be in the world was to be suspended among its places, and these places in turn structured spatial experience in all aspects and across all scales, all unfolding simultaneously within a coherently rendered system of expression.

Historical Background: Early Modern World Geography
The history of early modern world geography is one of the best-known topics in the humanities. It's also, I'll argue, profoundly misunderstood. While working on this chapter, my own sense of how early modern writers conceived the world was completely transformed. For this reason, I want to set aside theoretical exposition of the kind featured in the previous two case studies—I'll eschew discussion of spatial autocorrelation as a concept in geographic theory—and instead I'll review the background of the historical issues. My thinking on this topic came out of the quantitative analyses I'll present here, but before turning to those analyses I want to clear some common ground for interpreting the data.

The sixteenth and seventeenth centuries were an extraordinary time for geographical writing in Europe. Voyages across the Atlantic forced a massive revision in the world's topology. Instead of three continents—Europe, Africa, and Asia—a fourth had been discovered. The authority of ancient geographers like Ptolemy and Strabo were fundamentally compromised, and so the tasks of translating, publishing, and revising classical geography became urgent intellectual priorities—an important forerunner to the scientific revolution.[9] New maps and new books gave new shape to the world, ushering in a globalized era of unprecedented intellectual energy and colonial violence. Europe, too, had been changing for a long time.[10] As far back as the twelfth and thirteenth centuries, sea trade increased all along its coastlines, from the Baltic and North Sea to the Mediterranean. Commercial and cultural activities flowed through increasingly urban centers where tradespeople and merchants did more and more business.[11] Routes of travel improved and news traveled quickly, first by courier and letter and eventually in printed newsbooks.[12] European cities and towns became connected in a vast network of commodities, goods, and information. Faith in the power of a unified Christian political system was shaken. In 1453, the Ottoman Empire conquered Constantinople. In 1527, Rome was sacked. The Reformation quickly followed. A new European order emerged. Rather than principalities and minor fiefdoms joined in loose, shifting confederations, Europe came to be separated into something like modern nations—into culturally and linguistically distinct regions with sovereign monarchical authority over commerce conducted in their cities and towns.[13] This new vision of Europe would be codified in the Peace of Westphalia in 1648.

Further, economic and agricultural systems changed. (Because the sources I'll draw from in this chapter are all in English, my comments here focus in particular on England, but variations on this story with somewhat different chronologies could be told of other European nations.) The growth of towns across England depended on corresponding changes in the English countryside. Land enclosures carved traditional farming communities into areas of individually held property. Agricultural improvement and aristocratic estates transformed the English landscape to maximize productivity and profit.[14] Every part of England was subject to detailed measurement and description as country gentry—both new money and old—increasingly defined the lands over which they exerted authority as something else: ownable and saleable property.[15] While Spanish and Portuguese sailors were off discovering new worlds, back home England was cultivating itself as the world's first modern capitalist economy.

These massive cultural changes in the world system could not have happened without corresponding changes in the language of place. The early modern discourses of empire, nation, and capital are inextricable from changes in how people thought and wrote about the spaces they shared. Among the most innovative publications were travel narratives. Books like Richard Hakluyt's *Principal Navigations, Voyages, Traffics, and Discoveries of the English Nation* (1589) and Samuel Purchas's *Hakluytus Posthumus or Purchas His Pilgrimage* (1625) provided epic narratives of adventure, as English sailors, merchants, and privateers increasingly competed with their Spanish and Portuguese rivals. Travel books were written by pilgrims, merchants, colonialists, and ambassadors as well as by pirates and their captives.[16]

Closer to home, histories and geographical descriptions of Britain's counties and towns surveyed the nation in increasing detail. William Camden's magisterial chorography, *Britannia* (1586), gathered maps and prose descriptions of English towns, cities, and parishes. These descriptions covered county and parish history, but they also copiously surveyed local agriculture and trade. Camden's work was reprinted, adapted, and imitated throughout the following century.[17] As techniques of land surveying improved, so did maps and gazetteers. John Adams's extraordinary *Index Villaris* (1690) estimated the locations and basic demography of no fewer than 24,000 English towns, using the latest techniques for projecting the curvature of the Earth onto a two-dimensional cartographic plane.[18]

Such techniques were famously pioneered by sixteenth-century cartographers Gerhard Mercator and Abraham Ortelius, who produced large atlases that provided modern updates to Ptolemy's *Geographia*.[19] Like Ptolemy's, topographical dictionaries in the sixteenth and seventeenth centuries gathered encyclopedic descriptions of all places in the known world. They often included exotic tales of Asia, America, and Africa as well as of the Arctic and Antarctic zones, then called Terra Borealis and Terra Australis. Textbooks from the *Cosmographical Glasse* (1559) to *Cosmographia* (1679) provided chorographies of the cosmos that described the rises and falls of empires, that surveyed religions and cultures of various peoples, and that cataloged the flora and fauna of the world. The flavor of these books can be glimpsed in this description of Tonquin, from the ambitiously titled *Present State of the Universe* (1694):

> *Tonquin* is judg'd almost in equal extent with *France*. The *Tonquineses* say that the whole Kingdom contains above twenty thousand Cities and Towns; and many more there would be, but that many of the people choose rather to live on the Water, than on the Land, so that the greatest part of their Rivers is cover'd with Boats, which serve them instead of Houses.[20]

Such publications often veer toward the fantastical. For example, Peter Heylyn's *Cosmographie in Four Bookes* (1652) regales readers with tales of parts unknown, by which he refers not only to unexplored regions of the Earth, around the poles in particular, but also to places like Thomas More's Utopia, Francis Bacon's New Atlantis, and even to "Faerie Land" and the "New World in the Moon," which was "proposed as a fancie onely," Heylyn explains, "but is become a matter of a more serious debate."[21]

Spherical globes served as navigational tools and, perhaps more importantly, as aids to the imagination, helping readers visualize the Earth as a whole. In England, Joseph Moxon was the printer most active in popularizing globes to the new merchant class and to the middling-sort reading public.[22] Globes appeared in two kinds. The first and most familiar are terrestrial globes, which represent the Earth's surface as a sphere. Less familiar now are celestial globes, which display an exterior surface of the heavens, representing the constellations of stars that surround the Earth from a God's-eye perspective. The primary purpose of globes, in Joseph Moxon's words, was "to keep in memory the situation of Countries, and Order of the Constellations and particular Stars."[23] However, the globe was also an occasion for students and virtuosi to practice basic mathematical problems. Globes typically were constructed with lines showing the equator and the tropics, and they were adorned with metal wheels at the poles that allowed the lines of longitude to function as instruments to measure time. Textbooks published during this period tended to emphasize the globe's ability to track the movements of the sun and moon around the Earth, and so to calculate the time of day at any place. One such textbook offers instructions for how to "know the Length of the Day and Night in any place of the Earth at any time," and how to "know by the Globe when the Great Mogul of India, and Czar of Moscovia, sit down to Dinner."[24] Globes could also be used, somewhat more cumbersomely, to measure the distances between places. The great-circle distance that separates two cities could be estimated by extending a string from two points on a globe, then comparing the length of that string with any two coordinate points on the equator. Taking each equatorial degree to equal 60 English miles, as was conventionally assumed at the time, provides an estimate of the geodesic distance between any two points. Geographical dictionaries meant to accompany globes often included instructions for performing such calculations.

However, the continuous metric space defined by geodesic distance was not the usual mode through which geographical reality was experienced. Atlases and manuals for globe-reading betray a keen sense of their own novelty, as they very self-consciously invite readers to imagine themselves existing in space warped by the spherical Earth, the contours of which can be experienced only figuratively from some imaginary cosmic perspective. In more pedestrian books (which is to say, most books), the world remained a fundamentally social space, and it was presented to readers as an interconnected system of commercial, political, and historical activity. Practical reference manuals like Thomas de Laune's *Present State of London* (1681) cataloged businesses and guilds in the city, listed municipal officers, and provided details about local postal carriers, waggoneers, shippers, and stagecoaches. John Ogilby's *Britannia* (1675) collected special maps organized, not by latitude and longitude, but by the sequence of stops along each of England's major roads, showing what towns travelers would encounter along the way. Laurence Echard's *Newsman's Interpreter* (1692) and James Wadsworth's *Evropean Mercury* (1641) mapped places into networks by describing roads and travel routes that connected London to cities across the British Isles and Europe. Practical manuals like these differ from geographical dictionaries most obviously in their scope. Unlike the vast encyclopedias that attempt to describe the whole universe, such manuals provided detailed guides for readers, travelers, and merchants hoping to navigate the increasingly complex but comparatively smaller world-economy of Europe.

This raises a point that will be important to the analyses that follow. If historians look only at the official discourse of world geography during the period—at books by Mercator, Ortelius, Camden, and Ogilby—the Renaissance world will seem to be defined as a basically global entity, and the most important development will seem to be the advent of a global consciousness and a heightened awareness of the Americas, Africa, and eastern Asia.²⁵ But if the analysis is broadened to include other kinds of books, a very different picture comes into focus. The larger field of English print, especially newsbooks and other pamphlets, created an ever-thickening discourse devoted to politics, war, and commerce across England and Europe. Most books about geographical places were not really about *geography*, per se, but were instead on topics of history, news, and the politics of European statecraft. Books of this kind are perhaps too numerous and various to represent with a few epitomizing examples. On one spectrum are books of rich commentary that closely resemble those of world geography, like *Europæ Modernæ Speculum* (1666), which catalogs the "empires, kingdoms, principalities, seignieuries, and common-wealths of Europe in their present state, their government, policy, different interest and mutual aspect one towards another," as its title page explains.²⁶ Others are books describing political events happening in Europe's countries and city-states, accounts of battles, letters from abroad, and other pamphlets staking positions in the disputes of the day. Together these publications constitute a large and multifaceted discourse that directed English geographical attention persistently to the east and south.

Beyond Europe in the same direction lay the Near East, especially the lands of Egypt and Israel, where the legends of biblical antiquity continued to hold powerful appeal. Sermons directed readers toward this central region of the Ptolemaic *oikoumene*, where Old Testament legends and the story of Christ provided frequent topoi for English world-thinking. Like books of European statecraft, narratives and other references to biblical myth weren't usually about geography as such, but they consistently drew attention outside the boundaries of England and Europe. Many readers in England would have been more intimately familiar with the geography of ancient Judea than with present-day Ireland. Often, this extension eastward was meant to reflect recursively back home. The practice of typology, when applied to the modern world, mined biblical myth for analogies to present-day life and politics. In millennial rhetoric, world geography collapsed along a European axis, as ancient events in the lands of Israel, Babylon, and Egypt were interpreted as allegories of conflagration soon to embroil England, Rome, and the kingdoms of the modern European world.[27] At the same time, celestial objects like the sun, moon, and stars provided constant physical reminders of a heavenly dispensation under which the world of domestic life was lived. Spaces shared by animals, plants, women, and children were grounded in a profound mythology that called attention to worldliness by presenting itself as the world's encapsulating opposite, which, paradoxically, tended to be associated with places located in a comparatively narrow region surrounding Israel.

To summarize English geographical writing between the years 1500 and 1700 thus requires thinking across several different modalities simultaneously. Of undeniable importance were the new enterprises of colonial exploitation in the Americas and East Indies. They shook the authority of classical antiquity and motivated a huge, generations-long investment in measuring and mapping the globe, extending discourse outward in virtually all directions. Economic and political developments in Europe, however, directed attention back to England's neighbors, where the town-based commercial systems inherited from the Middle Ages had evolved into national territories and something like a common, international market for trade in goods. Under this view, geographical space was less an open field marked by latitude and longitude than a thick network of interaction. The same was also true closer to home, where towns, counties, and parishes were the focus of increasingly detailed description, not only in England but also across Ireland, Scotland, and Wales. These developments were all secular—in that they usually did not saliently presume a guiding providential agent—and we can see in them early seeds of moral orders that would dominate future centuries: the free market, national politics, religious denominationalism, &c. But throughout the sixteenth and seventeenth centuries, biblical geography continued to provide a powerful anchor to the world's geographical structure as well as paradigmatic models for domestic life, religious practice, and embodied experience.

For this reason, my account of early modern world geography will look very different from accounts offered by other scholars. The discipline of English literary history has a very strong—and, perhaps, inevitable—Anglocentric bias.[28] Great attention has been paid to the consolidation of Britain as a national entity and to the emerging ideologies of racial and gendered belonging that this nationalism required.[29] Of course, many scholars disavow this bias and try to resist it.[30] Historians of early American literature, in particular, have advanced an Atlantic model of the period's geography, showing how competing ideas of political community appeared along the western routes of trade and colonial exploitation.[31] Others have turned their attention even more broadly to the (retrospectively) global Anglophone world, emphasizing scenes of colonial encounter, not just in the Americas but also in Africa and across the Pacific in Asia. These studies all share a basically concentric model of world geography, where England sits at the national core and is surrounded by the sites of future empire. This vision of England's place in the world is best exemplified by Richard Helgerson's classic study, *Forms of Nationhood* (1992), which analyzed a Whiggish discourse of economic improvement, local to Britain, against a larger discourse of oceanic exploration and adventure. This vision can also be seen in the textbook *The English Literatures of America, 1500–1800* (1996), edited by Myra Jehlen and Michael Warner, with which I was trained as a graduate student. And it can be seen most clearly today in conferences and books that emphasize the history of empire, the Global South, and Global Anglophone literature.

When used as a framework for understanding early modern geographical thought in England, however, any national or global focus can be very misleading. Both suffer from two major blind spots. Considered in its entirety, early English print isn't Anglocentric. Even though it's all in English, it's actually Eurocentric. When describing the geographical ideas that informed English discourse, literary historians massively underestimate how much thought was directed across the channel to Italy, France, and other parts of Europe. Only rarely do the period's books describe the lands of the Atlantic or Pacific. Mostly they direct their focus south and east for news of battles, political intrigue, and doctrinal debate. Speaking of which: the other blind spot involves religion. Studies of Renaissance geography typically draw from only secular sources, but a significant portion of all the period's geography involved biblical geography, a discourse devoted to the contextualization, explication, and application of Christian myth. World history, and thus world geography, was understood to have happened mostly in the Mediterranean region, where discussions of Africa and Asia focus overwhelmingly on biblical antiquity. Put bluntly, when early modern English writers looked out to the world, they looked for two things: God and news. News came from Europe. God came from Israel. For most writers, everything else was mere curiosity, and any history of English world-thinking that doesn't foreground these basic concerns grossly misconstrues its topic. England wasn't the center of an Atlantic or global world; it was a geographically marginal actor in the economic and political system of Europe.

The early modern world was not shaped like a circle, but like a line extending from England to Israel, and at the center of that line was not London, but Rome.

Spatializing the EEBO Corpus

Data for this chapter was collected during the spring semester of 2018 with the help of a small team of undergraduate researchers at the University of South Carolina.[32] To curate data for the analyses required understanding how early modern books encode geographical information. This meant digging into the corpus to uncover its underlying spatial model—its basic organizing structure. At first glance, this premise may seem suspect. When compared to computerized geographical information systems, printed books and atlases can seem relatively unstructured, and indeed the layout and content of early modern geographical treatises can be idiosyncratic and somewhat arbitrary. However, the notorious heterogeneity and mutability of the period's geography masks a powerful underlying coherence and continuity. Although certain parts of the world underwent significant alteration—northern America, eastern Asia, and the whole of the southern hemisphere, most obviously—the areas where greater attention was paid remained remarkably stable. The basic topology of the Ptolemaic *oikoumene* proved flexible and durable as it underwent expansion. This topology divided the world into continents and continents into kingdoms (or other regional entities), and it populated those kingdoms with cities and towns as well as with geomorphological features like rivers, lakes, and mountains. This shallow hierarchy was built on a principle of containment. London was in England was in the British Isles was in Europe was in the world. And here's the crucial point: even when boundaries of continents and kingdoms shifted on maps, their basic topology remained very consistent.

This spatial hierarchy had advantages and disadvantages when used to organize world geography. It was well-suited for reproduction in printed books, which share a pretty similar (and similarly shallow) structure. Just as the world was divided into continents and nations, so too books were divided into books, volumes, and chapters, and that's precisely how geographical treatises tended to be laid out. Insofar as nations had coherent identities and stable(ish) boundaries, it made sense to break their descriptions into discrete textual segments. However, this one-to-one correspondence sometimes broke down. It often grouped countries that had little in common. Israel shared its history most directly with Egypt and Rome, but it usually got lumped in with China as part of Asia. Turkey and Russia didn't fit neatly into either of the continents they spanned. Similarly, the most significant political entity in English-language world history was the Roman Empire, but it couldn't be reconciled to the model in any straightforward way, nor could, for that matter, the newer colonial enterprises in the Americas and East Indies. As a consequence, many important historical and political features of early modern geography were distributed unevenly across what was otherwise a stable and coherent scheme.

The first step of data curation was to build a special list of place names, called a gazetteer, to reflect this hierarchical model. Modern gazetteers are often highly complex data objects that contain a wide variety of information, but our goals were much simpler. We wanted to find as many toponyms as possible, given limited time and resources; we wanted to be able to account for alternate spellings (common in the early modern period); and we wanted to know which places were *in* which, whether or not we knew their precise latitude and longitude. Luckily, we were not the first people to need this information. In fact, it was a pressing need for early modern readers as well—or, at least, it was perceived to be a need and justified publication of several reference works that compiled such information. The most important one, from which about two-thirds of our gazetteer is drawn, is Edmund Bohun's *Geographical Dictionary* (1693), which according to its title page represents "the present and ancient names of all the counties, provinces, remarkable cities, universities, ports, towns, mountains, seas, streights, fountains, and rivers of the whole world." Bohun was a controversialist and, briefly, licensor of the press, but his greatest work was this dictionary, which gathered together descriptions of thousands of places. Each description is written according to a formula that was meticulously planned and rigorously adhered to. Each begins by providing the place name, any alternate spellings, the place category (country, city, town, river, &c), and the containing location (fig. 3.2). When the document was transcribed by the Text Creation Partnership, the markup added was similarly formulaic, and so it

```
<p>
    <hi>Gothen, <hi>Gotha,</hi>
    </hi>, a fmall City in <hi>Thuringia</hi> in <hi>Ger<g ref="char:EOLhyphen"/>many,</hi> built by the <hi>Goths;</hi> which is now under the Duke of
    <hi>Gotha,</hi> a Branch of the Houfe of <hi>Saxony,</hi> whofe Caftle is
    <hi>Grimmeftein.</hi> This place was here<g ref="char:EOLhyphen"/>tofore very
ftrong, but in the time of <hi>Ferdinand</hi> I. it was deftroyed, and in later times
rebuilt, and cal<g ref="char:EOLhyphen"/>led <hi>Freidenftein.</hi> It ftands three
    <hi>German</hi> Miles from <hi>Erford</hi> to the Weft, and four from
    <hi>Eyfenach.</hi> § The Dukedom of <hi>Gotha,</hi> is a part of the <hi>
    <g ref="char:V">U</g>pper Saxony,</hi> under the Dominion of its own Duke; who is
a Branch of the Line of <hi>Weymar;</hi> and befides this, pof<g ref="char:EOLhyphen"
/>feffed of <hi>Altenburg</hi> in <hi>Mifnia, Coburg,</hi> a part of
    <hi>Hennenberg,</hi> in <hi>Franconia;</hi> and <hi>Ofterland</hi> in the <hi>
    <g ref="char:V">U</g>pper Saxony.</hi>
</p>
<p>
    <hi>Gothebourg,</hi> or <hi>Gotembourg,</hi> a very ftrong City with an Harbour
belonging to it, in the Province of <hi>Weftrogothia,</hi> at the entrance of the
    <hi>Baltick</hi> Sea, three <hi>German</hi> Miles from <hi>Bahuys</hi> to the
South, fixty fix from <hi>Stockholm</hi> to the South-Weft, and feventeen from
    <hi>Skagen</hi> (the moft Northern Point of <hi>Jutland</hi>) to the North-Weft.
In this City <hi>Charles</hi> IX. King of <hi>Sweden</hi> died, in 1660. § There is
another Town of the fame Name in <hi>New York</hi> (formerly called <hi>New
    Sweden</hi>) in <hi>America;</hi> built by the <hi>Swedes,</hi> but taken from
them by the <hi>Hollanders,</hi> and taken again from the <hi>Hollanders</hi> by the
    <hi>Englifh.</hi>
</p>
```

Figure 3.2. Example Text of an Early Modern Gazetteer. From Edmund Bohun, *Geographical Dictionary*.

was easy to write a short computer script to scroll through the document and gather this information. The same action was performed over several other books, mostly treatises on world geography, going back to William Cuningham's *Cosmographical Glasse* (1559). Across these source books, our process found approximately 15,000 unique toponyms, of which just over 6,000 are alternate spellings of 9,355 unique places. Alternate spellings include both orthographic variants, like "France" and "Fraunce," and alternate names, like "England" and "Albion." These places are connected by more than 11,000 "is contained by" statements, which locate almost all of them within a common spatial hierarchy.

Each entry in the resulting gazetteer takes the form of a statement representing the testimony of a specific historical source. The entries are not meant to provide an authority file, like a modern gazetteer, but a collection of historical testimonies. Our goal was not to create a single ground truth of Renaissance-era geography but to provide a framework under which its various and sometimes conflicting geographies could be described. Each statement includes a subject, predicate, and object. Predicates are restricted to naming three kinds of relation: category ("instance of"), correspondence ("is same as"), and containment ("is contained by"). Predicates are interpreted very generally. In table 3.1, Gothen

Table 3.1. Sample of a Gazetteer of Early Modern Spatial Relations. Data in this table is drawn from the XML source code in figure 3.2.

Subject	Predicate	Object	Source
gotembourg	is same as	gothebourg	A28561
gotha	is same as	gothen	A28561
gothebourg	instance of	city	A28561
gothebourg	is contained by	america	A28561
gothebourg	is contained by	westrogothia	A28561
gothen	instance of	city	A28561
gothen	is contained by	franconia	A28561
gothen	is contained by	misnia	A28561
gothen	is contained by	saxony	A28561
gothen	is contained by	thuringia	A28561

is listed as being contained by several regions of Germany (Franconia, Misnia, Saxony, and Thuriginia), even though it's physically located only in Thuriginia, because the duke who ruled Gothen also ruled in those areas. That's OK. Our goal wasn't to enforce early modern political boundaries but to trace networks of association among them.

In addition, a few books contained tables of latitude and longitude that could easily be translated into digital form. These sources contain 2,547 sets of geocoordinates providing locations for 2,448 places. Regional features like continents and countries are defined in the books as simple rectangles, as in statements like, "Egypt is situated between the 59th and 67th degrees of longitude and between the 21st and 31st degrees of latitude." In some books, the XML was laid out in a way to recover the coordinates automatically, but in many cases we transcribed these boundaries by hand. In the calculations that follow, I represent them as points by taking their centroid—the middle point of both latitude and longitude. Following seventeenth-century sources, I treat the Earth as a perfect sphere and assume that each degree is separated by an interval of 60 English miles. The result is an Earth not quite like the oblate, tomato-shaped Earth known to us today. Assuming 60 miles per degree, the diameter of this Earth comes out to exactly 21,600 miles, which is a bit smaller than today's estimate of 24,901 miles. Again, this is OK. We weren't trying to recover some objective truth of what the world was. Instead, we wanted to describe the world as it was understood at the time (fig. 3.3).

Once the underlying geographical models were complete, we were able to use them as instruments for measuring the texts of the EEBO corpus. Our last data-curation task began by building a list of keywords for study. We divided the collection into five roughly equal-sized historical segments (1500–1599, 1600–1639, 1640–1659, 1660–1679, and 1680–1699) and selected the 5,000 most-frequent words from each, resulting in a total list of 7,507 key terms. Across the 56,000 documents in the collection then available to us, we then counted how often each place was mentioned and how often each keyword was used.

As you'll see, identifying the places mentioned in each document allows for two things. First, we can trace references to places by year to see

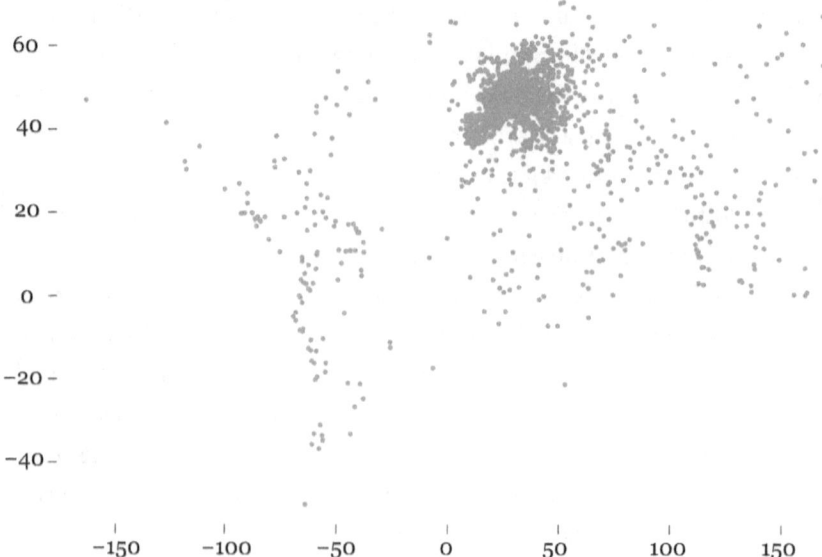

Figure 3.3. The World According to EEBO. Points of latitude and longitude in this graph are drawn entirely from early modern sources. From this perspective, EEBO's Eurocentric bias comes into clear focus. The outlines of Spain and Italy are clearly visible, as is the continuous landmass of France and western Germany. Other continents appear only in glimpses. Most of the Asian continent was covered by Tartary and China, but it's almost completely blank on this map, as is the continent now called North America. Except for the northern region, Africa, is unrecognizable. Australia, completely unknown.

how the scope of English world geography changed over time. Second, we can locate words within that geography, identifying which words were most commonly associated with which parts of the world.

Analysis (1): The Early Modern World in Aggregate—Continuity and Change

Which places did early modern writers mention most often? How did their interests change over time?

Across all of the Early English Books Online corpus, we found just over seven million references to the nine thousand places in our gazetteer. The most frequently mentioned places, in descending order, are England, Rome, Israel, London, France, Jerusalem, Egypt, Scotland,

Ireland, and Italy. Like many aspects of language, geographical discourse tends to be powerfully concentrated among a relatively small number of important terms. This top-ten list accounts for no fewer than two million of all geographical references—28% of the whole. Scaling out only a little higher, to the 100 most frequently mentioned places, the percentage doubles: the top-100 toponyms appear 3.9 million times, accounting for 56% of the total.

We encountered this kind of distribution in the first chapter. In a skew distribution, also known as a *power-law* distribution, values are distributed along a logarithmic scale (fig. 3.4). Like in economics, where the "top 1%" accumulate a disproportionate share of income and wealth, in language a small number of high-frequency places predominate. They're used as common touchstones that organize attention through redundant repetition. They provide constant points of reference throughout the entire sixteenth and seventeenth centuries. By contrast, other places receive far less attention. The median frequency for any individual toponym is just thirty-four. This means that, measured over two centuries, most places appear in EEBO on average less than once every five years. About eight hundred are used only once; another six hundred, just twice.

Table 3.2. Place References in EEBO. Total counts include spelling variations and alternate terms (e.g., England/Albion) for each place. Frequencies listed by 1,000s.

Place Name	Frequency
England	446.3
Rome	374.0
Israel	229.0
London	228.6
France	224.5
Jerusalem	141.2
Egypt	99.0
Scotland	94.1
Ireland	89.3
Italy	78.6

Table 3.3. Place References by Continent.

Africa		America		Asia		Europe	
Egypt	99.0	Virginia	6.2	Israel	229.0	England	446.3
Carthage	17.1	Mexico	5.1	Syria	42.5	Rome	374.0
Ethiopia	8.6	Brasil	3.2	Canaan	41.9	France	224.5
Barbary	5.4	Florida	2.6	Persia	26.4	Scotland	94.1
Malta	4.5	Jamaica	2.4	India	23.4	Ireland	89.3
Nile	3.3	Panama	1.8	Ephesus	19.4	Italy	78.6
Niger	3.1	Canada	1.6	China	15.9	Paris	70.6
Algiers	2.9	Cuba	1.5	Turkey	13.7	Spain	65.9
Lybia	2.4	Chili	1.3	Arabia	12.8	Germany	54.5
Guinea	2.4	Greenland	1.0	Media	10.9	Constantinople	44.9

Table 3.4. Place References in Select Countries: China, Greece, India.

China		Greece		India	
Canton	2.6	Corinth	24.7	Goa	4.4
Peking	1.1	Athens	21.6	Ganges	2.5
Cathay	1.0	Macedonia	13.5	Bengala	1.6
Puglia	0.6	Thrace	7.2	Calicut	1.5
Anian	0.5	Sparta	5.9	Agra	1.4
Macao	0.5	Thebes	4.9	Malacca	1.2
Nanquin	0.4	Cappadocia	4.2	Cambaya	0.8
Lao	0.3	Thessaly	4.1	Cananor	0.4
Philippine	0.3	Epirus	2.6	Indostan	0.4
Corea	0.3	Attica	1.9	Chersonese	0.3

Table 3.5. Place References in Select Countries: France, Germany, Italy..

France		Germany		Italy	
Paris	70.6	Saxony	10.8	Rome	374.0
Lyons	23.1	Munster	8.1	Venice	25.4
Flanders	21.3	Bavaria	5.6	Naples	24.0
Burgundy	10.1	Constantia	2.8	Geneva	22.1
Lorrain	8.8	Augusta	2.8	Florence	14.7
Valentia	4.9	Bonne	2.2	Mantua	9.4
Anjou	4.0	Basile	1.7	Genoa	7.6
Calais	3.6	Triers	1.7	Parma	7.1
Picardy	3.4	Hessen	1.5	Arno	5.2
Bourdeaux	3.4	Oder	1.5	Ferrara	4.6

Table 3.6. Place References in the British Isles.

England		Ireland		Scotland		Wales	
London	228.6	Dublin	16.5	Edinburgh	16.3	Anglesey	1.8
Bath	38.1	Galloway	3.7	Durham	9.1	Powis	1.8
Oxford	37.0	Cork	3.4	Hamilton	6.1	Denbigh	1.7
Canterbury	35.0	Derry	3.2	Ayr	4.7	Conway	1.4
Lancaster	28.2	Armagh	2.7	Glasgow	4.2	Knighton	1.2
Essex	24.0	Waterford	2.5	Montrose	3.7	Glamorgan	1.2
Kent	22.4	Kildare	2.3	Galloway	3.7	Shrop	1.0
Winchester	20.2	Tyrone	2.2	Berwick	3.1	Brecknock	0.9
Cambridge	19.6	Argile	1.8	Angus	3.0	Landaff	0.8
Lincoln	15.7	Kilkenny	1.8	Perth	2.9	Radnor	0.8

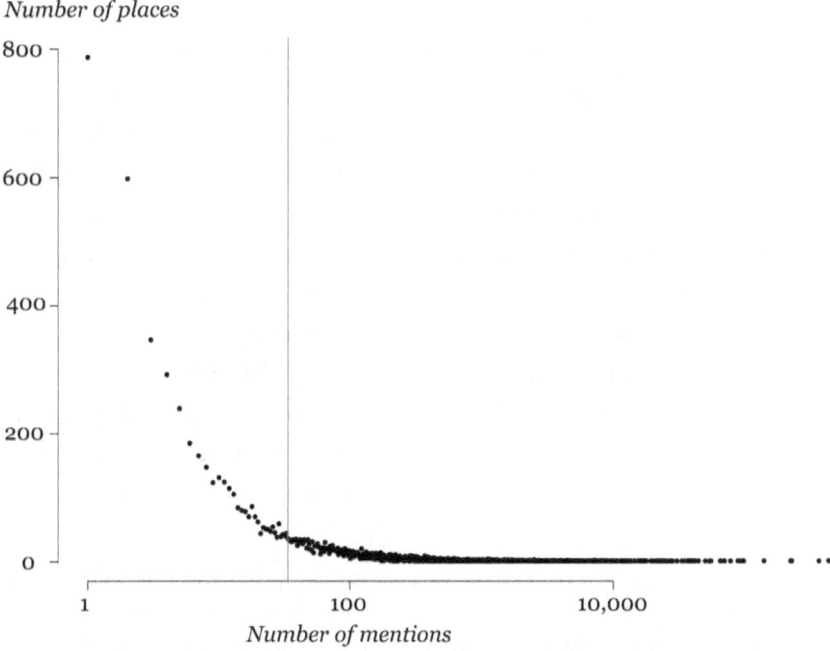

Figure 3.4. Power-Law Distribution of EEBO Place References. In the upper left, almost 800 places are mentioned just once, and another 600 are mentioned just twice. The vertical line shows the median—34 mentions. The "long tail" of the graph extends to the right, where a small number of places are mentioned hundreds of thousands of times.

(Which means in many cases that those places are found in Bohun's *Geographical Dictionary* but nowhere else, which could happen because he was transcribing place names from maps rather than from the textual bodies of books.) Of course, EEBO does not include all documents published during the period, and if the entire microfilm collection were transcribed the raw numbers would be higher. But the basic shape of the data would hold. Geographic language, like economic power, is marked by a strong core-periphery structure that separates a powerful center from the provincial outskirts. As we'll see, this tendency has important implications for the meanings attached to places and for the spatial structure of concepts.

Another important property of geographical language is its remarkable consistency. World geography changes very slowly. The list of most important places over EEBO looks pretty much the same across the two centuries, and indeed in most years when measured individually. Over our five periods, the list of most frequently mentioned places remains almost identical except for a few shifting positions here and there. The overall picture remains remarkably consistent. Not only do writers from year to year and generation to generation tend to focus on the same places, but they do so in roughly equivalent proportions.

However, some shifts do happen, and they'll seem familiar to scholars of the period. When compared to the sixteenth century, the seventeenth century world is bigger, more English, and (slightly) more secular. The most important change occurred in midcentury, when England displaced Rome in the top spot as EEBO's most-frequent toponym, a position it retained for the rest of the period. As seen year by year in figure 3.5,

Table 3.7. Top Five Most Frequently Mentioned Places, by Period.

1500–1599		1600–1639		1640–1659		1660–1679		1680–1699	
Rome	70.0	Rome	95.3	England	104.6	England	82.0	England	143.9
England	49.9	England	65.9	Israel	64.7	Rome	65.4	Rome	86.8
France	32.0	France	48.2	London	55.4	London	46.3	France	72.6
Israel	27.4	Israel	44.5	Rome	53.9	Israel	44.5	London	69.7
London	27.1	London	30.0	Jerusalem	36.7	France	36.3	Israel	48.0

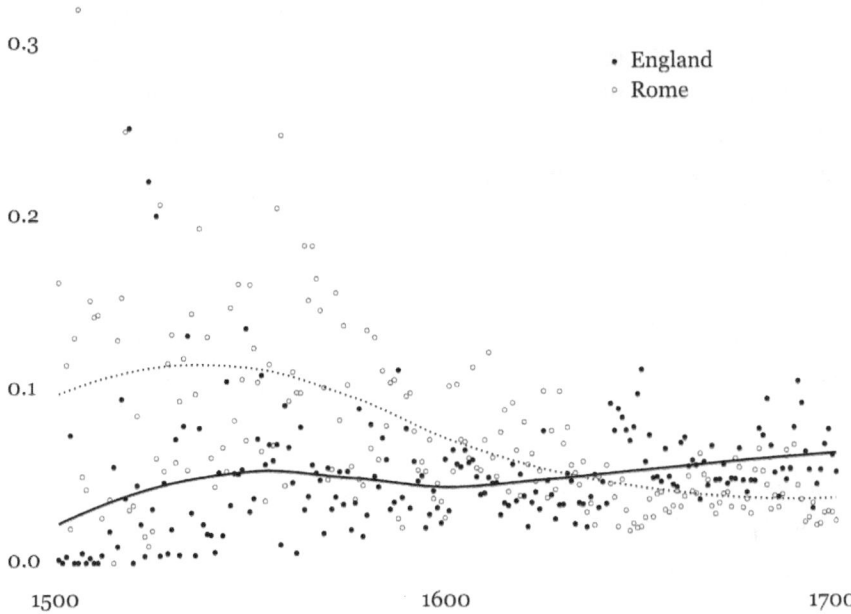

Figure 3.5. References to England and Rome in EEBO, 1500 to 1699.

this shift happened gradually but was punctuated by sharp responses to historical events. Spikes in references to England occur around the English Civil War of the 1640s and around the Glorious Revolution of the 1680s.

The larger trend that affected Rome's relative frequency also affected the other key places of classical and scriptural antiquity, each of which displays a similar pattern. Egypt, Israel, and Jerusalem all show declines in relative prominence over the later seventeenth century. By "decline," I don't mean that references to biblical geography actually decreased in raw terms—indeed, they remained among the most frequently used terms. Instead, greater attention paid to England and other places of the modern, secular world meant that references to biblical lands made up a smaller portion of the whole. Because terms like England, London, Scotland, Ireland, and Britain were all on the rise in the seventeenth century, terms like Rome, Egypt, Israel, and Jerusalem accounted for a smaller share of geographical discourse overall.

Even more generally, this shift occurred against a backdrop of geographical diversification. As the print marketplace expanded, more books were published annually, and so more and more places were written about every year. Over the period, the number of unique places mentioned in print each year increases linearly, more than doubling from one century to the next (fig. 3.6). As the world came to be more finely mapped and inventoried, English geographical writing followed along, and by the end of the seventeenth century it was common for several thousand distinct places to be mentioned each year.

This diversification reflects the globalization of self-consciously geographical discourse that occurred over the sixteenth century, even

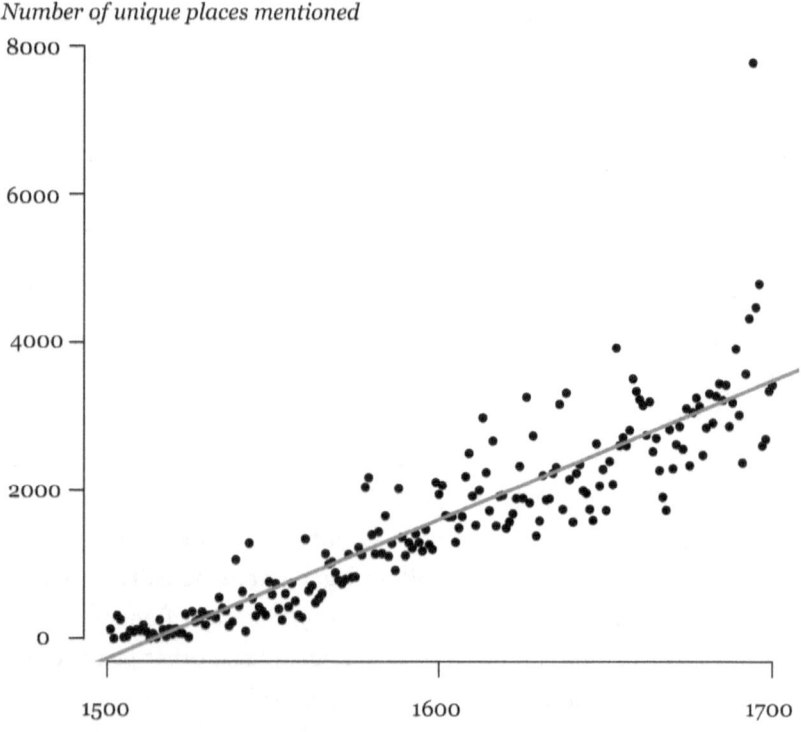

Figure 3.6. Unique Places Mentioned in EEBO, 1500 to 1700. The scope of English geography expanded through a neatly linear process. On average, 18.7 more unique places were mentioned each year than in the year previous. The outlier year in the upper right, 1693, is the year Bohun's *Geographical Dictionary* was published.

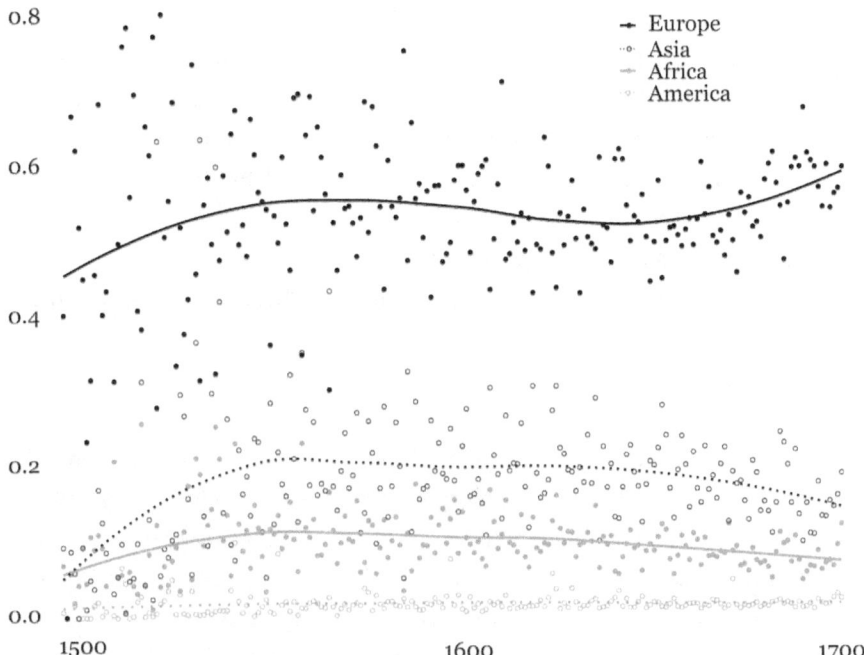

Figure 3.7. References to Places, by Continent. The total number of references to all continents and places contained within each continent, 1500–1700, including spelling variants for each place.

though England itself was not yet a dominant hub of international trade. The change was gradual, linear, and persistent. In 1500, what little geographical writing there was focused almost exclusively on Europe and the Mediterranean world, with only a few scattered references to Africa and Asia. By 1550, Europe had largely filled out, with increasingly diverse references to Anatolia, Arabia, and Persia as well as the occasional reference to America. By the end of the century, the early modern world had come into full view. Europe was a dense field, as were the Mediterranean coasts of Asia and Africa. Even outside this main zone, America and eastern Asia had evolved into regions of their own, each with multiple interconnected locales.

That said, English print remained fundamentally biased toward Europe and the Mediterranean world. European places dominate the corpus, consistently accounting for half or more of the total (fig. 3.7). Because it was the primary site of biblical myth, Asia is the next most common, usually making up about a fifth of all references. Africa follows Asia, with America trailing along the bottom, making barely a dent. Despite the enormous amount of attention paid to the American colonies by cultural historians of the period, American places consistently account for only about 2% or less of all geographical references in EEBO.[33]

Analysis (2): Mapping Conceptual Topographies

Places in the gazetteer are distributed primarily through Europe and the Mediterranean region of Asia and Africa. Counting all places equally, the average latitude and longitude of the gazetteer rests at 30 degrees longitude and 45 degrees latitude. The closest place to that spot is Brescia, Italy, a small town at the foot of the Alps between Milan and Venice. This spot marks a kind of absolute center of early modern geography, sitting at the longitudinal midpoint of the Mediterranean, but skewed north toward an economically expanding Europe. However, as we know, not all places are equal. Some are mentioned frequently and so co-occur with many words in the corpus; others appear only a few times. If we factor this into our calculations, EEBO's geographical center shifts dramatically to the south and east, to 33 degrees longitude and 41 degrees latitude, placing it just on the outskirts of Rome.[34] The distance that separates these points is about 270 English miles.

This distance reflects two competing imperatives English writers faced. On the one hand, there was a real need to catalogue the world-economy of Europe, naming and describing towns throughout Britain, France, and other European countries. Many of these locales were small and individually unimportant, so they barely register in the corpus, but their points flesh out the town-based geography that had developed since the Middle Ages. On the other hand, English writers remained fascinated with the Mediterranean world, where Rome, Israel, and Egypt continued to dominate English conceptions of world history. These competing imperatives meant that the spatial distribution of English print's geographical references pushed subtly but powerfully against its own underlying model of world geography, tilting it to the south and east like a tide pulled by the gravity of the moon.

The moon, in this analogy, was Israel. When I say that the center of the English world was Rome, you shouldn't interpret me to imply that Rome was always the center of attention. Sure, there was plenty of concern about popery and continued interest in the history of the Roman Empire, so Rome was mentioned often, but individual documents didn't typically refer to central Italy. Rather, the centroid represents a balance of geographical interests. Sometimes a sermon would talk about Jesus's life in ancient Judea or the exodus of the Jews from Egypt, or a pamphlet would express opinions about the politics of Scotland or Germany, or a traveler might describe adventures from Peru to Pegu. These various interests tend to balance out, and for this reason the footprint tends toward the center. Over the whole of EEBO, that center sits almost precisely on Rome.

To describe the *semantic footprint* of any term, I rely primarily on two measurements, each based on the geocoordinates of the places mentioned in any document or group of documents (fig. 3.8). The *centroid* shows the average latitude and longitude of places mentioned, weighted by frequency. The *range* shows the average distance each place reference

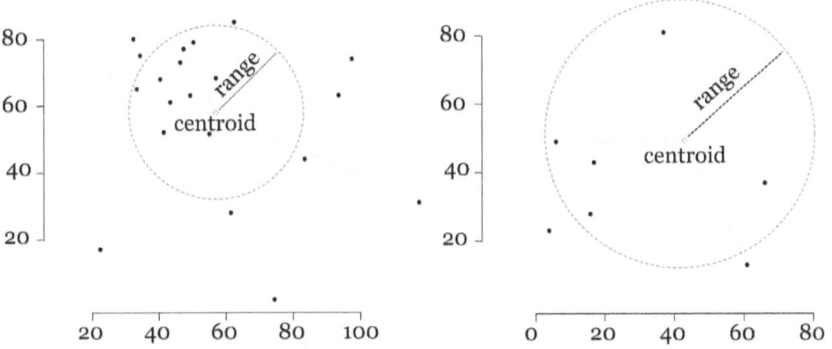

Figure 3.8. Comparing Dense and Sparse Semantic Footprints. The semantic footprint measures the distribution of places mentioned in a document or group of documents. The centroid represents the middle point of all references. The range is the average distance of each reference from the centroid. In documents about dense geographic regions like Europe (*left*), the range is relatively small because many places are near each other. By contrast, in the sparse case typical of America and Asia (*right*), the range tends to be relatively large.

sits from that centroid. The centroid and range reflect a document's geographic bias and provide a baseline for comparing it to others. Some books are densely focused on places that are near each other, while other books sweep more widely over the world. Footprints biased toward dense areas will tend to have a smaller range, while footprints biased toward the outskirts will tend to have a wider one.

My goal in this section will be to examine the semantic footprints of words. To do this, we represent the semantic footprint of a word as the footprint of all documents that use that word, weighted by the frequency of the word in each document. For example, books that use the word *sheriff* tend to focus on England and only rarely mention places outside the British Isles, so the centroid sits far to the north and west from Rome, very close to England, and the range is pretty small, just a few hundred miles (fig. 3.9). Similarly, the word *israelites* was a localized term, although

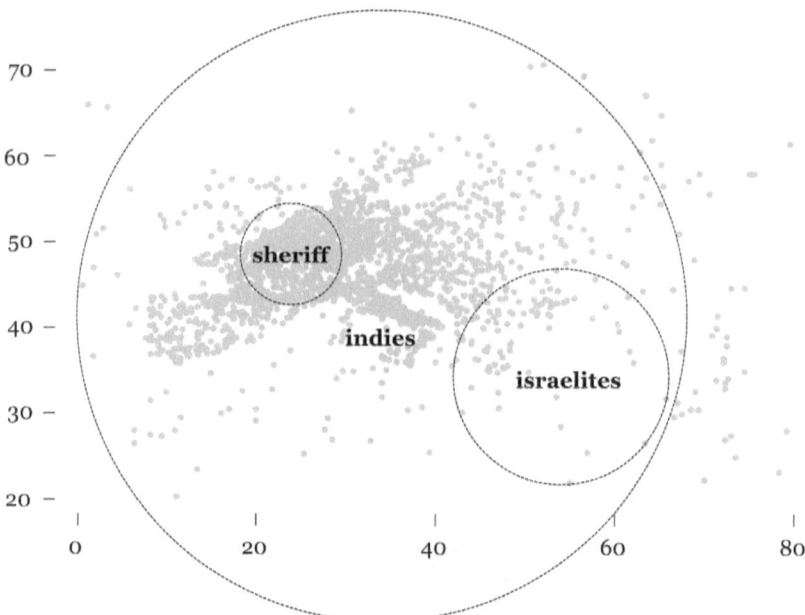

Figure 3.9. Semantic Footprints of *sheriff*, *indies*, and *israelites*. Terms like *sheriff* are tightly concentrated in the north and west. Terms related to biblical antiquity are skewed to the east and south, with larger but still relatively narrow ranges. Terms like *indies* have much wider ranges that tend to balance toward the center.

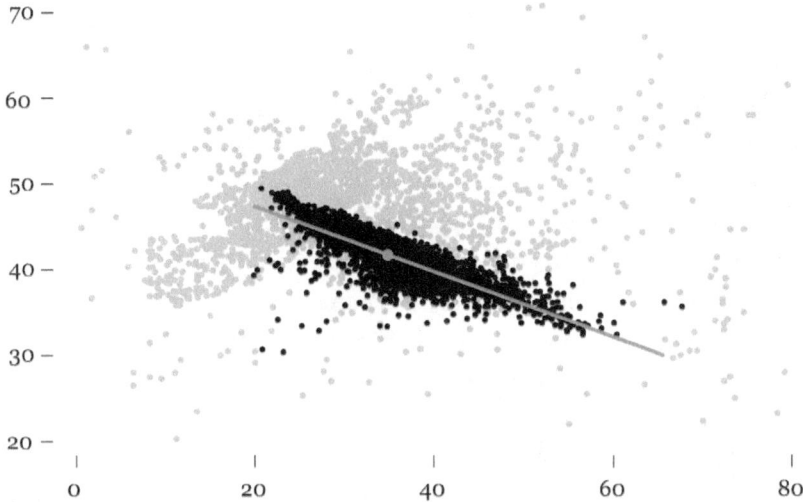

Figure 3.10. Centroid for Each Keyword in EEBO. The line across the middle displays a linear regression over the centroids for each of the 7,507 keywords. This line represents the fundamental geographic structure of EEBO, which consistently focused attention along a line extending between England and Israel.

its range is a little bigger because places in Asia tend to be spread out more sparsely. By contrast, the word "indies" was used to describe places far away, both to the east and the west, so it balances out near the center while expanding over a wide range of almost two thousand miles.

This tendency toward the norm is important. Words used in individual documents were as widely and as variously distributed as the underlying geographical structure allowed, but in aggregate they were constrained to a fairly narrow band. Figure 3.10 shows a plot of geographical places, with the corpus centroid near Rome highlighted, while also showing in black the centroid for each keyword. The highest frequency terms converge to the center, but others spread out. Early modern geography in English was distributed along a distinctly linear slope, pointing toward the British Isles in the north and west, passing near Rome (Italy is completely obscured in this map), and extending down to Israel and Egypt in the south and east. Through these points we can draw a line of best fit that organizes the early modern world along a single axis, like a fulcrum. This line accounts for the greatest part of its geosemantic variation, with England on one side, Israel on the other, and Rome in the middle.

At first, I was surprised how neatly EEBO's words fit this line, but in retrospect it should have been an obvious expectation. Places to the northeast and southwest had comparatively little impact on the corpus. Muscovy and Tartary occupied large swathes of land but contained very few concretely named places, so there's no reason for any keyword to be centered on them. In the other direction, sub-Saharan Africa remained largely unknown and the American colonies could do little to affect global patterns. Places like Brazil, Mexico, and Peru were objects of fascination but only rarely topics of discourse, so they pull only a small handful of highly specialized words toward themselves. For this reason, the two-dimensional spherical space of the globe can be neatly projected onto a single, one-dimensional line of spatial difference, where every word can be uniquely plotted.

We now have the tools we need to draw a topography of this complex conceptual space. The line of geographical best fit provides a useful base for examining the semantic footprints of individual keywords. Figure 3.11 plots longitude against range. The horizontal axis follows the line of best fit from west to east, with words located closer to England on the left and words tending toward Israel and Asia on the right. The vertical axis represents each word's range, with some confined to a narrow territory and others stretching over thousands of miles. From this perspective, the conceptual topography of EEBO is shaped like a lily, a trumpet, or a cornucopia. As words move farther east, the scope of their geographical reference expands linearly. For every longitudinal degree a word travels away from England, its radius expands on average by 34.1 miles. Words local to English politics sit at the base of a structure that extends through the European core, where most of the words cluster together. From there, moving farther eastward and outward, conceptual space splits and expands. Scriptural history floats back down, immune to the general expanding tendency. Keywords of scripture are unusually narrow in their geography, at least for words relating to places so far from England. Terms of the East Indies, like *cambaya*, *india*, *china*, and *quinsay*, are the

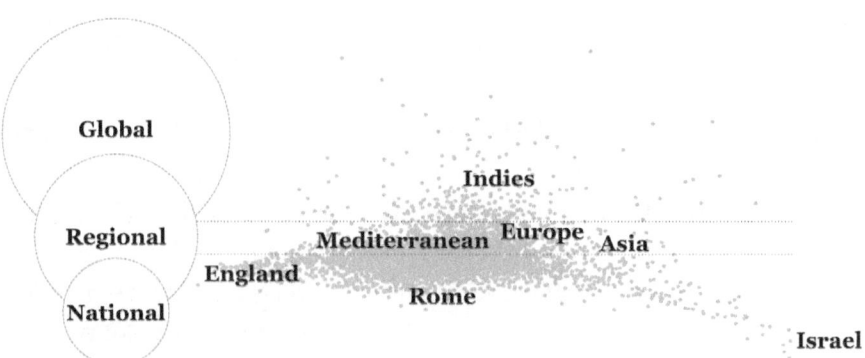

Figure 3.11. A Conceptual Topography of EEBO. The x-axis of this graph extends across the line of best fit from figure 3.10, displaying the longitude for each point along that line. The y-axis displays the range for each keyword. To adjust for the bias that causes words in the east to have wider ranges, the map is laid flat on its own line of best fit.

outliers in the upper right and top. These are the words both farthest away and most widely ranging in application. In the upper left are words relating to America, like *indians*, *chili*, and *andes*. These words skew westward like those of England but across a much wider space.

The conceptual topography of the early modern world is thus layered somewhat like the Earth's atmosphere. Near the ground, so to speak, is a troposphere where terms are used in tightly localized ways; in the middle is a mesosphere of regional concepts that range across the most common locales, and far above is an exosphere of far-out terms peculiar to the exotic lands of the Americas and East Asia. Across these layers, we can draw a lexical atlas that plots location against range, but tilted on the side to adjust for the longitudinal bias of the corpus. When reading over the atlas, the key thing to remember is that the x-axis represents each word's average position along the line of geographical best fit. Words biased toward England will be on the left; words biased toward Israel on the right. The y-axis reflects the range, so words toward the bottom are relatively local to their longitude, while words toward the top exist at a higher altitude, ranging more widely over the field of possible spaces.

CHAPTER THREE

Zone 1: National Concepts

When I survey this topography, I'll identify each region by its epitomizing toponym, then highlight the hundred or so words closest to that toponym in the chart. As we'll see, the language of place varies greatly from region to region, and as we survey them, we'll find not just different places but different psychologies of scale and different spatial modalities. I'll begin with the most tightly localized concepts, *england*, *rome*, and *israel*.

Farthest to the west of the early modern world is a compact semantic region that most prominently features England and other toponyms of northwest Europe. This area is narrow in extent, contained mostly between the 23rd and 30th degrees of longitude, with ranges as many as 200 miles less than typical. It's bounded below and to the immediate east with terms peculiar to France and above by Spain and other words that range more widely across Europe. At its most western tip is a political and geographical vocabulary exclusive to the British Isles. Throughout this region are scattered terms relating to European politics and statecraft, most notably the names of individual nobles, but also including

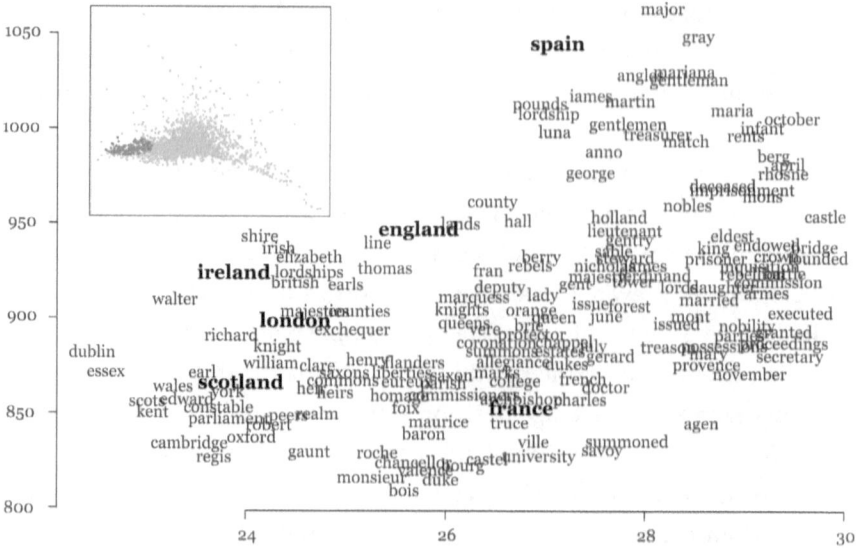

Figure 3.12. England. Terms related to England and its neighbors cluster closely together along the western frontier of EEBO. Most notable are names of countries and cities that gather together in a space distinct to the British Isles.

words describing judicial proceedings, battles, and titles like *baron*, *earl*, and *duke* as well as terms for local administrative units, like *shire*, *county*, and *parish*.

Of all regions in the conceptual space of the early modern world, here is where the idea of the nation-state is most clearly visible, indeed paramount. This configuration of terms represents a culmination of several centuries of social change. Political historian Saskia Sassen describes this change in strictly geographical terms as the "spatial demarcation of political authority."[35] In previous centuries, authority was dispersed among competing feudal and religious institutions. Over the course of the sixteenth and seventeenth centuries, Sassen argues, their authorities were either replaced by or consolidated under the collective sovereignty of states, which in turn came to be defined by the geographical boundaries that circumscribed their jurisdictions. This territorialization of authority gave nation-states unitary identities and thereby made them thinkable as discrete members of a continent-wide interstate system of diplomacy and commerce. The world-economy of Europe was born.

However, I want to emphasize one curious lexical consequence of this shift. The geospatial integrity of modern nation-states supported a way of talking about them that was, itself, free to disregard any sense of their physical geography as a continuous space of human movement. Once states were recognized as discrete entities, they could function in language like people, or like any other basically nonterritorial entity. As construed in the context of political discussion, states are not really regions on maps or three-dimensional zones through which people move. Instead, they're more like nodes in a network—points in a system of points. For example, consider the following 1689 proclamation, quoted in full, that announces William and Mary, already installed in England, as the new King and Queen of Scotland:

A PROCLAMATION, DECLARING WILLIAM and MARY KING and QUEEN of England, to be KING and QUEEN of Scotland.

Edinburgh April 11. 1689.

WHereas, the Estates of this Kingdom of *Scotland*, by their Act of the Date of these Presents, have Resolved, That *William* and *Mary*,

King and Queen of *England*, *France* and *Ireland*, Be, and Be declared King and Queen of *Scotland*, to hold the Crown and Royal Dignity of the said Kingdom of *Scotland*, to them the said King and Queen, during their Lives, and the longest Liver of Them; and that the Sole and Full Exercise of the Regal Power, be only in, and Exercised by the said King, in the Names of the said King and Queen, during their joynt Lives. As also, the Estates having Resolved and Enacted an Instrument of Government, or Claim of Right, to be presented with the Offer of the Crown, to the said King and Queen. They do Statute and Ordain, that William and Mary, King and Queen of *England*, *France* and *Ireland*, be accordingly forthwith Proclaimed King and Queen of *Scotland*, at the Mercat-Cross of *Edinburgh*, by the Lyon King at Arms, or his Deputs, his Brethren Heraulds, Macers and Pursevants, and at the Head-Burghs of all the Shires, Stewartries, Bailliaries, and Regalities within the Kingdom, by Messengers at Arms. Extracted forth of the Records of the Meeting of the Estates; by me

JA. DALRYMPLE, Cls.

GOD Save KING WILLIAM and QUEEN MARY.[36]

This proclamation perfectly exemplifies a conception of monarchical sovereignty that extends authority over discrete nation-states. The declaration covers all of Scotland, including "all the Shires, Stewartries, Bailliaries, and Regalities" Scotland contains. But notice what isn't on the page: any language that indicates a conception of space at the environmental scale. No references to houses, streets, hills, fields, nor any physical spaces through which human bodies might move, except for one point location, the Mercat Cross in Edinburgh, where the proclamation was to be publicly read. Nothing in the language of the proclamation renders space as a continuous field of action. It's most prominently marked by the names of political entities—England, Scotland, Ireland, France, Edinburgh—none of which need to be described. Because political authority had been spatially demarcated, the territorial integrity of states could be taken for granted and therefore didn't need to be represented in the documents that mentioned them. For this reason, this conceptual

CONCEPTUAL TOPOGRAPHY   147

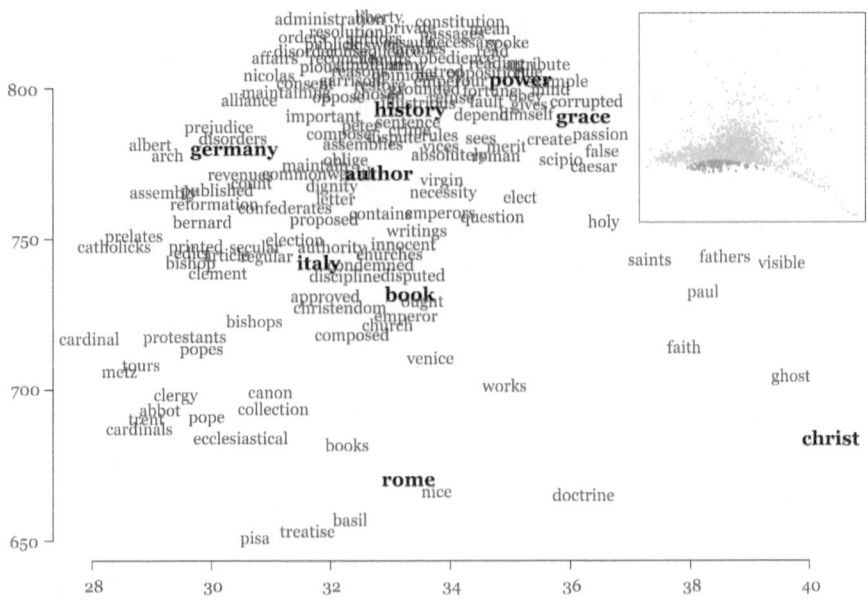

Figure 3.13. Rome. Rome marks the longitudinal midpoint of the world but sits near the bottom of this graph because of its relatively small range, compared to other words at its longitude.

region of the early modern world represents political space under a point-set topology, much like the hierarchical taxonomy of geographical containment, rather than as continuous physical territory, per se.

The conceptual region surrounding Rome is of much wider extent than the area surrounding England. It stretches from the 28th to the 40th degrees of longitude, where terms range between 100 and 500 miles less than typical. The word *rome*, itself, is among the outliers of the region, with an unusually narrow geographical application. (That's because it was so often mentioned only in reference to itself, rather than in relation to other places.) Rome is bounded to the west by a language of religious disputation that separates *rome* from *france* and to the east by terms of religiosity that point toward *israel*. Like the region surrounding *england*, *rome* is surrounded by toponyms: *pisa*, *basil*, *venice*, *italy*, and *germany*. However, the political space near *rome* was construed very differently. Whereas political terms that cluster near *england* tend to be very specific, made up primarily by the names of individuals and local institutions, the language surrounding *rome* emphasizes a much more general discourse of political discussion, centered on Italy but extending over a wider range, where the language of the public sphere marked a boundary that separated the conceptual space of religious and political debate from the rest of the corpus. Many words related to the world of the book trade fall in this region: *books, book, collection, letter, printed, published, author, reading, answer,* and *authors*. From west to east this region reflects the geographical biases of religious argument. Back toward France and England, printed books were more likely to focus on the institutional and social forms of religion, while toward Israel they emphasized terms of symbolic, abstract religious authority. This distinction can be epitomized by the differing positions of *treatise* and *doctrine* on either side of *rome*.

This region in EEBO's geosemantic space can therefore be understood to represent something like print culture—a conceptual space of information exchange where European history was known to unfold and where political values came under dispute. For example, notice how toponyms are situated among other words in this passage, taken from John Owen's *Some Considerations about Union among Protestants* (1680), which typifies discourse in this geosemantic region:

> The first Form of an Authoritative National Church-State amongst us, as in other places, was *Papal*: And the sole use of it here in *England*, was to embroyl, our Kings in their Government, to oppress the People in their Souls, Bodies, and Estates, and to sell us all, as branded slaves, unto *Rome*. These things have been sufficiently manifested. But in other places especially in *Germany*, whil'st otherwise they were all of one Religion, in Doctrine and Worship, all conform to the Church of *Rome*; yet in bloody contests meerly about this Authoritative Church State, many Emperours were ruined, and an hundred set Battels fought in the Field.
>
> At the *Reformation* this Church State, was accommodated, (as was supposed) unto the Interest of the Nation, to obviate the evils suffered from it, under the *other Form*, and render it of use unto the Religion established. Yet experience manifests that, partly from its

Constitution, partly from the Inclinations of them by whom it is managed, other evils have accompanied or followed it, which until they are removed, *the weakness of the* Protestant Interest through mutual Divisions, will remain among us.[37]

In this space, political authority is neither discrete nor absolute, but constantly questioned and contested. The attempt to create an "Authoritative National Church-State" was not local to any particular place but weaves among them. Germany was not yet a state, and the political abstraction with which Owen ends—the "Protestant Interest"—refers to something like a public in the Habermasian sense, rather than to a nation-state. In this passage, both space and time are a continuous, open field populated with historical events ("Battels fought in the Field") and kinds of persons ("Emperours," "People," and "Kings"). Under this framework, the European interstate system is tied together by religion and war, rather than by commerce, and so if we were to attach a label to this zone, we

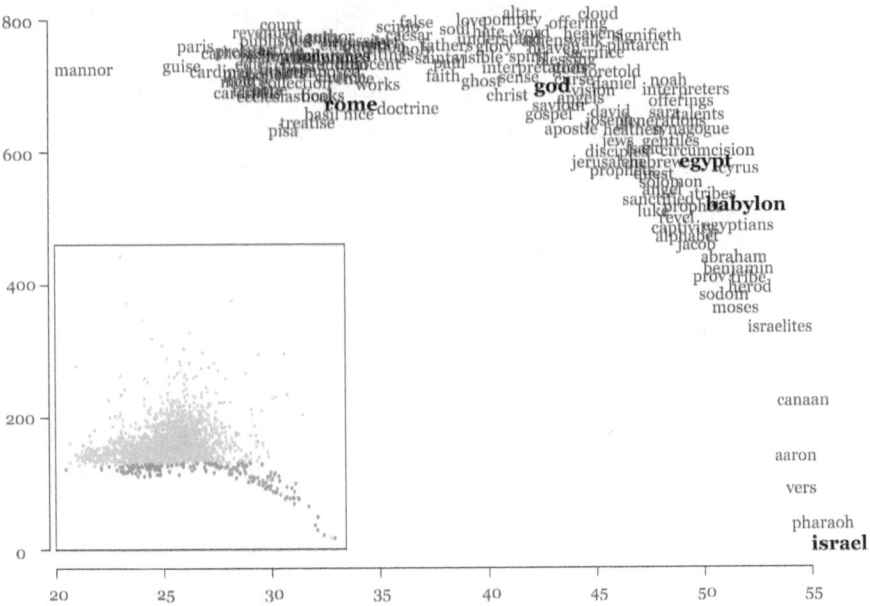

Figure 3.14. Israel. Terms related to Israel and biblical antiquity have special properties in the corpus.

wouldn't follow Braudel and Wallerstein in calling it "Europe." We'd call it "Christendom," a geoconceptual formation that endured long after the consolidation of its constituent nation-states. In much the same way that the international market bound together a world-economy, the international practice of religious dispute bound together a republic of letters.

Israel anchors a crucially important geosemantic region in the early modern world. Biblical antiquity dominates the outer edge of the corpus and, indeed, all local space east of Rome. This area extends from the 40th to the 60th degrees of latitude and is distributed along ranges from 500 to 1,300 miles smaller than typical. Terms of biblical antiquity sit far to the east but exhibit a geographical coherence similar to those of European countries: *israel, egypt, babylon,* and *jerusalem* anchor this space of Hebraic political and religious narrative. Like England, this region gathers together names of places, peoples, and prominent persons. But the people of biblical antiquity exist in a social space largely disjoint from Europe. The two regions are linked, not by geopolitical contiguity (as in the boundary that separates France from Italy), but by symbolic concepts of religious authority. Most notably, *god* and *christ*.

However, the other key feature of biblical geography is the prevalence of narrative prose. Whereas discussions of England and Europe often emphasized comparatively abstract debates about political authority or moral judgments about individual misconduct, biblical history tended to be grounded more solidly in environmental space. Consider this passage, from Nicolas Fontaine's *History of the Old and New Testament* (1699), which tells of the "Israelites Passing the Red Sea":

> PHARAOH seeing that the *Children* of *Israel* were escaped out of his *Hands,* and that the three Days they had demanded for to go and *Sacrifice* in the *Wilderness* were already past, and that there was no likelyhood of their Return; forgetting all the prodigious *Judgments* wherewith GOD had plagued him, and his habitual *hardness* of *Heart* getting the upper-hand of him, he resolves to pursue them.
>
> The *Israelites* seeing themselves in this danger, and engag'd in a *Desert,* where they had the *Sea* before them, and *Pharaoh*'s Army be-

hind them; these terrible *Objects* made that impression upon them, as made them forget their so late and miraculous *Deliverance*, together with the Divine Superintendency, which led them in the *Desert* with a *Pillar of Cloud by Day, and a Pillar of Fire by Night*. So they gave themselves up to *Murmurings* and *Complaints*, demanding in a peremptory way, of *Moses*, Whether it were for lack of *Graves* in *Egypt*, that he had brought them into that *Wilderness*, that they might find them there?[38]

The passage contains two toponyms: Israel and Egypt. Along with Jerusalem and Babylon, these place names appear so often together that they comprise an unusually tight geospatial frame of reference, compared to other places so far from England. Notice, though, how different the language is in this passage, compared to the passage cited previously in relation to England. Here, geographical concepts are portrayed as continuous fields of empty space through which subjects move. The "Israelites [see] themselves in danger," with the sea on one side and the Pharaoh's army on the other. In this space, history unfolds through action, where the Pharaoh and the Israelites can look toward each other, like opponents crouched in a field of contest. This empty space provides a formal frame for a variety of terms that would be less likely to appear in religious and political debate centered on European places. This will have important consequences when we examine the conceptual regions at higher altitudes. Because the discourse of Israel is so grounded in historical narrative, it exerts a powerful gravity on the more widely distributed regional concepts surrounding Europe and Asia.

Zone 2: Regional Concepts
Regional concepts range more widely than terms from nationally defined spaces. At this level, the ranges of semantic footprints tend to be several hundred miles wider than expected, based on their longitudinal centroids. I'll examine words surrounding *mediterranean*, *europe*, and *asia* (fig. 3.15).

The term *mediterranean* is one of very few toponyms in this central band of EEBO's geosemantic space. The terms that surround it are

152 CHAPTER THREE

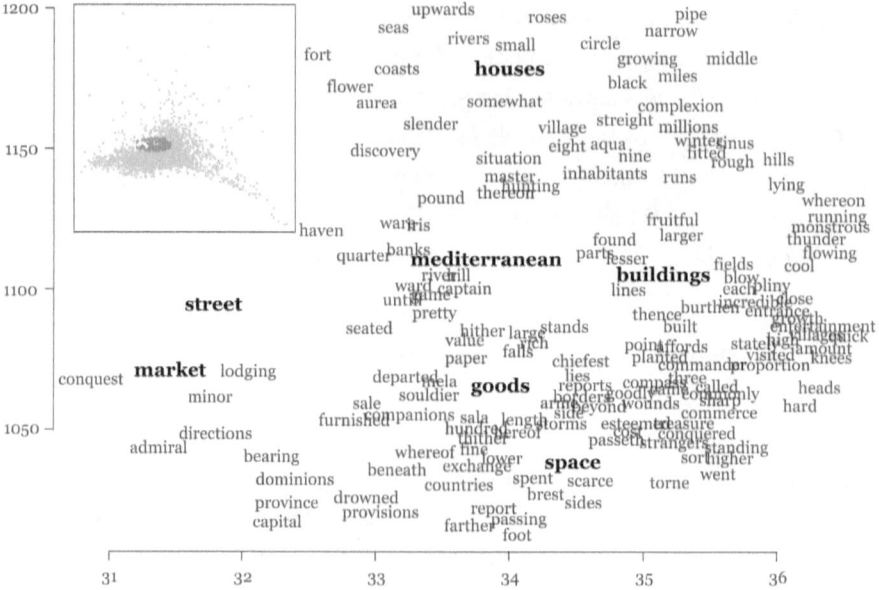

Figure 3.15. Mediterranean. Terms surrounding *mediterranean* were often used to describe places across Europe.

situated between the 31st and 36th degrees of longitude, placing them even with Rome. But they range much more widely, between two and four hundred miles more than typical for that longitude. The term *mediterranean* is bounded above by a general discourse of physical geography (*coasts, seas, rivers*) and below by terms that refer to political divisions without naming them individually (*dominions, countries*). In this region, words are centered in Europe, but they're distributed across a larger range than national concepts, so few relate to specific places. Instead, we find here a more general discourse of geographical description peculiar to Europe, where terms are still concerned with European war and statecraft but focus less on named institutions of power. Here we see the clearest indications of the built environment of the European world. References to things like *streets, houses,* and *buildings* surround the space, which is populated, not by geographically local figures like kings, but by *soldiers*. Of particular note is the language of commercial enterprise (*market, goods, exchange, commerce*) that sits alongside general reports of military occupation and action (*conquest, conquered*).

You might also notice the word *space* between the 34th and 35th degrees of longitude. The term's placement in this region is appropriate because here is where the corpus most directly reflects what Henri Lefebvre described as the social production of space, which involved the physical, economic, and ideological construction of European towns into environments that supported commercial activity and capitalist development. "The town was given written form," Lefebvre argues, as "representations of space derived from the experience of river and sea voyages were applied to urban reality."[39] Europe was subjected to detailed geographical description of the kind we tend to associate with accounts of exotic lands. For example, consider this passage from *An Accurate Description of the United Netherlands* (1691), written by an English diplomat in the later seventeenth century:

> The standing Forces of *Denmark* are well disciplined Men, and Commanded by good Officers, both Natives and Strangers, both French and Scots, as Major General *Duncan*, and Major General *Veldun*, both Scottish-Men, whom I saw at *Copenhagen*. The Soldiers as well as Courtiers are quartered upon the Citizens, a Custom which is likewise practised in *Sweden*, and tho' somewhat uneasie, yet not repined at by the People, who by the care and good Government of the King, find Trade much advanced. For his Majesty by encouraging Strangers of all Religions to live in his Dominions, and allowing the French and Dutch Calvinists, to have publick Churches, hath brought many Trading Families to *Copenhagen*, and by the measure he hath taken for setling Trade in prohibiting the Importation of Foreign Manufactures, and Reforming and new Modelling the East and West *India* Companies, hath much encreased Commerce, and thereby the Wealth of his Subjects; so that notwithstanding the new Taxes imposed upon all Coaches, Wagons, Ploughs, and all real and personal Estates, which amount to considerable Sums of Money; the People live very well and contented.[40]

"This language," Lefebvre explains, "was the *code of space*."⁴¹ And it's not hard to see why he would emphasize conceptual formations like these. The variety and richness of spatial concepts at work in this passage are difficult to enumerate because they're so complexly entangled. At one level are the named cities and countries of Europe, but rather than existing together in a simple point-set topology typical of the language of diplomacy and news, named places are in this passage very explicitly rendered as environmental fields that contain persons and objects. Yet, places are not mere passive containers. Instead, and as Doreen Massey might argue, in this passage Copenhagen functions as a site of action, variety, and mobility that participates in a wider spatial network of places that stretches all the way to India. Here, a place is an urban field available for military conquest, occupation, and governance, but it's also a scene of capitalist enterprise where the circulation of money supports global communication and trade. In this geosemantic region, the European world-economy described by Braudel and Wallerstein leaves the clearest imprint on the language of place.

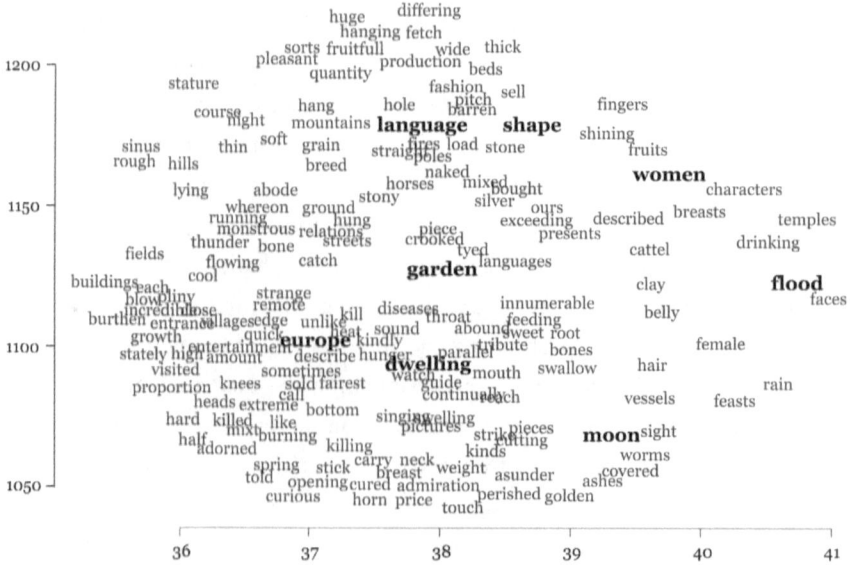

Figure 3.16. Europe. On the far eastern end of the *mediterranean* region is the conceptual field surrounding *europe*.

Terms surrounding *europe* are situated between the 36th and 41st degrees of longitude, ranging about 200 to 400 miles wider than typical (fig. 3.16). Perhaps curiously, the term *europe* sits on the conceptual outside of other terms relating to the European world-economy, and it represents the outer eastern edge of the region surrounding *mediterranean*. These words all sit relatively far to the east. They're less likely to be affiliated with named places of Britain and northern Europe and are more likely to be associated with narratives related to scriptural antiquity. As discourse moves into these more sparsely and widely ranging areas, terms shift in emphasis from the built environments of European towns toward spaces of domesticity and of the body. Here, language loses most of its explicitly geographical content and represents something like spatialized experience in general. It's here, on the outskirts of Europe rather than closer to home in England, that one finds a pastoral discourse of *dwelling*, as well as of rural life, of animal and human bodies, of women, of taste and touch, and of spatial extension itself.

In this region of EEBO's conceptual field, terms range widely across toponyms and so are not closely affiliated with any specific geographical places. However, they skew unmistakably to the east, where the daily lives of ancient Hebrews remained a constant source of reflection and commentary, but also in the modern world where aspects of material, everyday experience were presumptively alien and therefore required detailed description. Consider this account of the pagan religious practices of the "Ceremiss" tribe, now known in Russia as the Mari people, taken from *The Antient and Present State of Muscovy* (1698):

> They are a Nation barbarous, treacherous, and cruel, living upon Robbery, and addicted to Sorcery. . . . When they Offer their Sacrifices to God, they kill a Horse, an Ox, or a Sheep, some of the Flesh thereof, being roasted, and put into a Dish, and holding in the other Hand another Vessel fill'd with Hydromel, or some other Liquor. . . . They pay a great Veneration, even to Adoration, to the Sun and Moon, whom they believe the Authors of the Productions of the Earth. They make use of no Churches, Priests or Books, their Sacrifices and other religious Exercises, being performed near some Torrent

or another. Polygamy is used among them, even so as to Marry two or three Sisters at one time. Their Women and Maids are all wrapt up in a piece of coarse white Cloath, scarce any thing being to be seen but their Faces; The Men wear a long Coat, made of Linnen Cloath, under which they wear Breeches; they all shave their Heads; the young Men, who are unmarried, leaving however for distinctions sake, a long Tress of Hair, hanging upon their Back. Their Language is peculiar to themselves, having no relation with that of the other Neighbouring *Tartars*, or with the *Turkish* or *Muscovian Languages*, tho some of them, that are conversant with the *Muscovites*, have attained some knowledge of their Tongue.[42]

Anthropological descriptions like these focused attention on aspects of spatial experience that usually could be left implicit in books about more familiar places. What do people wear? How do they live and worship and eat? What animals do they raise? What languages do they speak? Notice, too, the presence of women, and with them all the attendant markers of domestic physicality: bodies and clothes, heads and faces, mouths and bones, fingers and touch. These things all bend far to the east, away from politics and markets and war, on the outskirts of Europe and toward the outer edge of the world. One of the most curious features of early modern English world-thinking is this strange tendency to locate intimacy and domesticity among distant and ancient places. Daily life enters English print from far away. Touch and taste, displaced onto exotic analogues.

The conceptual region surrounding *asia* makes up a sparse frontier where several different spatial modalities intersect (fig. 3.17). It is situated between the 38th and 46th degrees of longitude, with ranges between 800 and 1,000 miles above average. Its more localized terms overlap with the national spaces of *greece*, *persia*, and *sion*. To the west it is bounded by the language of *europe*. Thus, *asia* occupies the center of a diffuse space suffused with a discourse of religiosity that links Europe to human experience at its most general and most ideal. Here we find terms related to Christian universalism (*mankind, multitude*), family structures (*parents, children, wives, servants*), encounters with the divine (*miracle, miraculous, wonders*), terms of geographical totality (*world, earth, paradise*), and a

CONCEPTUAL TOPOGRAPHY 157

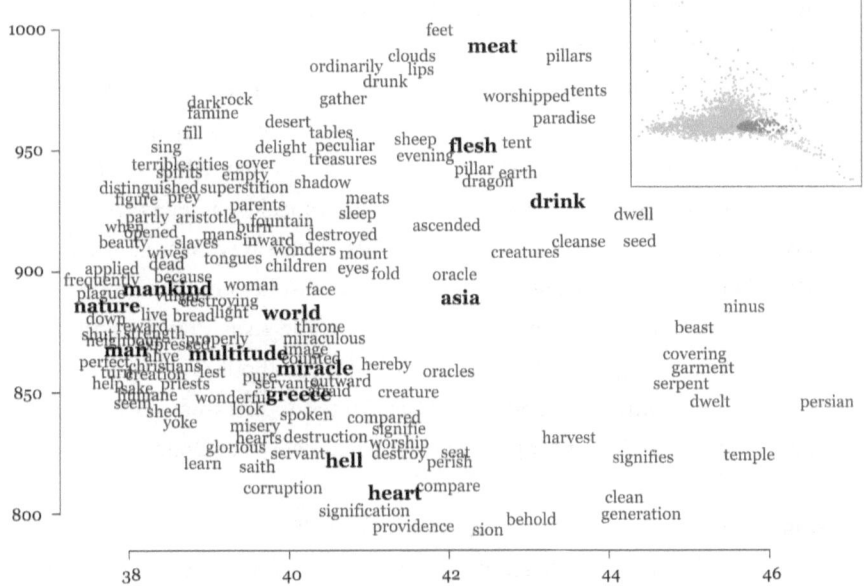

Figure 3.17. Asia. This geosemantic space separates the European world from biblical antiquity and divinity.

language of embodied subjectivity (*flesh, lips, feet, eyes*). In this sense, *asia* marks the point of intersection among several diverse but interwoven threads of early modern geographical thought: biblical antiquity, nature and mankind in general, and the body as a vehicle for divine witness.

The best examples come from scripture itself, where we find language related to Christian universalism and idealized embodied being. Notice the rich collection of toponyms found in this passage from Acts, quoted in Richard Baxter's *Paraphrase of the New Testament* (1685):

> And when the day of Pentecost was fully come, they were all with one accord in one place. And suddenly there came a sound from heaven, as of a rushing mighty wind, and it filled all the house where they were sitting.
>
> And they were all filled with the holy Ghost, and began to speak with other tongues, as the Spirit gave them utterance. And there were dwelling at Jerusalem, Jews, devout men, out of every Nation under

heaven. Then were at Pentecost Jews out of many Nations where they were dispersed, that came up to the Feast.

Now when this was noised abroad, the multitude came together, and were confounded, because that every man heard them speak in his own language. And they were all amazed and marvelled, saying one to another, Behold, are not all these which speak, Galileans? And how hear we every man in our own tongue, wherein we were born? Parthians, and Medes, and Elamites, and the dwellers in Mesopotamia, and in Judea, and Cappadocia, in Pontus, and Asia, Phrygia, and Pamphylia, in Egypt, and in the parts of Libya, about Cyrene, and strangers of Rome, Jews and proselytes. Cretes and Arabians, we do hear them speak in our tongues the wonderful works of God.[43]

Terms overrepresented in books about the New Testament tend to skew strongly to the East. Jerusalem, Judea, Mesopotamia, Libya, Egypt, Rome, and "every Nation under heaven"—these are the sites of divine witness, and therefore of the "world" as such. Although concepts like *mankind* were ostensibly universal, they weren't distributed evenly over early modern geography. Because of their association with scripture, terms like *mankind*, *world*, and *earth* were strongly associated with the eastern Mediterranean region, beyond the boundaries of Europe, but not so far away as India or China. The world was a fairly small place located somewhere among Greece and Asia. God might be ubiquitous, but God's ubiquity was confined to a relatively narrow region.

The universalizing ambitions of biblical world-making were expressed through narratives about groups of individuals—about "multitudes." Here, individuals are gathered together in a single house, where they stand "all amazed and marvelled" by a shared miraculous revelation from heaven. In the case of the Pentecost, this revelation takes a peculiar spatial form. Social differences that manifest through language are conceived in specifically geographical and national terms, as peoples from "every Nation" are able, however briefly, to understand each other in common. This geographical distribution is collapsed in the narrative (and on the page) by drawing those nations together and binding them in a shared lexical unit, where the multitude gathers to speak and hear of "the wonderful works of God." Thus, while the universal totality of "world" in early modern discourse might seem, on the surface, to transcend and erase national difference, it depended at all times on a lexicon of nations and cities that were named in the textual record of revelation and which together provided the framework over which universal transcendence could be described as such.

Perhaps strangely, this small place, where universal mankind took residence, was also the place of wives, slaves, and servants, of children and parents. Here is where domestic hierarchy was naturalized, so it was home to all persons excluded from politics and commerce. Here, an idealized collective self, *mankind*, parted ways from *men*, who were off somewhere else, back in Europe among monarchs and mayors, busy among soldiers and churchmen and books. Here, by contrast, in Asia, early modern print found *nature*, *creation*, and *providence*. Here were *meat* and *drink*. Here be *miracles*.

Zone 3: Global Concepts
Some terms were used most characteristically to describe places in America and the Far East. These terms range much more widely than most terms in the corpus.

Whereas the terms *earth* and *world* closely associate with the Mediterranean region of Asia, *globe* associates more strongly with geographical places further afield, and therefore with the Indies, both East and West (fig. 3.18). The conceptual region surrounding *indies* is situated primarily between the 30th and 50th degrees of longitude, while ranging between 1,200 and 2,400 miles above average. Here, words refer almost exclusively to topics involving navigation and trade (*voyage, commodities, ships*), specific sites of colonial encounter in the Americas and Asia (*india, china, puerto*), as well as to weather and climate (*winds, snow, summer*) and to geographical description (*ocean, islands, natives, trees*, and *fishes*), including the mathematical language for global geographical space (*meridian, latitude, minutes, degrees*, and *leagues*). Unlike the other regions of EEBO's conceptual topography, the Indies divide neatly into their respective

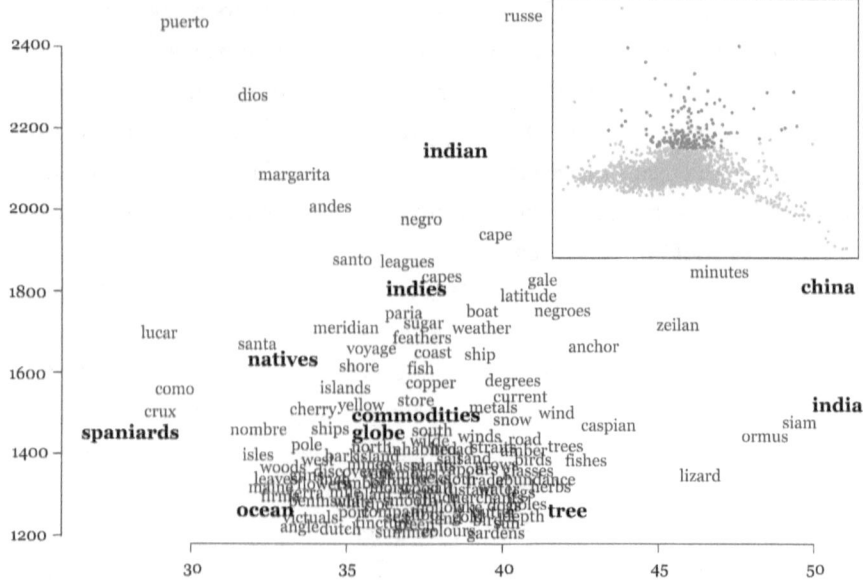

Figure 3.18. Indies The terms surrounding *indies* represent a wide-ranging global space of navigation, trade, and colonial exploration.

continents. To the west are words referring predominantly to places in America. To the east are words referring mostly to Asia. Words used in both contexts converge toward the center.

Of all the regions in early print's conceptual topography, this will likely be the most familiar to scholars, because this region has been subject to detailed commentary by historians interested in the ideological origins of the British Empire. Everything about the discourse at this altitude suggests places far away from home and activities far removed from domestic life. The language of adventure, travel, and cosmography dominates this space. A typical example of this mode can be found by selecting almost any page from William Dampier's *A New Voyage Round the World* (1697). Here is a characteristic passage:

> Between *Pulo Way* and the Main of *Sumatra* is another Channel of 3 or 4 Leagues wide: which is the Channel for Ships, that go from

Achin to the Streights of *Malacca*, or any Country to the East of those Streights, and *vice versa*. There is good riding in all this Semicircular Bay between the Islands and *Sumatra*: but the Road for all Ships that come to *Achin* is near the *Sumatra* Shore, within all the Islands. There they anchor at what distances they please, according to the Monsoons or Seasons of the Year. There is a small Navigable River comes out into the Sea, by which Ships transport their Commodities in smaller Vessels up to the City. The mouth of this River is 6 or 7 Leagues from *Pulo Rondo*, and 3 or 4 from *Pulo Way*, and near as many from *Pulo Gomez*. The Islands are pretty high Champion Land, the mould black or yellow, the Soyl deep and fat, producing large tall Trees, fit for any uses. There are brooks of water on the 2 great Islands of *Way* and *Gomez*, and several sorts of wild Animals; especially wild Hogs in abundance.[44]

Geographical descriptions of this kind are lexically distinct in how they combine three kinds of words. First, low-frequency toponyms like "Achin," "Malacca," and "Sumatra," at least some of which are usually associated with geocoordinates located far from Europe. Second, geomorphological terms naming water forms—that is, words like "river," "island," "bay," and "sea." Third, words naming categories of flora and fauna, like "trees" and "hogs." These nouns are all situated together in a paragraph where they represent a navigable, environmental space that can be directly plotted onto the cartographic spaces of maps. As a result, the language of travel was highly abstract, even when at its most colorful and most vivid. Everything Dampier describes is an instance of a type, every place a place on a map. But it was precisely that abstraction that allowed exotic locales to be conceived as sites of presumptively unrealized potential ripe for colonial exploitation. A faraway land is a place where the reader might visit, and where, if they do, they might sail their boats, walk around, check the consistency of the soil, find uses for trees, or tame wild hogs. These features of global discourse—abstraction, navigability, and potentiality—produced a lexical periphery far from the Mediterranean center.

Conclusion: Meaning Has a Spatial Component

Describing the world is no easy task. Yet, EEBO's vocabulary sorts into geographically and topically coherent zones, and if I were to describe how its authors, in aggregate, saw the world, I'd put it this way: Closest to home, England, France, and the other western nation-states existed in their own tightly bound space as outliers on the far side of Europe. The Mediterranean center represented a dense geographical and conceptual field where discourse most frequently tended, and where space was represented through a language of state politics, religious dispute, and commerce. On the far side of that main zone was Asia, a sparse region of discourse where the world was construed like a celestial object and guided by providence. In this world, geopolitical terms were displaced by universal conceptions of nature and mankind, which in turn supported a language of domesticity and the body. On the farthest eastern edge of Asia, Israel and the other biblical lands anchored a geography of God and Christ with narratives of divine witness and analogues to individual and familial being. Surrounding all of this, exploration and trade enwrapped the globe in a beautiful and violent and entirely exotic worldly abstraction.

Topics in discourse aren't like countries with borders or fences. There are no customs agents in lexical space policing distinctions between *here* and *there*. Readers might quibble with how I've divided early print's lexical space into zones, with what quotations I've chosen to exemplify those zones, or with how I've chosen to describe them. Nonetheless, I feel pretty confident that most readers will share my sense that there exists a sense of place within early modern print. Some places are geographical in the common meaning of that phrase, but such specificity often breaks down as the concrete topics of politics, geography, and history blend into philosophy, theology, and domestic life. The lexicon of scriptural history blends into a language of being that moves through God to inhabit body and earth. In the process, some conventional geographical regions are grossly distorted. Asia is a conceptual outlier that marks the outside of Europe, rather than a continent with coherent parts. Africa is almost completely absent except for Egypt, which is reduced to little more than a province of biblical antiquity. America is nothing more than a few very specialized terms scattered far and wide. In sum, the early modern world was a space of multiple independent geographies—political, economic, topographical, global, domestic, and celestial—all of which happened simultaneously in their various modalities, but all of which also remained mutually suspended over a common system of geographical coordination.

That's not to suggest that meaning is categorically determined by geographical location in the narrow sense. Indeed, no words—not even place names—are bound strictly to location. One risk of geospatial semantics is the risk of being taken too literally. Language's measurable tendencies should not be interpreted as truths that account for all instances. If they were, conceptual topography would look more like cartography. The world of early modern discourse would match more closely to the world as drawn by Mercator and Ortelius. But that's not how it happens. The spaces produced in language correspond to scales of experience that are only sometimes explicitly geographical. The Earth was a celestial object, not quite a geographical one. The heavens were not seen from everywhere equally, but nor were they confined to any place in particular. The spaces of domesticity, of the home and of the body, unfurled along lines of distinction that were commensurable to physical geography but not bound by it.

What does this analysis tell us about the language of place in general? The fact that place-word collocations organize a corpus like EEBO into legible topics is, in and of itself, powerful evidence for the basic idea behind geospatial semantics. This chapter's motivating theoretical argument is that geographical space and conceptual space are more closely related than most people realize. When scholars write about place, they tend to draw a fairly sharp distinction between a location and its sense of place. The former is mathematical and abstract; the latter humanistic and particular. But by the end of the early modern period, these two things weren't really that separate. *What* things were and *where* they were evolved together inside a common language, an organic whole where everything was connected to everything else, often in ways that are difficult to see when looking at individual examples. The geographical assumptions that guided early modern world-thinking—the heres and theres all authors held in mind while writing—were not always explicit or meant to imply hard and fast distinctions. Nonetheless, spatial difference became an important component of the language's semantic structure.

Words are proper to the places of their expression.

Language dwells.

CHAPTER 4

PRINCIPLES OF LITERARY MATHEMATICS

THE NASCENT FIELD OF CULTURAL ANALYTICS has exposed a gap in literary and historical theory. We have a rich vocabulary for describing texts and reading practices. By comparison, our shared vocabulary for describing corpora and their analysis remains very thin. Scholarship in the field has proceeded without any guiding methodological framework nor even a clearly defined set of questions for debate.[1] We need a theory of quantitative literary analysis. Such a discourse would ask: What kinds of things are the objects of textual computation? What mathematical forms are appropriate for their description?

In the information sciences, the social sciences, psychology, mathematics, and even in physics, scholars have developed quantitative models for the study of cultural phenomena and subjected those models to intense scrutiny.[2] But there has been little similar effort in the humanities, where discussions have been limited almost entirely to reflections about quantification in general and have included very little sustained analysis of any specific approach.³ Scholars too often argue *about* quantitative methods without being able to distinguish *among* them in even the most rudimentary ways. If we hope ever to advance the interdisciplinary project of learning to learn from corpora, as I described that project in this book's introduction, this will have to change.⁴

Within the field of digital humanities, a common mistake is made by virtually all commentators. They compare close reading with distant reading, or they contrast qualitative methods with quantitative ones. This leads to the question: "What are the benefits and pitfalls of quantitative methods? What can we *really learn* using them?" Whether this question is asked in an optimistic tone by scholars experimenting with new techniques, or whether it's asked skeptically (accusatorially) by critics, makes no difference. Either way, it's a very bad question—at least, it's a bad question to begin with because it skips to the end. By directing attention exclusively toward the outcomes of research, this question distracts from fundamental issues that must be clearly understood for corpus-based inquiry to be successful.

A much better question to begin with is this one: "What relations exist between the corpus and its source texts? Which quantitative models describe what aspects of those relations?" These questions are better because they connect the dots; they preserve the integrity of the provenance of meaning as it moves from evidence to claim. You have to be able to explain where your findings come from, what calculations they rely on, what features of the texts they're responding to, and what relation those features have to historical social practices. If you can't answer these questions, you won't ever really learn anything through computational methods. You might occasionally be impressed by virtuoso performances of scholarly panache (perhaps even your own), but you won't learn much.

The purpose of this chapter is to model a different approach. Rather than argue laterally among other researchers and critics, I want to focus attention down to the corpus itself, then reason out from there. My argument will begin by presenting what I believe to be the organizing assumptions of cultural analytics, beginning with this basic premise: that variations in a corpus of historical documents will likely correspond meaningfully to the histories of the people who produced those documents. I call this the *distant reading hypothesis*. From there, I'll highlight what I believe to be the most important concepts in quantitative literary analysis, and I'll describe their most direct applications to corpus-based inquiry. Literary mathematics is math applied to literary problems; it is the practice of representing critical concepts using formal expressions that describe relations among literature's countable features. With distant reading, the goal is to use computation in service of literary history, and mathematical models become instruments for evaluating and describing historical variation.[5]

Such research includes three basic steps. Given any collection of texts, the first step is to identify their formal structures. The second step is to describe the distribution of difference across those structures. The last step is to evaluate the significance of those differences. How are texts formed? How are some different from others? Which differences are most significant or surprising? These three broad categories of critical inquiry—form, difference, and significance—correspond loosely to three kinds of quantitative reasoning—discrete mathematics, matrix algebra, and statistics. Literary mathematics uses computation in service of theory, focusing on the models themselves as newly invented constructs and with the goal of better understanding what quantifiable marks the cultural past has left on the surviving record.

The Distant Reading Hypothesis

What reason do we have to believe corpus-based inquiry is trustworthy? What relation exists between our maps and our graphs, on one side, and the cultural past we purport to study, on the other? How does discourse move from there to here? To answer these questions, we need something like a general hypothesis of distant reading—something like a correspondence theory for the corpus. Franco Moretti provided no such thing when he coined the phrase "distant reading," but, now that this paradigm has been taken up by others using more rigorous computational methods, I believe that a few founding assumptions can be identified and are worth making explicit.

Text-based cultural analytics is premised on the belief that what one observes in a corpus corresponds meaningfully to things outside the corpus. Those "things" might just be the source texts themselves—as in, say, a study of a small corpus of novels—but very often scholars hope to extend their inquiries through their sources to recover something generally true about the cultural past. This hope is based on an implicit commonsense historicism. The documents that survive in archives like the British Library were produced by historical agents engaged in social practices. Novel writing is a social practice; so is theatergoing, medicine, civil war, domestic service, party politics, natural philosophy, and so on. These practices all produce various kinds of documentation in their wake, and in many cases the documents were carefully preserved and cataloged in libraries. When we gather that documentation together, transcribe it, and systematically count its features, we can reasonably expect that the features we count will reflect, in one way or another, important and meaningful aspects of the original practice. Actions of the past will echo through our data. This strikes me as the basic premise of distant reading, which I offer here in the form of a proposition:

> *If a social practice produces documentation, and if that documentation is preserved, transcribed, and collected into a corpus, variation in the corpus will tend to correspond meaningfully to differences in that practice.*

You might notice what this proposition doesn't say. It doesn't say that corpus data will provide anything like the objective truth of the past. It doesn't say that a corpus will represent history completely or accurately. It doesn't even say that we can know anything about the past. I'll get to that in a moment. Right now, I'm just saying much more narrowly that differences in *what people were writing about* will likely correspond with variation in *what people wrote*. This idea is very similar to what sociolinguists call the "context of situation."[6] Just as a corpus of flight manuals from across the twentieth century will probably exhibit variation related to changes in aviation, and just as a corpus of political blogs will likely differ where authors are progressives or conservatives, so too any corpus will tend to differ, here or there, based on the various concerns and activities of the original authors and readers.

You'll notice, too, that this proposition rests on two very important conditions, both of which are well known to historians and corpus linguists. Like the records from which its drawn, a corpus is a textual artifact; it inherits all the limitations of its sources. Any voices that have been silenced in the past will also be difficult to trace in a corpus, because social practices that don't produce documentation by definition can't result in corpora. The same principle holds for issues of preservation and transcription. Corpus-based historical inquiry depends entirely on the work of archivists, editors, technical editors, transcribers, and catalogers, whose work is necessarily fallible. Their fallibility can take the form of a simple mistake-making, but such work is necessarily ideological and so also reflects biases and assumptions about how persons and other things should be classified. At stake here is both the "representativeness" of the corpus, as representativeness is traditionally conceived, and the "representativeness" of the categories used to classify metadata and to inform analysis.[7] Variation in a corpus can correspond with a historical practice only insofar as that practice generated a record of itself and as that record was preserved and digitized, and also only insofar as the metadata accurately accounts for the phenomena of interest.

These issues are all important and remain vital areas of scholarship. The curatorial work involved in identifying, collecting, and transcribing records of marginalized peoples is perhaps the most important work happening in digital humanities right now. However, the point I'm making here is the complementary opposite. Yes, scholars should be extremely cautious when using a corpus to make claims about anything that exists outside the corpus. However, that caution should not blind scholars to the enormous amount of information corpora often contain about the social practices that generated the source documents. The distant reading hypothesis, as I've called it, says that, whether or not some group of authors and readers *were representative* of the past in general, a corpus drawn from their texts *will likely represent* at least some of their concerns and activities. The corpus will correspond meaningfully (not comprehensively, but meaningfully) with the histories of the people who produced the documents. This assumption is implicit in the project of recovering lost voices and building corpora of marginalized peoples.

We intuit that a corpus will likely provide good evidence for something. The question that follows is twofold: (1) Why do we believe this? and (2) Once we tease out the reasoning behind this belief, what does our answer suggest about the best practices for analyzing and interpreting that evidence?

Five Underlying Assumptions

Variation in a corpus will tend to correspond meaningfully to the histories of the people whose discourse is recorded in the corpus. Therefore, true statements made about the corpus are likely to correspond to true statements about the past. This proposition rests on five underlying assumptions:

1. *Documents are meant to be read.* The lexical and structural features of documents included in a corpus will tend to be consistent. These consistencies suggest that the source texts addressed a more or less coherent readership with shared expectations and concerns. The more heterogeneous the corpus, the more varied the implied readership.
2. *Documents are written and published purposefully.* Although the documents of a corpus are expected to be broadly similar, most will also exhibit unique properties that correspond to the intentions of their authors and publishers. Words are not distributed randomly; most represent deliberate choices made by intending persons whose intentions are implied in the features of the documents they authored or published.
3. *Digital transcriptions will tend to be accurate.* In most cases, transcriptions will represent the words and punctuation of their source texts in the correct sequences.
4. *Metadata will tend to be accurate.* The authors, publishers, and dates and places of publication will be recorded accurately for most source texts, and the terms used for classification will be appropriate.

5. *Errors and exceptions will tend to be random.* There will exist errors in the transcriptions and the metadata, and there will be anomalies in the source texts, but those errors and anomalies will tend to be distributed randomly and sporadically.

If these five conditions hold, we can safely presume that measurements of a corpus will correspond meaningfully with at least some concerns of the source texts' authors, publishers, and readers. The first two assumptions suture the source texts to their original contexts; the next two connect the texts to the corpus; and the last accounts for errors in the data and anomalies in the sources. Anomalies include elements in the source text that may cause a break in any of the other relationships, such as false imprints (which create inaccurate metadata) or compositor's errors (which aren't written purposefully).[8] If any of these conditions don't hold—if, for example, the transcription errors make the textual data unreliable, or if during data curation the catalogers have imposed false, biased, or otherwise misleading classifications—the connection between the past and the corpus is severed.

For reasons that will become clear, corpus-based inquiry requires maintaining a rigorous distinction between the transcriptions and the metadata. Words on a title page are different from words on the other pages; when digitized, they exist differently in the topology of the corpus. Indeed, in quantitative literary analysis the boundary that separates data from metadata serves as a proxy for the boundary that separates discourse from historical reality as such. Corpus methods do not assume that source texts represent reality. Instead, they assume that metadata situate documents in historical relation to each other. Documents labeled with the same author are likely to have been written by the same person; if labeled with the same printer, they are likely to have been printed at the same house; if labeled with the same year, they were probably first published at more or less the same time. These samenesses are distant reading's enabling fiction. They are purely ideological. The past is an idea we impose on the corpus when we take for granted a meaningful distinction between documents and the bibliographies that describe them.

The result is a kind of metaphysical ambivalence that suspends digital literary studies between an almost naive-seeming historicism, on the one hand, and, on the other, an austere posthumanism. In corpus-based historical inquiry, "the past" is a presumed reality that exists prior to the texts and that motivates research. It's our true object of study. It's what we want to know about and learn from. It's spatiotemporally continuous with ourselves. But in terms of how quantitative analyses are actually conducted, the past functions very differently. It has no existence outside the corpus. It's a structuring principle that organizes documents in relation to each other. The past is an ideological construct that allows us to sort documents into sets based on their metadata.

In turn, grouping documents into sets allows scholars to describe variation in a corpus and to ascribe meaning to that variation. Without metadata, a corpus would be an arbitrarily gathered collection of documents. Still useful to linguists, perhaps, but useless for literary history because researchers would have no principled way to distinguish one group of documents from another and therefore no way to situate either the source texts or the corpus data within any historical frame.

Variation Defined
Several times in the preceding discussion I have used the term "variation," but I have so far left that term undefined. Elsewhere, I have said that the purpose of quantitative literary analysis is to describe "the distribution of difference." For me, these two phrases mean the same thing. I use the word "variation" when I hope to be understood while making a point about something else. I use the phrase "distribution of difference" when trying to specify the concept more clearly.

Variation can be broken down into two parts. The first is "difference." Things have different properties and are categorized differently. We say that apples are different from oranges and that rain is different from snow. The second is "distribution." Things have different positions and are situated differently in relation to each other. If we ask where rainfall is heavy and where it's light, we're describing geographical distribution. If we look at a patch of land and ask how its annual rainfall is being affected by climate change, we're looking at temporal distribution. However, distribution need not have an explicitly spatiotemporal component. If we look at a group of workers and compare their salaries, we're examining the distribution of income. If we count how many times a word appears in each book of a collection, we're examining the distribution of that word.

The term *variation* refers to these two forms of contrast when brought together into a single composite thought. When I look at my arm, I see variation in my skin. Differences in tone and texture are distributed from my fingertips to my elbow. When I think back to the past, I remember that my skin used to be less spotted and less wrinkled, and I refer to such variation as *change*. But when I look across the classroom at my students, and I compare them to myself, I see that this variation isn't necessarily spatial or temporal. Sure, they'll get older too, but for now we all exist together in the same time and place. Nonetheless, skin has very different properties depending on the person. My point is simply to say: Any time we talk about variation, we're talking about how properties correlate with positions. We're talking about how differences are situated in the world. We're asking *what* is *where* (or *when*, or *among whom*). "Change over time" is nothing but variation described over temporal metadata.

In the context of corpus-based inquiry, variation describes a relationship between the data and the metadata, between the observable properties of documents and the structural tags used to label those documents, in whole or in part. Typically, this means comparing transcriptions with bibliographies. Indeed, we can say that the fundamental task of quantitative literary analysis is to describe how differences in textual data correlate with differences in textual metadata. Scholars use bibliographies to sort documents into groups—by date, by author, by genre—and then use the transcriptions to show how textual features differ according to those factors. When working with a corpus like EEBO that has been transcribed using the Text Encoding Initiative (TEI) to differentiate among textual parts, it's possible to make more finely grained comparisons. Markup provides tags for sections and chapters in prose books, or for acts and scenes in plays, and these tags can be used to identify intratextual variation. In any case, "variation" refers to an identified correspondence between differences in the textual data (typically, the lexical sequences or frequencies) and the textual metadata (title, author, date, and so on). Variations of this kind are sometimes called "patterns" or "trends." I refer to them as distributions of difference.

Quantitative literary analysis assumes that variations tend to be meaningful. Upon first hearing, this might sound like a naive assumption. It's easy to imagine random variations that don't mean anything. But if features of a corpus cluster together in some way that persistently corresponds with values in the metadata, those clusters almost certainly suggest something true about the past. It's actually hard to think of a variation that would cluster significantly without suggesting something meaningful in a corpus of historical documents. If books by one author use a very different lexicon from books by another, those authors probably had very different concerns, or they were from different speech communities, or they collaborated with different printers. If the discourse of one year is different from that of another year, something probably changed or happened differently at those times. Variations usually mean something for the simple reason that words on a page are rarely random. They're put there on purpose by people who meant them.

What Variations Mean
Whether such variations are interesting to us as cultural historians . . . that's a different matter entirely. What is meaningful is not necessarily remarkable. However, before we can evaluate the significance of any observed variation, we must first have a general guiding notion about what kinds of variation we expect to observe under what conditions.

The most important discovery made in the library and information sciences during the twentieth century was to show that language operates according to mathematical regularities and that, on the basis of those regularities, documents could be identified and classified automatically using computers. All other advancements in the field are founded on this idea, which is known as the "distributional hypothesis." Zellig Harris first defined this idea by claiming that "difference in meaning correlates with difference in distribution." It is now more often stated in simpler terms: "Similar words tend to appear in similar contexts." This aphorism posits two kinds of similarity that exist together in a mutually informing dialectic that is basically tautological. Words are similar if they appear in similar documents; documents are similar if they contain similar words. When Gerard Salton, Karen Spärck Jones, and other scholars developed computational techniques for automatic indexing and information retrieval, they proposed that these similarities would correspond closely with the subjects of articles and books; documents with similar words would likely be about the same things. Mathematical procedures were designed to identify synonyms for search queries and to supplement bibliographical metadata with automatically generated subject tags.

For corpus-based historical inquiry, the distributional hypothesis has a broader meaning with a more widely ranging application. It suggests a general correspondence between words and actuality that manifests as a relation between a corpus's transcriptions and its bibliography: *Similar words tend to appear in documents with similar metadata*. This small change in the phrasing of the distributional hypothesis entails many corollaries with broad ramifications. Similar words will be used by similar authors, at similar times, when describing similar things in similar places. Consequently, we expect a broad correlation between the lexical contents of discourse and the historical situation within which discourse was produced. We expect this correlation to hold both in general and in narrowly localized settings.

Further, the clustering effects that one finds in language have analogues in other domains of social activity. Because we assume that metadata tend to be accurate, we can behave as if named entities in bibliographies share properties with real things in the world, and we can describe relations among them accordingly. Even though "Dryden, John, 1631–1700" is just a value in EEBO's metadata, we can describe its relationship to "Shadwell, Thomas, 1642?–1692" as if that relationship is between persons. We expect values in the metadata to be distributed in ways reminiscent of real-life social networks. Principles of social interaction like *homophily*—the tendency of people to prefer the company of others who are like themselves—will likely hold when describing values in the author and publisher fields of library catalogs. Bibliographical metadata will likely take forms similar to those of other social formations. Theories developed in the field of network science will likely hold when applied to bibliographies.

We can assume that dates of publication represent values on a real timeline. Documents labeled 1590 were first published about twenty years after books labeled 1570, and this interval is roughly comparable to similar intervals we experience in our own lives. We can take for granted that London was a real place, with buildings and streets and a geographical location. London was closer to Cambridge than to Dublin, closer to Dublin than to Rome, and closer to Rome than to Jerusalem. Principles of geographical interaction like *spatiotemporal autocorrelation*—the tendency, at any given time, of nearby places to have more in common with each other than they have with faraway places—will likely hold when situating the discourse contained in the corpus among the times and places mentioned in its metadata. Geographical metadata in a corpus will likely take forms similar to those observed in physical reality. Theories developed in the field of quantitative geography will likely hold when applied to the study of geographical writing.

For these reasons, the words, persons, and places most relevant to a historical practice are likely to concentrate together in a corpus of documents that record that practice. Variations in the corpus that correspond with the metadata in this way will tend to be trustworthy and, when discovered, are likely to seem intuitive. Against this baseline expectation, variations can be meaningful in three ways: (1) If the correspondence holds and the variation feels intuitive, its representation in the corpus will provide a trustworthy index to, and additional details about, the historical practice at issue. (2) If the correspondence fails, and the variation is shown to be correctly measured but still feels counterintuitive, we are given reason to believe that our understanding of the metadata is incomplete or inaccurate; that is to say, we've learned "something new" about the historical phenomenon. (3) Where variation is discovered that is simply unaccounted for in our understanding of the metadata, and therefore can be neither intuitive nor counterintuitive, we've learned a new way to categorize the past.

The case studies offered in the preceding chapters provide examples of each of these kinds of meaningful variation. A detailed network of the early modern book trade reveals clusters that look a lot like historical periods. Its basic structure has a familiar shape. Such a model can be used to identify locally important figures and to delineate careful and rigorous comparisons while conforming, on the whole, to received notions about the London book trade. However, some of the findings previously presented were meant to challenge conventional wisdom. In chapter 3, for example, I showed that early modern writing about the world was profoundly at odds with how scholars represent the period's "world geography." Scholars whose arguments depend on close readings of Camden or Mercator have greatly distorted our understandings of these topics. Because quantitative surveys are likely to provide very different pictures from close readings of canonical texts, which are by definition idiosyncratic and unrepresentative, variations of this second kind are most likely to be interesting to, and may sometimes prove controversial among, specialists who otherwise care little for computation.

However, if we choose to approach these topics with more self-confidence and a curious spirit (and therefore a higher capacity for creative, rather than merely critical, thinking), we are likely to find variations of the third kind most interesting. Each of the case studies offers examples meant to demonstrate new ways of categorizing the past. To define breaks between historical periods as "structural holes" in metadata networks is to understand periodization in a fundamentally different way. To regularize and systematize theories of intertextuality through aggregation and quantitative analysis is to advance an altogether different conception of meaning. To ask how words are situated in geographical space is to introduce an entirely new line of inquiry to conceptual history.

Scholars should be more creative in how they think about computation. But that creativity should not manifest as unprincipled experimentalism that treats computers as magic hats or black boxes. Instead, it means taking the corpus seriously as an object of analysis by engaging theories for its description that have developed in other disciplines. This imperative suggests another. Findings that reveal new ways of categorizing and understanding the past are discoverable and cognizable only through formal expressions that describe the underlying structures of literary data. Those expressions are necessarily mathematical.

But here's the problem: the mathematics involved in literary computing are very complicated—more so, in fact, than standard applications in many quantitative research fields. The math required for econometric analyses or medical trials is often limited to linear regressions, analyses of variance, and significance tests. By contrast, statistics play a comparatively small role in literary computing, because corpus-based inquiry tends to synthesize operations from many branches of mathematics simultaneously. We use graph theory to describe networks, geospatial analysis to analyze maps, linear algebra and information theory to describe word frequencies—and of course statistics to evaluate significance. The sheer variety of mathematical concepts brought to bear on research in digital humanities can be bewildering. There is no previously existing body of quantitative theory that brings together and explains the fundamental concepts needed for analyzing culture through corpora.

In what follows, I will try to meet this need. Of course, I cannot treat any aspect of this topic except in the most cursory way. However, I will try to explain how the most important concepts relate to each other and to the demands of historical inquiry. The central task of quantitative literary analysis is to describe variation in a corpus by finding meaningful relationships between documents and their metadata. This task involves identifying formal structures in the data, describing differences that appear across those structures, and evaluating the significance of those differences.

Form: Sets, Topologies, and Graphs

What are the basic elements of a corpus? What relation do those elements have to each other? These are the most fundamental questions of corpus-based inquiry because they establish the formal structure of the corpus and determine how its parts will be counted. To answer these questions, I will describe what I call the *ordinary topology of the corpus*. Less precisely, we might call this the *form* of the corpus. Key concepts for describing formal structures can be found in branches of discrete mathematics, including set theory, graph theory, and point-set topology.[9] Often, scholars doing digital work use these concepts more or less unknowingly while designing data structures and research plans, describing them as "choices" made while preparing data for analysis.[10] As a practical matter, it's possible (and at first, probably easier) to make such choices while ignoring general principles. However, better specifying the form of the corpus will help to clarify the larger field of possibility within which these choices get made. The technical and intellectual challenge is to identify topological forms and to invent analytical procedures that navigate among them.[11]

The Topological Space of the Corpus

A corpus can be understood as having the properties of a *topological space*. Topological spaces are spaces that may lack measurable distances but that nonetheless involve relationships of continuity and containment.[12] A topological space implies a sense of "hereness" and "thereness" without necessarily specifying how far "here" is from "there."

Consider these two examples:

First, compare a street map of New York with a subway map. The street map will be drawn carefully to scale and will embed all the streets, parks, and buildings within that scale. If you get out a ruler, you can measure the distance that separates Battery Park from Central Park, and the distance you measure will relate meaningfully to the distance you'd experience if walking the city. A street map is therefore a metric space. By contrast, a subway map cannot be measured in this way. You can use a subway map to identify routes through the city, but the distances that separate any two points on such a map are not meant to correlate meaningfully to measurable physical distances. There's no scale to a subway map.

Second, compare a book with the text it contains. In descriptive bibliography, measurable distances are very important. They determine the size and thickness of the paper as well as the sizes of fonts, illustrations, figures, and so forth. The space of the page is a metric space. By contrast, textual space typically is not measured in this way. In *Paradise Lost*, it would be strange to get out a ruler and try to specify how many millimeters separate Book 1 from Book 9. However, it's perfectly reasonable to say that they're separated by Books 2 through 8. Just like the names of stops along a subway route, the different labels of textual parts specify their locations in relation to each other.

To understand variation in a corpus, you need to be able to describe the topological space over which its textual features are distributed. A topological space includes a collection of basic elements and a system of subsets that situate those elements in relation to each other. The total collection of all elements is called the *underlying set*. The organizing subsets are called the *topology*. The underlying set of a corpus is the set of all tokens it contains. The topology of the corpus is the system of attributes we use to categorize those tokens. Examples of attributes used to categorize tokens include word type, document title, author, and date. Each of these attributes corresponds to a different class of subsets in the corpus.

It's worth pausing over this point to appreciate its strangeness. One weird thing about the underlying set is that it can't be observed directly. Tokens are *literary noumena*: instances, existents, property-less entities. They're perceptible only as examples of *literary phenomena*: as instances of something, as having some property, as exemplifying some general category. This means the basic elements of the corpus are impossible to describe or represent. Every token is perceptible and therefore countable only as an instance of a type or as a part of some larger whole. It exists, but its existence can only be registered as an instance of one of its properties. Another difficulty is caused by our tendency to reify these properties—these types and wholes—as actually existing things, which interferes with our ability to recognize how they overlap with and penetrate each other. Because we experience reality and therefore textuality through its phenomenal characteristics, students and researchers new to the field can find it difficult to conceptualize texts as mere attributes of some underlying, property-less existence. However, in the context of corpus-based inquiry, it is a mistake to think of words or documents as having any real existence of their own. The most difficult-to-grasp threshold concept in quantitative literary analysis involves resisting the reification of word types and document titles to see that, in the context of a corpus, words and books exist only as overlapping sets. What we think of as the real stuff of literary history (words, texts, persons, dates, and such) are actually just attributes that define subsets of tokens.

At bottom, this is a problem of counting.[13] If the preceding discussion seems overly abstract, consider a typical scenario. Although in shorthand we might say that the play *Much Ado About Nothing* uses the word *loue* eighty times, a more precise phrasing would say instead that eighty tokens in the corpus have the following attributes: they are contained in a document of the title *Much Ado About Nothing* and they are instances of the type *loue*. These eighty tokens comprise the intersection between several very different sets. Title is crucial because it connects the metadata to the tokens, which therefore inherit other information as well: they were all authored by "Shakespeare, William. 1564–1616," and they were all printed by Valentine Simmes for Andrew Wise and William Aspley in London in the year 1600. Each of those eighty tokens are instances of all of these things. They're instances of words, yes, but they're also countable instances of persons, times, and places.

What I am describing here is a fundamental similarity and commensurability between two things that we tend to think of very differently: properties of words and properties of texts. Properties of words include their various spellings, their parts of speech, or their inclusion in idiomatic expressions. Properties of texts include their internal divisions and external factors like author, date, or genre.[14] In a corpus-based inquiry, these properties all exist as attributes of tokens. The difference between them is that properties of words tend to be distributed paradigmatically, here and there throughout the corpus, while properties of texts organize tokens syntagmatically. Tokens of the type *loue* will appear discontinuously in lots of different documents. By contrast, tokens of the title *Much Ado About Nothing* will constitute a continuous string with lots of different types.

What Can and Can't Be Counted in a Corpus

The topology of a corpus chosen by the researcher determines what textual features can and can't be counted. In mathematics, topological spaces allow any combination of their subsets, but in practice the topology of a corpus is not quite so flexible. The distributions of tokens in a corpus tend to obey regularities that suggest additional constraints beyond those that define topological spaces in general. These constraints can be boiled down to several rules related to counting tokens.

Consider the situation in which we count words by a specific author. Authorship is an attribute, and "Shakespeare, William. 1564–1616" is a value of that attribute. The subset of tokens that share this value constitute an observable *feature* of the corpus—words written by Shakespeare—and the number of tokens in that subset is the *frequency* or *count* of the feature. For features that are unified by a single value, this definition is clear enough. The frequency of the word *loue* is the count of all tokens spelled l-o-u-e. The word count of *Much Ado About Nothing* is the count of all tokens in that title. The number of words published in 1600 is the count of all tokens contained in documents published on that date. Clear enough.

The matter becomes more complicated when we start thinking about how we might analyze the data. Sometimes we want to lump things together. We might want to know more than just how many words were published in 1600; we might want to know how many appeared in total over the first decade of the 1600s. We'd be taking the union of ten sets: { 1600 ∪ 1601 ∪ 1602 ∪ 1603 ∪ 1604 ∪ 1605 ∪ 1606 ∪ 1607 ∪ 1608 ∪ 1609 }. Other times, instead of lumping things together, we want to parse them more finely. We might want to know, not how many words were published in 1600, but how many words published that year were written by Shakespeare. We'd take the intersection of two sets: { 1600 ∩ "Shakespeare, William. 1564–1616" }. In either case, the frequency of the phenomenon would be the number of tokens in the set we're left with after the operation is complete.

In most cases, operations like the ones I've just described are the only valid ones. The union of two sets is only possible when two metadata values have some implicit commonality. The year 1600 presupposes that it's part of a decade, even though the decade itself is not recorded in the metadata, and so it's reasonable to treat the tokens of that decade as a single composite whole. A scholar might have reason to believe that two or more authors share some important property. Perhaps they were part of the same social clique, or they had the same profession. Therefore, it might be reasonable to add the works of those authors together. Spelling variations or word forms might be collapsed. There could be reason to treat *love, loue, loved, loued, loving, louing*, and such all as a single group. A group of words might be related conceptually, and so perhaps you'd want to count, not only *loue* and its variants, but also the variants of *hate*. Across these examples, it's possible and reasonable to take the union of sets because they share an implicit common value that, through stemming, becomes recorded in the metadata. The frequency remains the number of tokens that share some value in a common attribute, whether or not that value was explicit prior to analysis.

Without a common value, unions are not valid. Scholars would never add all of Shakespeare's tokens to all the tokens published in 1600. The two subsets might intersect—Shakespeare might have published some words in 1600—but they aren't conceptually commensurable categories, so there's no qualitative historical concept their union could ever approximate. It would be a nonsense set because there's no category that { "Shakespeare, William. 1564–1616" ∪ 1600 } could ever stand for. The same holds for combining word types with texts. You'd never take the union between *loue* and *Much Ado About Nothing*. Sure, you could count the two features and add those counts together, but their sum would not have any meaning. There's no historical phenomenon that "all the tokens spelled l-o-u-e plus all the tokens in *Much Ado*" could ever refer to. Such a metadatum could never be indexical (to return to distant reading's founding assumptions) because it has no analogue in historical actuality. The resulting set would not be empty; it would simply have no meaningful correspondence with the past.

On the other hand, intersections are nonsensical when metadata are disjoint by definition. Word form is the most obvious example. There will be no token that is of the type *loue* and also of the type *love*. Every instance of a word has exactly one type. Their intersection, { *loue* ∩ *love* }, would always be an empty set, no matter the corpus. Of course, if we stem the words, we could take the union of these disjoint sets and count them as a single, stemmed word type. But the intersection between them will always be empty. This principle also holds true for the document identifier. Two texts might have a lot in common. They might even quote each other extensively. They might be identical, word for word. But there won't be any tokens that are in one document and also in any other. In the course of ordinary research, no tokens will be labeled with more than one type or more than one document.

Intersections between sets are valid and nonempty when there exist tokens that share the characteristic values of both sets. Because the corpus is made of documents, and each document is an ordered sequence of words, every token will have, at a minimum, a type, a document, and a position. For this reason, the simplest and most common form of counting is to find the intersections among word types and document titles. The basic shape of a corpus is determined by the relationships among such values. Some sets are both disjoint and commensurable; they divide the corpus into similar parts. Others are incommensurable and not disjoint; they provide points of connection that make differences recognizable. To study variation in the corpus is to study how tokens are situated across overlapping but incommensurable structures of kind and place. To exist is to be the point of intersection between incompatible realities.

Corpora like EEBO that are rigorously annotated have complex topologies defined by relationships beyond this simple minimum. However, my goal here is to outline only the ordinary case. In most cases, a literary topology will identify historically meaningful variations if it conforms to these rules for validity. Such, at least, are several principles that seem true to me. The study of literary topology would debate such principles by showing how different data structures express different literary-historical concepts by identifying different kinds of variation. The goal is to preserve the integrity of the interpretive provenance that connects variation in the data to differences in the past while, at the same time, discovering new and more sensitive frameworks for describing variation as such. Possibly there is some understanding of the past within which {"Shakespeare, William. 1564–1616" ∩ 1596} makes sense as a thing that actually existed. More likely, scholars would decide that concepts like authorship and temporality require additional constraints or otherwise more sophisticated forms of expression than I have offered here.

Topologies enter the study of cultural history at the point of data curation and design. How does the corpus look differently when distributed over, say, the spaces of sentences, paragraphs, and full texts, and how does this vary among authors or across historical periods? The basic method begins by identifying multiple candidate categorical schemes, then analyzing their structure and evaluating their most significant points of overlap and divergence.

However, topological considerations in corpus-based inquiry are not restricted to organizing subsets of tokens. Within the metadata by itself, social and geographical forms can be studied in much the same way. (The complete topology of EEBO is extraordinarily complex.) Two research areas with the most direct applications to literary history include network science and geospatial topology.[15] Many aspiring digital humanists first encounter literary mathematics when they draw their first network graph or their first map of historical data. However, in graph theory, a graph isn't something you can look at.[16] A *graph* is a particular kind of topological structure that organizes objects, called *nodes* or *vertices*, into pairs connected by *links* or *edges*. Across these simple connections, nodes join together into large, complex networks.[17] The goal of network science is to correlate the local formation of individual links with emergent patterns reflected in a network's overall structure.[18] In geospatial topology, features like cities and countries may or may not have fixed boundaries, but they often have discrete structures that are nonetheless well defined. Regardless of its precise area, London is in England, and England sits adjacent to Scotland and Wales. Geospatial topology provides a mathematical framework for such putatively qualitative concepts, providing the basis for much work in geographical information science.[19] When combined, network science and GIS enable the study of discrete structures distributed over geographic space, whether those structures are physical networks like roads, socially stipulated entities like political territories, or lived practices like kinship and communication.[20]

The study of networks is well underway in literary history. Studies have appeared that use graphs to represent connections among people in publication or epistolary networks, or connections among characters in novels and plays.[21] So too, mapping.[22] The most sophisticated and promising areas of research cross multiple topological domains to learn how the distributions of things and people affect the distribution of ideas, and vice versa.[23]

The first task of distant reading is to identify countable proxies for qualitative concepts. Rhetorically effective arguments often suppress this aspect of the research, preferring to emphasize intuitive connections across the qualitative and quantitative domains. That is unfortunate, because here's where the heavy intellectual lifting usually occurs. General topology is the abstract theory of such structures, applied in fields where scientists and mathematicians are tasked with reconciling measurements across different coordinate systems, like differential geometry, geodesy, cartography, and physics.[24] In software engineering, these topics arise when designing conceptual models that establish data categories and relationships.[25] When applied to corpora by linguists and computer scientists, these questions are central to experiment design; much research in computation and language hinges on the question of how corpora can be divided and how resulting measurements can be correlated.[26] Analogized to literary studies, such research would identify new topologies that expose different aspects of the cultural record. Such questions strike to the heart of literary theory: How do texts exist in time? How are persons connected to words? Across what apparent discontinuities are real continuities imaginable, even necessary? Comparative analyses of literary topologies would help to clarify these issues, both as a practical matter for scholars designing research projects and more generally for people interested in the questions themselves.

Difference: Matrices and Metric Spaces

A *matrix* is a rectangular array of numbers with fixed rows and columns, like a table or a spreadsheet.[27] Matrices are the most common and most important structure for analyzing data. Indeed, the topological issues discussed in the previous section can all be defined in terms of matrices; that is to say, any topology over a corpus can be defined by the matrices it makes available for analysis. Given any two attributes in the topology, each value in the matrix represents the number of tokens at each point of intersection between those attributes. Usually, scholars are interested in describing how paradigmatic word forms are distributed over syntagmatic stretches of the corpus. The simplest format just divides the corpus by title and creates a *term-document matrix*, where words are taken as the rows, documents as the columns, and the value of each cell records the frequency of each word in each document.[28] Social-network data can be described similarly; in a typical *bipartite network* represented by an *incidence matrix*, the rows represent people and the columns stand for events that connect them, like social meetings they attended or, in the case of citation-network studies, academic papers in which they are mutually cited.[29] Geographical data is stored in matrices where the rows represent places and the columns contain statistical measurements, like census or climate records.[30] Sometimes rows are referred to as *observations* and columns are called *variables* or *attributes*. Tabular data can be organized in any number of variations depending on the adopted topology, and complex topologies often imply systems of related matrices.

Virtually all forms of quantitative analysis involve computing over matrices at some point or another, and so if there's one area of general mathematics that digital humanists should review as part of their training, it's matrix algebra.[31] The central idea of matrix algebra is to represent numbers in the form of a fixed sequence, sometimes called a *vector*. Vectors can be multiplied together by adding the products of their respective elements, reducing them to a single value. The *dot product* (or inner product) takes this form:

$$a \cdot b = a_1 b_1 + a_2 b_2 + \ldots + a_n b_n$$

where a and b represent two sequences of numbers of the same length, n.[32] Each a is multiplied against its corresponding b, and the sum is taken over the whole. The inner product is useful analytically because it represents the variation between any two vectors. If two rows of a matrix have a lot in common, the inner product between them will be high. If not, it'll be low. For example, if you were analyzing a term-document matrix representing a corpus of genre fiction, and you compared the rows for *detective*, *police*, and *dragon*, you'd likely find that the inner product between *detective* and *police* is higher because they're used frequently in many of the same novels; the big *a*'s get multiplied by the big *b*'s. By contrast, *detective* and *dragon* would be lower, because they tend to appear in different kinds of books; the big *a*'s are lost when multiplied against low *b*'s. Most of the fantasy words get canceled out by zero values in detective fiction, and vice versa.[33]

The Dot Product as a Fundamental Concept
Thus, the dot product measures the degree of alignment between any two vectors of numbers, showing how much any two observations have in common when defined over the same variables. In terms of the topological space of the corpus, the dot product compares any two commensurable subsets—words against words, documents against documents—when measured over the subsets with which they are mutually incompatible but across which they both intersect. The dot product is the formal expression of "variation" and "distribution of difference." Under this expression, "difference" and "distribution" become in fact the same compound concept. Each is simply the transpose of the other, in exactly the same way and for the exact same reason that any matrix can be rotated 90 degrees without losing information or distorting any of the relationships it describes.

Why is the dot product so important? Previously, I described the corpus as a topological space, and I contrasted that space with the physical space of the page. Books occupy a metric space, I argued, because you can measure pages from top to bottom. By contrast, texts cannot be measured this way, and I used this contrast to introduce the notion of a topological space that lacks any function for measuring distance. However, the dot product adds something new. By reducing two vectors to a single value that describes their overlap, the dot product becomes a distance function, and the matrix over which it's computed represents a continuous metric space. This space has nothing in common with physical space, of course.³⁴ You can't measure how many inches separate Shakespeare from Jonson in EEBO. However, if Shakespeare and Jonson are observed over fixed variables—over the words used in their plays, for example—then it is possible to take their inner product and so to characterize how much overlap they share. Shakespeare and Jonson probably share more words than, say, Chaucer shares with Dickens. They'll be closer in semantic space.³⁵ As a distance metric, the dot product suggests that the rows and columns of a matrix exist along some implied continuum of possibility, and so matrices are sometimes said to exist over *inner product spaces* or, more generally, *latent spaces*.³⁶ A latent space is a metric space that organizes a topology without being explicit in that topology's definition.

Most research uses some version of the dot product for this purpose. Cosine distance, a popular metric, is just normalized to the unit vectors. Euclidean distance works, not by multiplying each element of the vectors, but by taking the differences between them, then multiplying those differences against each other. In statistics, variance and covariance are just riffs on the dot product. Entropy is basically the dot product of a vector against the logarithm of itself. The Pythagorean theorem just multiplies a two-dimensional vector with itself. Even the arithmetic mean is really a dot product, because it multiplies a set of values against their weights. Once you understand this basic operation, you'll find it everywhere. The inner product is the master concept of all data science. Anything that involves computing over matrices involves the dot product. Some distance metrics can get quite complicated and exotic, but they all share the same basic structure: combine the respective elements, then combine the combinations into one value.³⁷ This final value represents the proximity between any two objects in your data's latent space. Such proximities are analogous to qualitative judgments about variation because they measure how differently two phenomena are distributed over a common set of variables. The dot product is comparison, formally expressed.

Matrix Decomposition
Just as any two matrices of similar shape can be multiplied together to create a third, so too any matrix can be decomposed into its component

parts. Matrix decomposition exists in slightly different forms depending on context, but you'll see it referred to as *principal component analysis*, *matrix factorization*, or *singular value decomposition*.[38] Multiplying two matrices together creates a detailed picture of their points of overlap. Decomposing a matrix exposes its underlying structure.

When applied to a corpus data, singular-value decomposition is called *latent semantic analysis*.[39] Beginning with a table of word frequencies in books, decomposition identifies three component matrices: one of words, showing their relative axes of difference, another of books, showing theirs, and a third that represents the size of each latent dimension. This latent matrix is called the *spectrum* because it organizes the system along a scale of gradually decreasing intensity. Each level in this spectrum is marked by a special number called an *eigenvalue* that sets the scale; the large eigenvalues point to areas where the system exhibits widest variation. Partitioning a matrix along the axes of its spectrum identifies groups of objects that appear together in meaningful patterns. When computed over words, the spectrum exposes hidden axes of meaning that structure *semantic spaces*. The phrase *semantic similarity* refers to the proximities among words and documents in such spaces.

Matrix decomposition supports many other kinds of analysis as well. In the study of networks, spectral partitioning uses the second-smallest eigenvalue to separate a graph into modules.[40] In image processing, it's a crucial step in tasks like zooming, compression and decompression, and pattern recognition (including face detection).[41] Similarly, in geospatial modeling, principal component analysis finds regions in the data; that is, it finds points that share similar statistical profiles and so sit near each other in latent space, whether or not they sit together in physical space.[42] All of these applications share a common theoretical base. All are computed over matrices that represent data in prescribed rectangular structures. Once placed in such an array, the numbers of any given row or column are never quite identical to themselves, because the matrix itself is an elaborate proposition about their mutual interrelation. Every vector of numbers carries the latent possibility of its comparison and recombination along countless possible axes. In this way, matrix decomposition formalizes dialectical reason by systematically toggling among parts to create varying snapshots of the wholes they constitute.

New machine-learning algorithms like topic models and word-embeddings are designed to mimic this procedure efficiently for semantic analysis.[43] For large datasets, computing all the necessary linear combinations can be too much for a desktop machine, so software engineers have devised various shortcuts using randomized sampling. These methods are much more complicated than latent semantic analysis, but through an unfortunate twist in the history of literary criticism, this area of research was introduced to scholars through such software packages. Not only were literary historians insulated from the mathematics behind the software, but they were also misled to believe that these very complicated operations are the most immediately appropriate math for their critical questions. If you're trying to understand topic modeling, the worst place to start is with topic modeling.[44] Simple matrix factorization was always the motivating inspiration for those algorithms, and matrix algebra has a long intellectual tradition across many disciplines.

Exploring applications of this paradigm to the cultural record should be an explicit priority for the digital humanities. Possible lines of general inquiry might ask: What matrices are appropriate for studying semantic, social, geographical, and temporal networks? How can they be combined and decomposed, and with what effect? To what qualitative differences are latent distances analogous? What spaces organize what kinds of meaning? What is the shape of history?

Significance: Information and Probability

Discrete structures describe the forms of literary data. Metric spaces describe the distribution of differences across those forms. Statistical models describe the significance of those differences. What does it mean for something to be significant, interesting, or surprising? These questions, too, can be asked quantitatively.

A *probability space* shares much in common with a topological space, but one key difference is worth noting.[45] Valid topologies ensure continuity by requiring that all unions and intersections be included. In a probability space, continuity is not required. Instead, every subset must be paired with its complementary opposite. If you want to say how likely a coin toss will come up heads, you also have to say how likely it will come up tails. What are the odds you'll roll snake eyes? The precise opposite of the odds you'll roll anything else. Every countable subset in a probability space exists in relation to its countable opposite, its *complement*.[46] With classes of events like coin tosses and rolls of the dice, this complementarity seems obvious—too obvious to be mentioned, really, which is why introductory books and lectures on statistics usually suppress this central idea, even though the general foundations of probability theory begin with it.[47] It's confusingly abstract. Any statement declaring how likely something is requires a taken-for-granted categorical background of other somethings, distinct from the first but similar enough to belong to a common class of events. Thinking probabilistically always means thinking categorically. Evaluating significance means contrasting instances of one kind from instances of a class of kinds.

The key idea of statistical reasoning is thus to compare each value in the data against the observed variation within which it is embedded. Every element in the sequence is thus understood as a composite entity with two parts: an *expected value* and an *error*. Any value, X_i, can be represented as a relation between its expected value, $E[X]$, and the difference that separates this expectation from the observed data, $X_i - E[X]$. Taken together, it looks like this:

$$X_i = E[X] + (X_i - E[X])$$

which, if you parse carefully, you'll see is just the tautological statement, $X_i = X_i$, with an $E[X]$ added and subtracted on one side. In most cases, the expected value is just the average. This way of thinking about numbers treats every observed value as a compound entity that includes both the average and each value's deviation from that average. If you say that a man is 73" tall, you're saying how far the top of his head is from the ground. If you say that he's 3.9" taller than average, you're comparing him against a baseline of categorically similar others. His height is 73 = 69.1 + (73 − 69.1).

The funny thing about the "expected" value is that you never really expect it. You never expect someone to be exactly 69.1" tall. That's just your best guess based on the average of what you've seen so far, and his actual height, 3.9" above that estimate, is how much you were wrong by. That's the strange thing about statistics. You never actually expect anything to be the expected value, and the actual data you correctly observe is your error.

That strangeness masks an important epistemological premise. It holds that experience is a composite of expectation and error. To learn about the world is to formulate a general idea and then to experience systematically all the ways your idea is wrong. In the context of data analysis, this means finding ways to represent variation that capture general patterns in order to show how each value differs from that pattern. Usually, this means combining the above calculation, $X_i = E[X] + (X_i - E[X])$, with the dot product. Core concepts of statistical comparison, like *variance*, *covariance*, and *correlation*, are all just versions of the dot product, except that those calculations take as their elements the errors, $X_i - E[X]$, rather than the observed values.

Probability spaces thus share a lot in common with vector spaces. Despite the very different notation and very different jargon, probabilities are similar to vectors. Both organize elements into interlocking categories. A *discrete probability distribution* is just like a vector, except, instead of showing the raw frequency for each variable, it shows the relative or proportional frequency. All this means is that you divide each value by the total and represent it as a percentage. Rather than say Shakespeare used *loue* eighty times in *Much Ado About Nothing*, you say that he uses *loue* 0.12% of the time. A *joint probability distribution* is just like a matrix, except that every value is divided by the sum of the matrix as a whole. It's like asking: If you selected any token at random from the corpus, what are the odds you'd get one that is both from *Much Ado about Nothing* and of the type *loue*? As we'll see, these extra steps of processing do nothing to interfere with operations over the matrix—normalizations of this kind adjust the scale of each vector without destroying its basic shape—but the subjunctive mindset implied by probabilistic thinking invites creative comparisons across various categorical baselines, any of which might reveal significant structures in the observed data.

Before looking at such a baseline in detail, let's pause for a moment to think about two calculations commonly performed over probability distributions, to develop a slightly deeper sense of how this field of mathematics differs from matrix algebra. Remember, the inner product represents two sequences of numbers by multiplying their corresponding elements and taking the sum of the products. *Entropy* and *relative entropy* work in a similar way.[48] Given a length-n sequence of proportional frequencies, entropy is calculated by taking the sum of each element multiplied by the logarithm of itself:

$$H = -(p_1 \log p_1 + p_2 \log p_2 + \ldots + p_n \log p_n)$$

and relative entropy, like the dot product, weaves two sequences of values together:

$$D(p||q) = -(p_1 \log(p_1/q_1) + p_2 \log(p_2/q_2) + \ldots + p_n \log(p_n/q_n))$$

These calculations differ from those of matrix algebra in one important respect: the logarithm is inserted at each point. By taking each value and representing it as the exponent of some base, the logarithm has the effect of smoothing out variation along the sequence by measuring it against an underlying scale. It also responds to large values of p: as p approaches 1, its logarithm approaches 0, so distributions with high values concentrated in just a few elements will exhibit lower entropy, while more evenly distributed values exhibit higher entropy. This metric is sometimes called the quantity of *information* in a system.[49] Relative entropy measures how much variation one vector contributes to another, so is sometimes called *information gain* or, because of its similarity to a more conventional distance metric, *divergence*.[50] The key point to take away here is to notice how similar these metrics are to calculations common in linear algebra, but also to see that they further describe the level of variation in a system while identifying areas where that variation is most densely concentrated.

In this way, descriptive statistics analogize significance to deviance. Something is significant insofar as it differs observably from the categories constructed to define it. To evaluate significance involves a two-step process. First you generate an expected value based on averages over whole classes of data, then you compare those expected values to the actual, observed frequencies.[51] For example, the most significant values in a matrix can be identified by taking the *positive pointwise mutual information*, sometimes abbreviated as PMI or PPMI.[52] Given a matrix of Shakespeare's plays, you begin by calculating two probability distributions, one of plays and another of words. Of all tokens in the corpus, what percentage appear in *Hamlet*? What percentage are of the type *ghost*? Each categorical value is multiplied together to return the *expected value* for each cell in the table, $p(x)p(y)$. You might find that the expected value for *loue* in *Much Ado About Nothing* is merely 0.03%. By taking the logarithm of the ratio between the *observed value*, $p(x, y)$, and this expected value, you get the PMI score, in this case as $\log(.0012 / .0003) = \log(4) = 0.6$. When the actual value is lower than the observed value, the logarithm turns negative, and in the final step of processing all negative values are disregarded and set to zero. PMI becomes PPMI. The algorithm is complete. You started with a matrix of simple word counts, and PPMI returned a matrix showing which terms are most significantly overrepresented where. Every value in the new matrix reflects the outcome of a complex series of interconnected reasoning about how Shakespeare's works are structured. Rather than mere data, each value becomes an explicit historical claim.

This calculation and others like it, such as TF-IDF, are useful in many interpretive contexts.[53] They're often performed prior to matrix decomposition in semantic analyses and have been shown to dramatically improve results. In information science, to "improve results" means to perform better at complex tasks like guessing the correct answers on vocabulary tests or returning the right books in a library catalog search. When scholars use these methods for distant reading, to improve results means to delineate more clearly categories of words, groups of authors, and genres of books.[54]

However, insofar as attention turns away from evaluating texts within genres and toward evaluating the genres themselves, the question of statistical significance shifts in subtle but important ways. How do we know whether the categories we use to describe literary texts are adequate to explain them? Statisticians describe this problem as *uncertainty*.[55] If there's one group of mathematicians most preoccupied with questions involving belief and inference, it's statisticians. Their goal is to evaluate the trustworthiness of data-driven claims, given that, in most cases, such claims are extrapolated from samples but generalized to whole populations.[56] In voter opinion polls, clinical trials, and other experimental contexts, researchers try to explain what's true about everybody while constrained to observing just a few people. Under a classical, frequentist paradigm, statistical tests imagine an ideal universe where experiments can be performed infinitely many times, then estimate the likely shape of data in that imaginary world, based on actual data collected in this one. Under a Bayesian framework, scholars begin with a subjective, *prior* expectation about the likelihood of events, then update those expectations by comparing them against new observations.[57] In either case, statistical findings are evaluated in the end based on how well they predict future events.

Because so much of the intellectual scaffolding of statistics deals with questions of uncertainty and prediction, it may seem far outside the bounds of literary scholarship. If there's uncertainty in literary studies, it's usually about what texts mean, not about what words they contain. How do you predict the literary past? If you could, why bother?

The reason comes back to questions of explanatory sufficiency. Some literary features might appear most significant under statistical analysis, but are those features actually sufficient to differentiate among literary kinds? If, say, words like "detective" and "suspect" are overrepresented in detective fiction, do those words provide, in and of themselves, a trustworthy indication of what we want to know? If not, what statistical properties are sufficient? To answer questions like these, scholars begin by curating a special subset of the corpus, called a *training set*, with all relevant metadata carefully noted. Statistical models of the training set are compiled, then used as a baseline for comparing other documents in the corpus. If the statistical model of a training set accurately predicts the metadata of books not included in it, there's good reason to believe that the model provides a trustworthy and accurate representation of the literary phenomenon at issue. For this reason, the goal of literary prediction is not to predict the future, but to evaluate whether quantitative models adequately represent the qualitative properties they claim to analogize.

In computer and information science, the line of inquiry I've been describing is called *machine learning*. Closely related to Bayesian statistics, machine learning offers a complex theory of how beliefs are tested and how information is incorporated into knowledge.[58] To better integrate these theories into our understanding of humanities computing, we need intellectual histories of statistical theory that are oriented directly to problems of literary-critical and historical explanation.[59] We also need more and better case studies in machine learning to compare how different conceptions of probability and information produce differently interpretable results when tested against cultural data. Most broadly, this line of inquiry tackles a question nestled among the thorniest problems exposed by literary computation: What theories of literature and history are implied by the statistical concepts like bias, probability, and uncertainty (when applied to corpus data) and how might distant-reading projects shed new light on those concepts' fundamental premises? Given what we've learned and will continue to learn about corpora, how should we revise our account of the relation between textuality and actuality?

Conclusion: From Text, to Structure, to Claim

Literary mathematics names the point of contact between cultural analytics and literary theory, where scholars connect the measurable with the meaningful. Whereas quantitative literary analysis is instrumentalist and results-oriented, literary mathematics is theoretical and concept-oriented. This distinction is neither hard nor fast and would break down if taken too literally—people doing cultural analytics are doing literary math, and vice versa—but it names a difference in emphasis that feels tangible enough.

The main purpose of this chapter has been to chart a path through corpus-based inquiry and to articulate a chain of reasoning that would lead researchers from text, to structure, to claim. I began by advancing the idea that historical documents are basically trustworthy. I do not mean "trustworthy" in the historian's sense of "credible" or the statistician's sense of "representative." Rather, I mean more simply that people write about the things they think about and care about, and therefore those things, that thinking, and that caring are likely to be recorded in the books they produce, if they produce any. Traces left by the social production of any shared historical actuality are likely to reflect important aspects of that actuality. I call this premise "the distant reading hypothesis." Source documents will tend to correspond to the lives of the people who wrote, published, and read them, and therefore discourse varies along the contours of social difference, and these variations are likely to register in the corpus, one way or another.

This premise suggests in turn that quantitative literary analysis should take as its central practice the study of variation. To study variation quantitively requires thinking across three broad categories, which correspond, not to particular methods or fields of inquiry, but to general concepts in literary studies: form, difference, and significance. To study *form* under the paradigm of literary mathematics is to discover or invent new ways of describing how literary objects are situated within corpora. As a critical practice, it involves designing data models that support quantitative analysis by making it possible to count literary features while ensuring that such features relate validly to the past. To analyze variation is to describe the distribution of *difference* across the data. This usually means converting a discrete representation of a corpus, network, or map into a metric structure over which fine-grained comparisons can be made. In latent space, persons of social networks can be shown to join something like communities, towns can be shown to occupy something like regions, books can be shown to coalesce into something like genres, and words can be shown to indicate something like concepts. Lastly, the *significance* of any literary feature is determined by constructing a detailed picture of its defining categories, then contrasting the feature against those categories. Global metrics like averages, deviations, and entropies, as well as more complex measurements like linear regressions and analyses of variance, reveal what to expect in a system and expose where variations are most surprising or, perhaps, most interesting. Taken together, these concepts constitute a vast, heterogeneous, and highly sophisticated body of theory that remains almost wholly unknown to literary scholars but will prove crucial to studying the digital collections now available.

CONCLUSION

SIMILAR WORDS TEND TO APPEAR IN DOCUMENTS WITH SIMILAR METADATA

IMAGINE THE FOLGER LIBRARY IN WASHINGTON, DC. Close your eyes and picture the building. Now start taking things away. First, remove the building itself and all of its surroundings. Imagine the contents of every room of the library suspended in midair against a white screen. Remove the artwork from where the walls had been. Now strip away the furniture: the lockers, chairs, tables, and cabinets. Remove everything until nothing is left but books, and while you're at it throw away all the modern books, too. Just picture the old ones—the collected holdings of the Folger—levitating motionlessly in front of you, as if by magic. Next, strip the covers from the books and undo their bindings. Strip off the title pages. Wash away the dust and the centuries of grime. Now, remove the paper—every molecule of every page—but leave the ink. Just remove the paper around each letter of each word. Then get rid of the punctuation, the illustrations, and the printers' ornaments. Smooth out the letters so all the typeface looks the same.

Imagine what that would look like. The words hovering in front of you would have no collective form and few identifying marks. You'd have no way to read them and no way to know where one book ends and another begins. You'd have in front of you neither texts nor books, just a big cloud of words. Yet, as formless as they'd appear when viewed as a whole, if you somehow could go through them systematically one by one, you'd see that they have a latent structure. They wouldn't be scattered randomly. Some words would cluster among others, and together they'd form groups and patterns, woven together like threads of a tapestry. If you could read them, you'd say the clusters each suggest a subject, a theme, or maybe a topic or concept. When words cluster this way, we can call them *similar*.

Now, start over again and imagine everything the same, with the books suspended in midair. But this time, don't take away the title pages. Instead, throw everything else away—the whole text of every book—and keep only the title pages. What would you have left? Just a big cloud of book titles and authors' names as well as the names and locations of the printers and booksellers, and the dates of publication. This cloud would be sparser by far than the cloud of words you had before, and it too would have an amorphous, lump-like shape. However, underneath this apparent formlessness, the words would again reveal a similar latent structure. People didn't collaborate randomly. Some printers' and publishers' names would appear together frequently. Names that cluster together in this way suggest something like groups or communities, and these relationships, in turn, would correspond with typical date ranges. When metadata values cluster this way, we can call them *similar*, too.

Now imagine these two ink clouds and all the relationships they imply; superimpose them in your mind, one on top of the other. You'd see that relationships of each kind correspond closely with those of the other. Clusters of words would overlap closely with communities of names. The metadata networks would extend through this word space, not like a "form" containing "content," but like a skeleton or frame holding the other pieces in place. The textual contents of books and the historical facts of their production and circulation are closely related. When counted and compared, they will likely correlate with one another. Put simply: *Similar words tend to appear in documents with similar metadata.*

If you remember nothing else from this book, I ask you to remember this phrase. It represents my attempt to encapsulate into a single proposition a whole host of innovative ideas pursued by researchers from a wide range of disciplines, including most especially linguistics, network science, and quantitative geography. Linguists approach this idea by studying word collocation and meaning. Network scientists study how information moves through organizations and loosely connected communities. Geographers study the uneven distribution of material things, like manufactured goods, and immaterial things, like cultural practices. Across all these kinds of research, there has been revealed a fundamental commensurability between the attributional properties of things (what they *are*) and the relational properties of their distribution (what they're *among*). And because those things (whatever they are) must be recorded in documents to be known at all, this principle applies most directly and most fundamentally to textuality itself. The idea is a profound one. It suggests something like a cosmic ordering principle for all things, or at least the closest we'll ever get to such a principle. Most importantly for my purposes in this book, it suggests an underlying commensurability and interdependence between textuality and historicity.

Just as important for researchers, the distributional hypothesis, as I've expanded it here, suggests a set of general procedures for quantitative modeling and analysis. We can think of a corpus, not just as a collection of digitized books or newspapers, but also as a vast network of collocation among words, people, places, and times. The contents of textual objects and the facts describing their production and distribution can now be represented as a unified whole. Computer-mediated discourse reconciles the categorical divide between text and context by representing textuality and contextuality as a single object and in the process transforms both. Instead of an archive that gathers real books written by real people, you have a structured system where books and people exist together in a dense fabric of mutual interrelation. When gathered into a corpus, no document exists on its own as a single entity. Each is part of a larger body structured by historical facts. Bibliographical metadata (like title, date of publication, author, and so on) organize the corpus into sets of documents. Lexical metadata (most importantly, word forms) identify paradigmatic relations across those sets. Every element in every document exists within this self-contained system of relations, and every token marks a point of intersection between such sets. The fundamental constituent unit of a corpus is not the document or the word, but the token—the *instance* that marks an *incidence* between language and history. Taken together, these incidences constitute the topology of the corpus—the form and structure over which meaningful variations can be discovered and described.

The whole purpose of this book has been to share this vision of the corpus and to explain how its representation of textuality opens new avenues of research. If the hunch that motivates distant reading is true, variation in any corpus will tend to correspond with differences in the social practices that produced the documents recorded in that corpus. But to follow through on this hunch requires stating those relations more precisely in terms implied by the corpus itself: thus the phrase, "Similar words tend to appear in documents with similar metadata." Books tagged as sermons and biblical commentaries are more likely than other kinds of books to contain tokens of the type, *christ*. Treatises on natural law will be more likely to intersect with *government*. Further, the similarities that exist among documents come in many varieties, not just subject or genre, and a glance across any library catalog suggests many possible axes of comparison. Books published in 1641 will have more words in common with books from 1642 than they'll have with books from 1520. Books published in London will be like each other in ways they're unlike books from Venice. These kinds of tendencies will have many exceptions, of course, but the overall patterns will hold. It's obvious that they must, and every case study in this book—and, indeed, as far as I know, every experiment in corpus linguistics—confirms the rule. The distributional hypothesis is practically a natural law of human discourse.

Still, the idea that similar words tend to appear in similar documents remains, I think, a very strange one. And it's worth keeping strange. Early on, corpus linguists were too quick to naturalize it, too quick to take it as given and assume they knew what it meant. Each of its key phrases is vague in ways that invite further exploration:

Similar words. Our notion of lexical or semantic similarity remains underdetermined and poorly explained. In practice, it means that two words share a common distribution over the corpus, but as the case studies presented in earlier chapters are meant to show, the measurements that determine "similarity" can be performed in different ways that capture different kinds of conceptual connection. However, we have few clearly articulated principles for choosing among metrics or comparative procedures. At bottom, this is because we continue to lack a satisfactory account of what it means for words to be related conceptually to one another. Linguists and conceptual historians offer many guiding theories. Too many, really. Throughout the twentieth century, both fields developed elaborate theoretical regimes that made sweeping claims on small evidentiary bases, and their accounts often rest on assertions about the speaker's mind that are difficult and perhaps impossible to confirm. The task of sifting through their work and figuring out which ideas hold up and remain useful when modified for empirical research, and which can be relegated to intellectual history, is a huge one. Perhaps I was wrong, in chapter 2, to focus on Kristeva's description of Bakhtin. Perhaps I ought to have gone back instead to Koselleck's notion of the "semantic field." Maybe to Chomsky or Jackendoff? All their ideas need to be reconsidered in light of new evidence. Accounts of meaning that start from other premises will reach different conclusions and produce different insights. This research remains in the infancy of its new phase.

Tend to appear. The phrase "tend to appear" refers to a statistical test of any kind that describes the distributions of values within some dataset. The ambiguity of the phrase is useful because it licenses an open-ended curiosity toward measurement, but that open-endedness also highlights the challenge such research faces. We continue to lack a robust understanding of the quantitative models that describe tendencies in cultural data. To say that one thing has a tendency to appear near another is to propose a statistically measurable relation between them. But what statistics are the right ones to use? As a field, the digital humanities operate piecemeal with little sustained discussion about what quantitative methods are appropriate for studying which cultural topics. Historical network research has a small but growing body of theory behind it, as do computational semantics and historical GIS. Very little discussion attempts to generalize across this hodgepodge or to adjudicate among proposed techniques. To this end, we should engage research in the information sciences with open minds and a willingness to experiment while maintaining careful attention to the provenance of explanation that moves from text to data, from data to statistical extrapolation, and from results to interpretation. The key step too often passed over is the central one, where formal, mathematical expressions are used to describe variations in textual data. The tendencies or "patterns" discovered in corpus-based inquiry gain meaning only when articulated through mathematical formulas that identify the relationships being evaluated. The formal vocabulary we might borrow or adapt from mathematics is enormous and needs to be tested against known cases in order to be understood at all. This work, too, is only beginning.

In documents. Even the word "documents" disguises ambiguity. In the context of computation, a document might be an entire book, but it might also refer to paragraphs, sentences, or snippets drawn from books. It could refer to newspaper articles, blogs, tweets, or any other textual genre. This means that any quantitative approach to social or conceptual explanation ultimately rests on a theory of textual forms. Yet, the critical tradition we have inherited from literary theory reaches in many directions, only some of which will be directly relevant to quantitative studies. Unpacking the relationship between genre and other kinds of textual metadata will require a great deal of thought. For the purposes of computation, we might not need or even want to know the differences between literary categories like "naturalism," "realism," and "sentimentalism," but we'll need clear-eyed attention to other formal categories, like the differences between sentences, context windows, paragraphs, and chapters. I do not believe we have an adequate vocabulary for describing syntagmatism in all its varieties, nor a strong sense of how relationships among words differ across syntagmatic scales.

Similar metadata. The phrase "similar metadata" is the most compacted part of this book's central claim, and it has the most widely ranging implications. The problem it raises is that "metadata" can be anything. Authors are people, and so our ideas about similarities among them will be informed by a broad and often vaguely conceived sense of what it means for persons to be related. They might be related in the sense of a familial connection or a professional affiliation. They might be collaborators or members of a shared community. Or they could share socially stipulated attributes like gender or race. These similarities will manifest differently in a corpus in ways that are difficult to anticipate in general. Other metadata might seem simpler to deal with, but they introduce their own complexities. Time is ostensibly the simplest case. Years are "similar" if they're near each other chronologically, and this assumption informs the use of time-series graphs to represent change over the x-axis. But years could also be similar if they feature repeating events, like elections or wars. We would expect, in a corpus of news reports from the years 2010 to 2020, to find similarities between 2012, 2016, and 2020 that set those years apart from the others. But we don't have any general theory for formulating such expectations. Much sociological information, like changes in demographics or economic activity, would operate in a corpus-based inquiry as temporal metadata. What variations in a corpus are likely to correlate with periods of economic growth? It's a difficult question. There is a generic logic to historical temporality that remains poorly understood. Questions of geography pose similar challenges. Places are similar to each other if they are spatially approximate, but places are also functional entities with generic properties, and it's largely unknown how those properties will manifest in various corpora. For this reason, the phrase "similar metadata" is meant to describe a point of intellectual connection between textual studies and the other social sciences, because we cannot develop a coherent and sufficient understanding of these new textual forms without articulating some underlying notions about relations among the source texts, and those notions could come from any number of disciplines, from sociology to geography, and from psychology to economics.

Here, then, is the point with which I'd like to conclude. The intellectual merit of corpus-based research will depend entirely on its interdisciplinary character, and so humanists who hope to do good work must be willing to engage ideas from outside their fields of specialty and even from outside the digital humanities. In the social sciences, scholars have developed rich technical vocabularies for describing similarities among the things they study. In the information sciences, an elaborate framework for describing measurable relationships of many kinds is available to be borrowed from and adapted. What has been learned in the past several decades is that texts have structural features that respond to sociological and historical conditions in measurable ways. This discovery marks a major advancement in our collective knowledge about language and textuality. Theorists during the nineteenth and twentieth centuries could only imagine this possibility and so were far too quick to dismiss it as impractical techno-utopianism. They were far too confident in drawing bright lines between what can and can't be measured. The fundamental task of cultural analytics and of computational social science is to imagine and create data structures across which research from various domains can become commensurable and therefore comparable and newly knowable. In so doing, researchers in those fields will bring the intellectual disciplines into a better and more informative conversation.

NOTES

Introduction

1. Henry E. Brady, "The Challenge of Big Data and Data Science," *Annual Review of Political Science* 22, no. 1 (2019): 297–323, 298.

2. Michael Laver, Kenneth Benoit, and John Garry, "Extracting Policy Positions from Political Texts Using Words as Data," *American Political Science Review* 97, no. 2 (2003): 311–31.

3. Jonathan B. Slapin and Sven-Oliver Proksch, "A Scaling Model for Estimating Time-Series Party Positions from Texts," *American Journal of Political Science* 52, no. 3 (2008): 705–22; Sven-Oliver Proksch et al., "Multilingual Sentiment Analysis: A New Approach to Measuring Conflict in Legislative Speeches," *Legislative Studies Quarterly* 44, no. 1 (2019): 97–131; and Tamar Mitts, "From Isolation to Radicalization: Anti-Muslim Hostility and Support for ISIS in the West," *American Political Science Review* 113, no. 1 (2019): 173–94. For overviews of the field, see Justin Grimmer and Brandon M. Stewart, "Text as Data: The Promise and Pitfalls of Automatic Content Analysis Methods for Political Texts," *Political Analysis* 21, no. 3 (2013): 267–97; and John Wilkerson and Andreu Casas, "Large-Scale Computerized Text Analysis in Political Science: Opportunities and Challenges," *Annual Review of Political Science* 20, no. 1 (2017): 529–44.

4. Charles E. Osgood, "The Nature and Measurement of Meaning," *Psychological Bulletin* 49, no. 3 (1952): 197–237.

5. Thomas K. Landauer, "LSA as a Theory of Meaning," in *Handbook of Latent Semantic Analysis*, ed. Landauer et al. (Mahwah, NJ: Lawrence Erlbaum Associates, 2007), 3–34. In the same volume, see Susan Dumais, "LSA and Information Retrieval: Getting Back to Basics," 293–322. A more recent application of semantic modeling to the science of meaning can be found in Gabriel Grand et al., "Semantic Projection: Recovering Human Knowledge of Multiple, Distinct Object Features from Word Embeddings," *arXiv preprint arXiv:1802.01241* (2018).

6. Corpus-based research in these fields is abundant. See, for example, John W. Mohr and Petko Bogdanov, "Topic Models: What They Are and Why They Matter," *Poetics* 41, no. 6 (2013): 545–69; Kyung Hye Kim, "Examining US News Media Discourses about North Korea: A Corpus-Based Critical Discourse Analysis," *Discourse and Society* 25, no. 2 (2014): 221–44; Debarchana Ghosh and Rajarshi Guha, "What Are We 'Tweeting' about Obesity?: Mapping Tweets with Topic Modeling and Geographic Information System," *Cartography and Geographic Information Science* 40, no. 2 (2013): 90–102; Frank Fagan, "Big Data Legal Scholarship: Toward a Research Program and Practitioner's Guide," *Virginia Journal of Law and Technology* 20, no. 1 (2016): 1–81; Nick Obradovich, et al., "Expanding the Measurement of Culture with a Sample of Two Billion Humans," *NBER Working Paper Series* (Cambridge, MA: National Bureau of Economic Research, 2020). For a theoretical overview of quantitative theory for cultural sociology, see John W. Mohr et al., *Measuring Culture* (New York: Columbia University Press, 2020).

7. Franco Moretti, *Distant Reading* (London: Verso, 2013); Lev Manovich, "The Science of Culture?: Social Computing, Digital Humanities, and Cultural Analytics," *Journal of Cultural Analytics* 1, no. 1 (2016), https://doi.org/10.22148/16.004; Andrew Piper, "There Will Be Numbers," *Journal of Cultural Analytics* 1, no. 1 (2016), https://doi.org/10.22148/16.006.

8. Laver, Benoit, and Garry, "Extracting Policy Positions," 326.

9. The year 2013 was an annus mirabilis for quantitative literary theory. That year saw the publication of Franco Moretti's *Distant Reading*; Matthew L. Jockers's *Macroanalysis: Digital Methods and Literary History*; Ted Underwood's *Why Literary Periods Mattered*; and Peter de Bolla's *The Architecture of Concepts: The Historical Formation of Human Rights*.

10. See Ted Underwood, *Distant Horizons: Digital Evidence and Literary Change* (Chicago: University of Chicago Press, 2019) and Andrew Piper, *Enumerations: Data and Literary Study* (Chicago: University of Chicago Press, 2018).

11. Katherine Bode, *A World of Fiction: Digital Collections and the Future of Literary History* (Ann Arbor: University of Michigan Press, 2019).

12. Sarah Allison, *Reductive Reading: A Syntax of Victorian Moralizing* (Baltimore: Johns Hopkins University Press, 2018); and Daniel Shore, *Cyberformalism: Histories of Linguistic Forms in the Digital Archive* (Baltimore: Johns Hopkins University Press, 2018).

13. See Kim Gallon, "Making a Case for the Black Digital Humanities," in *Debates in the Digital Humanities*, ed. Matthew K. Gold and Lauren F. Klein (Minneapolis: University of Minnesota Press, 2016), 42–49; Kim Gallon, *The Black Press Research Collective*, http://blackpressresearchcollective.org/about/; Hoyt Long and Richard Jean So, "Literary Pattern Recognition: Modernism between Close Reading and Machine Learning," *Critical Inquiry* 42, no. 2 (2016): 235–67, and "Turbulent Flow: A Computational Model of World Literature," *Modern Language Quarterly* 77, no. 3 (2016): 345–67; Nicole M. Brown et al., "Mechanized Margin to Digitized Center: Black Feminism's Contributions to Combatting Erasure within the Digital Humanities," *International Journal of Humanities and Arts Computing* 10, no. 1 (2016): 110–25; and "In Search of Zora/When Metadata Isn't Enough: Rescuing the Experiences of Black Women through Statistical Modeling," *Journal of Library Metadata* 19, no. 3–4 (2019): 141–62.

14. See Dennis Yi Tenen, "Toward a Computational Archaeology of Fictional Space," *New Literary History* 49, no. 1 (2018): 119–47; Mark Algee-Hewitt, "Distributed Character: Quantitative Models of the English Stage, 1550–1900," *New Literary History* 48, no. 4 (2017): 751–82; and Peter de Bolla et al., "Distributional Concept Analysis," *Contributions to the History of Concepts* 14, no. 1 (2019): 66–92.

15. For the full list of contributors to the Torn Apart project, see the project's credits at https://xpmethod.columbia.edu/torn-apart/credits.html. This work is described in Roopika Risam, *New Digital Worlds: Postcolonial Digital Humanities in Theory, Praxis, and Pedagogy* (Evanston, IL: Northwestern University Press, 2018).

16. See, for example, Ian N. Gregory and Andrew Hardie, "Visual GISting: Bringing Together Corpus Linguistics and Geographical Information Systems," *Literary and Linguistic Computing* 26, no. 3 (2011): 297–314; Anouk Lang, "Visual Provocations: Using GIS Mapping to Explore Witi Ihimaera's *Dear Miss Mansfield*," *English Language Notes* 52, no. 1 (2014): 67–80; Patricia Murrieta-Flores and Naomi Howell, "Towards the Spatial Analysis of Vague and Imaginary Place and Space: Evolving the Spatial Humanities through Medieval Romance," *Journal of Map and Geography Libraries* 13, no. 1 (2017): 29–57; Catherine Porter, Paul Atkinson, and Ian Gregory, "Geographical Text Analysis: A New Approach to Understanding Nineteenth-Century Mortality," *Health and Place* 36 (2015): 25–34; and Peter M. Broadwell and Timothy R. Tangherlini, "WitchHunter: Tools for the Geo-Semantic Exploration of a Danish Folklore Corpus," *Journal of American Folklore* 129, no. 511 (2016): 14–42.

17. See Ruth Ahnert and Sebastian E. Ahnert, "Protestant Letter Networks in the Reign of Mary I: A Quantitative Approach," *ELH* 82, no. 1 (2015): 1–33; Heather Froehlich, "Dramatic Structure and Social Status in Shakespeare's Plays," *Journal of Cultural Analytics* 5, no. 1 (2020), doi:10.22148/001c.12556; James Jaehoon Lee et al., "Linked Reading: Digital Historicism and Early Modern Discourses of Race around Shakespeare's Othello," *Journal of Cultural Analytics* 3, no. 1 (2018), doi:10.22148/16.018; and Anupam Basu, Jonathan Hope, and Michael Witmore, "The Professional and Linguistic Communities of Early Modern Dramatists," in *Community-Making in Early Stuart Theatres: Stage and Audience*, ed. Roger D. Sell, Anthony W. Johnson, and Helen Wilcox (London: Routledge, 2017), 63–94.

18. For my overview and response to recent controversies in cultural analytics, see Michael Gavin, "Is There a Text in My Data? (Part 1): On Counting Words," *Journal of Cultural Analytics: Debates* 5, no. 1 (2020), https://doi.org/10.22148/001c.11830.

19. Tony McEnery and Andrew Hardie, *Corpus Linguistics: Method, Theory, and Practice* (Cambridge: Cambridge University Press, 2012), 1.

20. Adam Kilgarriff advances a similar argument in "Language Is Never, Ever, Ever, Random," *Corpus Linguistics and Linguistic Theory* 1, no. 2 (2005): 263–75.

21. The word *interpretation* is particularly debilitating because of how it promises to explain the meaning of data when visualized without needing to consider whether the underlying mathematical operations are appropriate, or even how they work. I believe this to be the central flaw of Franco Moretti's later work. This flaw can also be thought of as the flip side of his loose and unprincipled use of data, which Katherine Bode objects to in "The Equivalence of 'Close' and 'Distant' Reading; or, Toward a New Object for Data-Rich Literary History," *Modern Language Quarterly* 78, no. 1 (2017): 77–106.

22. For a virtuoso performance of computationally assisted close reading, see Martin Paul Eve, *Close Reading with Computers: Textual Scholarship, Computational Formalism, and David Mitchell's Cloud Atlas* (Stanford, CA: Stanford University Press, 2019).

23. Stanley Fish has argued that "the purpose of literary interpretation is to determine what works of literature mean; and therefore the paradigmatic question in literary criticism is 'What is this poem (or novel or drama) saying?'" *Professional Correctness: Literary Studies and Political Change* (Oxford: Clarendon Press, 1995), 25. Fish has been a longtime critic of computational literary analysis and has published many essays in its opposition. For an early example of this particular genre of scholarly performance, see "What Is Stylistics and Why Are They Saying Such Terrible Things about It?" chap. 2 in *Is There a Text in This Class? The*

Authority of Interpretive Communities (Cambridge, MA: Harvard University Press, 1980).

24. Theodor W. Adorno, *Prisms*, trans. Samuel Weber and Shierry Weber (Cambridge, MA: MIT Press, 1967), 33.

25. For an introduction and overview of the concept of homophily, see Charles Kadushin, *Understanding Social Networks: Theories, Concepts, and Findings* (Oxford: Oxford University Press, 2012), 18–21.

26. See Paul F. Lazarsfeld and Robert K. Merton, "Friendship as a Social Process: A Substantive and Methodological Analysis," in *Freedom and Control in Modern Society*, ed. Morroe Berger (New York: Van Nostrand, 1954), 18–66.

27. For the classic theoretical treatment of this idea, see Zellig Harris, "Distributional Structure," *Mind* 10 (1954): 146–62.

28. This history is narrated in W. John Hutchins, Machine Translation: Past, Present, Future (Chichester, UK: Ellis Horwood, 1986).

29. J. R. Firth, "A Synopsis of Linguistic Theory, 1930–1955," in *Studies in Linguistic Analysis* (Oxford: Oxford University Press, 1962), 11.

30. For an overview of spatial autocorrelation and techniques for its measurement, see A. Stewart Fotheringham, Chris Brunsdon, and Martin Charlton, *Quantitative Geography: Perspectives on Spatial Data Analysis* (Thousand Oaks, CA: Sage Publications, 2000), chap. 5.

31. Waldo Tobler, "A Computer Movie Simulating Urban Growth in the Detroit Region," *Economic Geography* 46, no. sup1 (1970): 234–40.

32. There is no specific essay I am quoting here, but this instrumentalist assumption—which presumes textual computing is useful only for how it is used—is prevalent throughout the humanities.

33. At the time of publication, the supplementary website is located at www.literarymathematics.org.

34. *R: A Language and Environment for Statistical Computing* (Vienna: R Foundation for Statistical Computing, 2021), https://cran.r-project.org/.

35. See Bonnie Mak, "Archaeology of a Digitization," *Journal of the Association for Information Science and Technology* 65, no. 8 (2014): 1515–26; and Michael Gavin, "How to Think about EEBO," *Textual Cultures* 11, no. 2 (2017 [2019]): 70–105.

36. See, for example, Ian Gadd, "The Use and Misuse of Early English Books Online," *Literature Compass* 6, no. 3 (2009): 680–92.

37. Alexandra Hill estimates book loss by genre in her essay "Lost Print in England: Entries in the Stationers' Company Register, 1557–1640," in *Lost Books: Reconstructing the Print World of Pre-Industrial Europe*, ed. Flavia Bruni and Andrew Pettegree (Leiden: Brill, 2016), 144–59. For a general account of the issue of representativeness in corpora, see Douglas Biber, "Representativeness in Corpus

Design," *Literary and Linguistic Computing* 8, no. 4 (1993): 243–57. A concise overview of scholarship on the topic of historical corpora in particular, including EEBO, can be found in Merja Kytö's and Päivi Pahta's "Evidence from Historical Corpora up to the Twentieth Century," in *The Oxford Handbook of the History of English*, ed. Terttu Nevalainen and Elizabeth Closs Traugott (Oxford: Oxford University Press, 2012), 123–33.

38. See, for example, Anupam Basu and Joseph Loewenstein, "Spenser's Spell: Archaism and Historical Stylometrics," *Spenser Studies* 33 (2019): 63–102; John R. Ladd, "Network Poetics: Studies in Early Modern Literary Collaboration" (PhD thesis, Washington University, 2019); Catherine Medici, "Using Network Analysis to Understand Early Modern Women," *Early Modern Women* 13, no. 1 (2018): 153–62; Rachel Midura, "Conceptualizing Knowledge Networks: Agents and Patterns of 'Flow,'" in *Empires of Knowledge: Scientific Networks in the Early Modern World*, ed. Paula Findlen (New York: Routledge, 2018), 373–77; and Ingeborg van Vugt, "Using Multi-Layered Networks to Disclose Books in the Republic of Letters," *Journal of Historical Network Research* 1, no. 1 (2017): 25–51.

Chapter 1

1. Robert Herrick, *Hesperides, or, The Works Both Humane & Divine of Robert Herrick, Esq.* (London: Printed for John Williams, and Francis Eglesfield . . . 1648), *Early English Books Online Text Creation Partnership*, 2011, http://name.umdl.umich.edu/A43441.0001.001.

2. John H. Miller and Scott E. Page, *Complex Adaptive Systems: An Introduction to Computational Models of Social Life* (Princeton, NJ: Princeton University Press, 2007), 46.

3. Albert-László Barabási, *Network Science* (Cambridge: Cambridge University Press, 2016), 23–24.

4. M. E. J. Newman, *Networks: An Introduction* (Oxford: Oxford University Press, 2010), 17.

5. Manuel Castells, *The Rise of the Network Society* (Malden, MA: Blackwell Publishers, 1996), 1:500.

6. Duncan J. Watts, *Small Worlds: The Dynamics of Networks between Order and Randomness* (Princeton, NJ: Princeton University Press, 2000), 162. See also Duncan J. Watts and Steven H. Strogatz, "Collective Dynamics of 'Small-World' Networks," *Nature* 393 (1998): 440–42.

7. Barabási, *Network Science*, 24–25.

8. For the classic treatment on the role of analogy in scientific discourse, see Mary B. Hesse, *Models and Analogies in Science* (Notre Dame, IN: University of Notre Dame Press, 1966). See also Devin Griffiths, *The Age of Analogy: Science*

and Literature between the Darwins (Baltimore: Johns Hopkins University Press, 2016).

9. Kate Davison writes, "The metaphorical use of 'networks' is longstanding, a distinctive feature of recent work is the tendency to apply techniques developed in the field of network analysis." "Early Modern Social Networks: Antecedents, Opportunities, and Challenges," *American Historical Review* 124, no. 2 (2019): 456–82, at 457.

10. Christopher D. Kilgore, "Rhetoric of the Network: Toward a New Metaphor," *Mosaic: A Journal for the Interdisciplinary Study of Literature* 46, no. 4 (2013): 37–58, at 38, emphasis original.

11. I join Mark Erickson in calling greater self-awareness on this point: "We need . . . to notice the metaphors that we are using, and to clearly describe them as such." "Network as Metaphor," *International Journal of Criminology and Sociological Theory* 5, no. 2 (2012): 912–21, at 919.

12. Caroline Levine, *Forms: Whole, Rhythm, Hierarchy, Network* (Princeton, NJ: Princeton University Press, 2017), 113.

13. Davison, "Early Modern Social Networks," 466.

14. Erickson writes, "This is the core question . . . by deploying the network metaphor, by seeing the world as being just network, what are you not seeing? To borrow their metaphor—what falls through the gaps in the mesh?" "Network as Metaphor," 917–18.

15. This brief historical overview borrows most directly from John Scott, *Social Network Analysis*, 3rd ed. (Los Angeles: Sage, 2012); and the introduction to Ileana Baird, ed., *Social Networks in the Long Eighteenth Century: Clubs, Literary Salons, Textual Coteries* (Newcastle upon Tyne, UK: Cambridge Scholars Publishing, 2014).

16. Paul F. Lazarsfeld and Robert K. Merton, "Friendship as a Social Process: A Substantive and Methodological Analysis," in *Freedom and Control in Modern Society*, ed. Morroe Berger (New York: Van Nostrand, 1954), 18–66.

17. See Scott, *Social Network Analysis*, 19–29.

18. Described in Scott, *Social Network Analysis*, 26–27.

19. See Scott, *Social Network Analysis*, 34–38.

20. See Nancy Howell Lee, *The Search for an Abortionist* (Chicago: University of Chicago Press, 1969); and Mark S. Granovetter, "The Strength of Weak Ties," *American Journal of Sociology* 78, no. 6 (1973): 1360–80.

21. Watts, *Small Worlds*, 241, emphasis removed.

22. Barabási, *Network Science*, 126.

23. See, for example, Anna D. Broido and Aaron Clauset, "Scale-Free Networks Are Rare," *Nature Communications* 10, no. 1 (2019): 1–10.

24. See Alexis Weedon, "The Uses of Quantification," in *A Companion to the History of the Book*, ed. Simon Eliot and Jonathan Rose (London: Blackwell Publishing, 2008), 33–49; Michael F. Suarez, "Towards a Bibliometric Analysis of the Surviving Record, 1701–1800," in *The Cambridge History of the Book in Britain*, ed. Michael F. Suarez and Michael L. Turner (Cambridge: Cambridge University Press, 2009), 37–65; and Michael F. Suarez, "Book History from Descriptive Bibliographies," in *The Cambridge Companion to the History of the Book*, ed. Leslie Howsam (Cambridge: Cambridge University Press, 2014), 199–218.

25. See Anupam Basu, Jonathan Hope, and Michael Witmore, "The Professional and Linguistic Communities of Early Modern Dramatists," in *Community-Making in Early Stuart Theatres: Stage and Audience*, ed. Roger D. Sell, Anthony W. Johnson, and Helen Wilcox (London: Routledge, 2017), 63–94. For useful overviews and efforts to conceptualize historical publishing networks, see in particular Leo Lahti et al., "Bibliographic Data Science and the History of the Book (c. 1500–1800)," *Cataloging and Classification Quarterly* 57, no. 1 (2019): 5–23. Catherine Medici highlights network theory's applications to feminist history in particular in "Using Network Analysis to Understand Early Modern Women," *Early Modern Women* 13, no. 1 (2018): 153–62. A very similar line of inquiry looks, not at the bibliographic metadata of book publishing, but at historical correspondence. See Dan Edelstein et al., "Historical Research in a Digital Age: Reflections from the Mapping the Republic of Letters Project," *American Historical Review* 122, no. 2 (2017): 400–424; and Ruth Ahnert and Sebastian E. Ahnert, "Protestant Letter Networks in the Reign of Mary I: A Quantitative Approach," *ELH* 82, no. 1 (2015): 1–33.

26. Davison, "Early Modern Social Networks."

27. Sometimes, historians invoke the language of network analysis explicitly, as in Mark Knights's account of the bookseller John Starkey, who brokered distinct strands of political writers and publishers during the period. See "John Starkey and Ideological Networks in Late Seventeenth-Century England," *Media History* 11, no. 1–2 (2005): 127–45. Jason Scott-Warren proposes "network" as an alternative to other terms: "Scholars have tended to employ a range of terms as if they were straightforwardly interchangeable; manuscripts communities are by turns 'spheres,' 'circles,' 'peer groups,' 'elites,' or 'coteries.'" "Reconstructing Manuscript Networks: The Textual Transactions of Sir Stephen Powle," in *Communities in Early Modern England*, ed. Alexandra Shepard and Phil Withington (Manchester: Manchester University Press, 2000), 19.

28. A counterexample can be found in Mark Algee-Hewitt, "Distributed Character: Quantitative Models of the English Stage, 1550–1900," *New Literary History* 48, no. 4 (2017): 751–82.

29. Heather Hirschfeld writes, "Indeed, it is possible to categorize the activities of members of the book trade, just as it was possible to categorize the activities of scribes, as a brand of collaborative literary endeavor. Such a categorization may be understood as a loose construction of the term collaboration, which simultaneously and consciously enlarges the definition of author to printers, publishers, and booksellers." "Early Modern Collaboration and Theories of Authorship," *PMLA* 116, no. 3 (2001): 609–22, at 614. It is not my goal in this chapter to reflect at any length on what relation exists between copublication and other forms of human interactivity, but it's worth pointing out that literary scholars have for a long time considered textual exchanges, like those recorded in EEBO, as a kind of social relation. I refer here most specifically to Jeffery Masten's *Textual Intercourse: Collaboration, Authorship, and Sexualities in Renaissance Drama* (Cambridge: Cambridge University Press, 2007). For Masten, relationships among authors are implicitly or intrinsically erotic, insofar as they produce abstract forms of relationality through a kind of shared being that comes into existence. I would argue that relationships, like those modeled in EEBO's metadata, are "queer" in the loosest and most expansive sense of queerness, not that they imply (nor exclude) homosociality and homoeroticism, but that they disrupt a naturalized, commonsensical notion of being-among-others and being-in-oneself.

30. Within the imprint, stationers' names are not regularized or stored in separate fields. To get around this problem, a simple pattern-matching algorithm searched over each imprint, extracted name words of printers and booksellers, then found matches (or near matches, in cases of spelling variation) in the British Book Trade Index. The algorithmically generated dataset required some hand correction because about 5 percent of initial hits were false matches.

31. To avoid confusion, several caveats about this data need to be kept in mind. First, these numbers necessarily entail some margin for error. Authorship attributions in the EEBO metadata are imperfect and incomplete. False or incomplete imprints are invisible to this process. Printers and booksellers identified only by their initials were often impossible to narrow to a single possible candidate, and so had to be discarded. As a result, many imprint attributions that would have been obvious to Restoration readers are not represented in the model. Further, while it was fairly easy to identify obviously false matches generated by the algorithm, differentiating among stationers is not always easy, especially in cases when, for example, a son or widow takes over a stationer's business, when two stationers have very similar names, or when relatives appear together on an imprint. The British Book Trade Index includes many duplicate entries, and although the algorithm was designed to avoid duplication, there are certainly

cases where a single stationer's publications are divided among multiple nodes in the network. The network does not have the same level of precision and accuracy as library-catalog metadata. However, such precision is not necessary for its purpose here. The network is not meant to describe the precise number of real participants in the early modern print marketplace. Instead, the model represents a sample of that historical population as represented through EEBO; so, although my descriptions of the network will include ostensibly precise numbers, those numbers always have meaning only in relation to each other as parts of an imperfectly sampled whole.

32. Roland S. Burt defines "structural holes" as "the separation between nonredundant contacts." *Structural Holes: The Social Structure of Competition* (Cambridge, MA: Harvard University Press, 1992), 18. Connections are "nonredundant" if one person serves as a bridge node between otherwise disparate groups.

33. Barabási, *Network Science*, 135.

34. Though visualized using simple linear binning, the degree exponent was estimated using the "fit_power_law" function in the "igraph" R package, according to principles outlined in M. E. J. Newman, "Power Laws, Pareto Distributions and Zipf's Law," *Contemporary Physics* 46, no. 5 (2005): 323–51; and Aaron Clauset, Cosma Rohilla Shalizi, and M. E. J. Newman, "Power-Law Distributions in Empirical Data," *SIAM Review* 51, no. 4 (2009): 661–703.

35. Franco Moretti, "Network Theory, Plot Analysis," *Pamphlets of the Stanford Literary Lab*, Pamphlet 2, (Stanford, CA: Stanford Literary Lab, 2011), 3–4.

36. An overview of Jugge's career can be found in H. R. Tedder and Joyce Boro, "Jugge, Richard (c. 1514–1577), Bookseller and Printer," *Oxford Dictionary of National Biography*, 2008, https://doi.org/10.1093/ref:odnb/15160.

37. For a detailed history of their troubled partnership, see Maria Wakely, "Printing and Double-Dealing in Jacobean England: Robert Barker, John Bill, and Bonham Norton," *The Library* 8, no. 2 (2007): 119–53.

38. Jason Peacy describes efforts to control the press under Cromwell in "Cromwellian England: A Propaganda State?" *History* 91 no. 2 (2006): 176–99.

39. For the later seventeenth century, see Robert L. Haig, "New Light on the King's Printing Office, 1680–1730," *Studies in Bibliography* 8 (1956): 157–67.

40. I respond here most directly to the thesis advanced by Steve Pincus in *1688: The First Modern Revolution* (New Haven, CT: Yale University Press, 2009).

41. Ted Underwood, *Why Literary Periods Mattered: Historical Contrast and the Prestige of English Studies* (Stanford, CA: Stanford University Press, 2013), 170. See also Jo Guldi and David Armitage, *The History Manifesto* (Cambridge: Cambridge University Press, 2014), especially chap. 4.

42. Underwood, *Why Literary Periods Mattered*, 169.

43. See Micah Mattix, "Periodization and Difference," *New Literary History* 35, no. 4 (2004): 685–97. Mattix claims that period terms "obscure" differences among authors "by superimposing a predetermined schema that is reductive" (686). In making this claim, he responds most directly to Marshall Brown, "Periods and Resistances," *Modern Language Quarterly* 62, no. 4 (2001): 309–16; and borrows from Robert Rehder, "Periodization and the Theory of History," *Colloquium Helveticum* 22 (1995): 117–36. My conclusions here answer with a definitive "yes" the question posed in Steven N. Zwicker, "Is There Such a Thing as Restoration Literature?" *Huntington Library Quarterly* 69, no. 3 (2006): 425–50.

44. Ronald Burt's analysis is directed primarily toward the roles played by individuals within organizations. My use of the phrase to describe patterns of book publication adapts the concept, much like Mark A. Pachucki and Ronald L. Breiger adapt the term in their essay, "Cultural Holes: Beyond Relationality in Social Networks and Culture," *Annual Review of Sociology* 36, no. 1 (2010): 205–24.

45. See the relevant entries in the *Oxford Dictionary of National Biography*.

46. For Charlewood's role in printing Q1 of Sidney's *Astrophil and Stella*, see J. A. Lavin, "The First Two Printers of Sidney's *Astrophil and Stella*," *The Library* 5, no. 3 (1971): 249–55; and MacDonald P. Jackson, "The Printer of the First Quarto of 'Astrophil and Stella' (1591)," *Studies in Bibliography* 31 (1978): 201–3.

47. David Scott Kastan, "Humphrey Moseley and the Invention of English Literature," in *Agent of Change: Print Culture Studies after Elizabeth L. Eisenstein*, ed. Sabrina Alcorn Baron, Eric N. Lindquist, and Eleanor F. Shevlin (Amherst: University of Massachusetts Press, 2007), 105–24.

Chapter 2

1. Magnus Sahlgren and Fredrik Carlsson, "The Singleton Fallacy: Why Current Critiques of Language Models Miss the Point," *arXiv preprint arXiv:2102.04310* (2021).

2. In particular, see Emily M. Bender and Alexander Koller, "Climbing towards NLU: On Meaning, Form, and Understanding in the Age of Data," in *Proceedings of the 58th Annual Meeting of the Association for Computational Linguistics* (2020): 5185–98. A similar argument is advanced in Sean Trott et al., "(Re)Construing Meaning in NLP," *Proceedings of the 58th Annual Meeting of the Association for Computational Linguistics* (2020): 5170–84; and in Yonatan Bisk et al., "Experience Grounds Language," *Proceedings of the 2020 Conference on Empirical Methods in Natural Language Processing* (2020): 8718–35. All three essays argue that real understanding comes from mental representations of experience that inform language, rather than from structures of language within itself. In making this argument, all three rely on conventional linguistic theories of meaning and construal. For

an overview of semantic theory that places statistical models of word meaning within the context of the discipline of linguistics more generally, see Dirk Geeraerts, *Theories of Lexical Semantics* (Oxford: Oxford University Press, 2009).

3. Juan Luis Gastaldi, "Why Can Computers Understand Natural Language?: The Structuralist Image of Language behind Word Embeddings," *Philosophy and Technology* 34, no. 1 (2020): 1–66, at 25. Emphasis removed.

4. Gastaldi, "Why Can Computers Understand Natural Language?" 58, 62.

5. For a concise description of Kristeva's early ambitions for semiotics, see her essay, "Le Lieu Sémiotique," which introduces the collection she edited with Josette Ray-Debove and Donna Jean Umiker, *Essays in Semiotics / Essais de Sémiotique* (The Hague: Mouton, 1971), 1–7.

6. Julia Kristeva, "Word, Dialogue, and Novel," in *The Kristeva Reader*, ed. Toril Moi (New York: Columbia University Press, 1986), 34–61. For a more detailed account of the relationship between Bakhtin and Kristeva, see Graham Allen, *Intertextuality* (New York: Routledge, 2000), chap. 1.

7. Although "intertextuality" has a much broader application than "dialogism," Kristeva would always credit Bakhtin with the idea. In a 1985 interview, she acknowledged that "the concept of intertextuality . . . does not figure as such in the work of Bakhtin," but argued that "one could deduce [it] from his work." *Julia Kristeva Interviews*, ed. Ross Mitchell Guberman (New York: Columbia University Press, 1996), 189.

8. For an early essay that identifies and explores this connection, with more emphasis on Barthes's version of Kristeva's ideas, see Mark Olsen, "Signs, Symbols, and Discourses: A New Direction for Computer-Aided Literature Studies," *Computers and the Humanities* 27, no. 5 (1993): 309–14.

9. M. M. Bakhtin, *The Dialogic Imagination: Four Essays*, trans. Caryl Emerson and Michael Holquist (Austin: University of Texas Press, 1981), 280.

10. Bakhtin, *Dialogic Imagination*, 276.

11. In his summary of Bakhtin's theory, Allen puts it this way: "The most crucial aspect of language, from this perspective, is that all language responds to previous utterances and to pre-existing patterns of meaning and evaluation, but also promotes and seeks to promote further responses. One cannot understand an utterance or even a written work as if it were singular in meaning, unconnected to previous and future utterances or works." *Intertextuality*, 19.

12. Bakhtin, *Dialogic Imagination*, 279.

13. Bakhtin, 281.

14. Bakhtin, 275.

15. Kristeva, "Word, Dialogue, and Novel," 37.

16. Kristeva, 37.

17. In her gloss of this passage, Mary Orr remarks, "What is therefore so stunningly new in Kristeva's work here is the advancing of a theory of *translinguistics*, and the transformative operations at work in any cultural transfer, whether intra- or interlingually. It is but a short step from this to notions of transference and counter-transference and the realm of the pre-linguistic and the pre-semiotic in her later 'psychoanalytic' works." *Intertextuality: Debates and Contexts* (Malden, MA: Polity, 2003), 27.

18. Kristeva, "Word, Dialogue, and Novel," 27.

19. Kristeva argues that intertextuality explains "the overdetermination of a lexeme by multiple meanings which it does not carry in ordinary usage but which accrue to it as a result of its occurrence in other texts." *Kristeva Reader*, 28.

20. Michael Riffaterre calls this *"retroactive reading"* or *"hermeneutic reading"*: a process of "reviewing, revising, comparing backwards . . . as [the reader] moves through the text he comes to recognize, by dint of comparison simply because he is now able to put them together, that successive and differing statements, first noticed as mere ungrammaticalities, are in fact equivalent, for they now appear as variants of the same structural matrix." *Semiotics of Poetry* (Bloomington: Indiana University Press, 1978), 5–6. It is rarely clear, in literary criticism of this vein, when scholars are talking about literary reading practices and when they are talking about features of the literary text. In places, Riffaterre (and perhaps Barthes, though I'll stick with Riffaterre here) hazily recognizes this gap and attempts to resolve it through fantasy, imagining that poems somehow compel the reading practices he pretends to impose on them: "In a response rendered compulsive, and facilitated by this familiar model, as soon as the reader notices a possible substitutability, s/he automatically yields to the temptation to actualise it." "Compulsory Reader Response: The Intertextual Drive," in *Intertextuality: Theories and Practices*, ed. Michael Worton and Judith Still (New York: Manchester University Press, 1990), 56–78, at 77.

21. Roland Barthes, "Death of the Author," in *Image, Music, Text*, trans. Stephen Heath (London: Fontana Press, 1977), 142–48, at 148.

22. See Gérard Genette, *Palimpsests: Literature in the Second Degree*, trans. Channa Newman and Claude Doubinsky (1982; Lincoln: University of Nebraska Press, 1997). For a discussion of Genette and how his textual theories relate to those of Bakhtin, Kristeva, and Barthes, see Allen, *Intertextuality*, 95–115.

23. Kristeva, "Word, Dialogue, and Novel," 57–58.

24. Julia Kristeva, *Σημειωτική: Recherches pour une Sémanalyse* (Paris: Editions du Seuil, 1969), 189–90. Cited and translated in Alan Sokal and Jean Bricmont, *Fashionable Nonsense: Postmodern Intellectual's Abuse of Science* (New York: Picador, 1998), 45–46.

25. See Warren Weaver, "Machine Translation," in *Readings in Machine Translation*, ed. Sergei Nirenburg, Harold L. Somers, and Yorick Wilks (Cambridge, MA: MIT Press, 2003), 13–18; and Erwin Reifler, "The Mechanical Determination of Meaning," in *Readings in Machine Translation*, 21–36.

26. Margaret Masterman, "Mechanical Pidgin Translation," in *Readings in Machine Translation*, 177.

27. Zellig Harris, *Methods in Structural Linguistics* (Chicago: University of Chicago Press, 1951), 22.

28. According to Harris, "The transformations operating on the kernels yield the sentences of the language, either by modifying the kernel sentences of a given set (with the same modification for all kernels in the set) or by combining them (in fixed ways) with other kernel sentences." *Methods in Structural Linguistics*, vi–vii.

29. Chomsky first developed these views in *Syntactic Structures* (1957), written while employed by MIT on its machine-translation initiative. Yehoshua Bar-Hillel compares Harris's and Chomsky's approaches in "The Present Status of Automatic Translation of Languages," in *Readings in Machine Translation*, 50–51.

30. Indeed, computational linguists tended to work with extremely small corpora during most of the later twentieth century. Yorick Wilks, Brian M. Santor, and Louise M. Guthrie report on a conference from the early 1990s in which researchers in natural language processing admitted that their systems contained, on average, thirty-six words. See Wilks, Brian M. Santor, and Louise M. Guthrie, *Electric Words: Dictionaries, Computers, and Meanings* (Cambridge, MA: MIT Press, 1996), 2.

31. Zellig Harris, "Distributional Structure." *Mind* 10 (1954): 146–62.

32. J. R. Firth, "A Synopsis of Linguistic Theory, 1930–1955," in *Studies in Linguistic Analysis* (Oxford: Oxford University Press, 1962), 11.

33. Weaver, "Machine Translation," 13.

34. Bar-Hillel, "Automatic Translation of Languages," 74. For what it's worth, Google Translate manages the sentence just fine, because increased computing power allows it to compile statistical profiles not just of words but of whole phrases.

35. The problem of data sparseness is a serious one for corpus-based word-sense discrimination, as Nancy Ide and Jean Véronis argue in "Introduction to the Special Issue on Word Sense Disambiguation: The State of the Art," *Computational Linguistics* 24, no. 1 (1998): 17. They point out that the Brown Corpus of one million words, released in 1967, contains only eight instances of the word *ash*, and that common meanings of the word are underrepresented or excluded altogether. For researchers today, the easy availability of massive online sources, like

Wikipedia, lessens this problem significantly, but it remains an issue for many humanists, whose datasets are often much smaller.

36. Victor H. Yngve recounts such an experiment in "Early Research at M.I.T.: In Search of Adequate Theory," in *Early Years in Machine Translation: Memoirs and Biographies of Pioneers*, ed. W. John Hutchins (Amsterdam: John Benjamins, 2000), 44.

37. For contemporary accounts of this development, see Nancy Ide and Donald Walker, "Introduction: Common Methodologies in Humanities Computing and Computational Linguistics," *Computers and the Humanities* 26, no. 5-6 (1992): 327-30; and Kenneth W. Church and Robert L. Mercer, "Introduction to the Special Issue on Computational Linguistics Using Large Corpora," *Computational Linguistics* 19, no. 1 (1993): 1-24. For a retrospective overview, see Tony McEnery and Andrew Hardie, *Corpus Linguistics: Method, Theory, and Practice* (Cambridge: Cambridge University Press, 2012).

38. This view is echoed, without the algebraic formalization, by Werner Hüllen: "The essential gain to be had from thesauri is, therefore, the awareness that the lexis of a language is a huge semantic web in which every unit (word) is dependent on many others, or—carrying the idea to an extreme—where each unit is determined by every other one. The lexis of a language has no central point and no periphery, it is an endless functioning of interdependencies." *Networks and Knowledge in "Roget's Thesaurus"* (Oxford: Oxford University Press, 2009), 140-41.

39. See Margaret Masterman, *Language, Cohesion, Form*, ed. Yorick Wilks (Cambridge: Cambridge University Press, 2005).

40. Masterman, R. M. Needham, and Spärck Jones recognized this similarity early on; see Masterman, R. M. Needham, and Karen Spärck Jones, "The Analogy between Mechanical Translation and Library Retrieval," in *Proceedings of the International Conference on Scientific Information* (Washington, DC: National Academy of Sciences, 1959), 917-35. Spärck Jones adapted the lattice network for this purpose in later articles and in her book-length study, *Automatic Keyword Classification for Information Retrieval* (London: Butterworths, 1971).

41. H. P. Luhn, "A New Method of Recording and Searching Information," *American Documentation* 4, no. 1 (1953): 14-16, at 14. Writing in 1987, Gerard Salton describes the significance of this early work: "It was suggested, in particular, that instead of assigning complex subject indicators extracted from controlled vocabulary schedules, single term descriptors, or key words, could be used that would be assigned to the documents without context or role specification. These single terms could then be combined in the search formulations to produce complex phrase specifications and chains of synonyms . . . the coordinate keyword

indexing methods eventually became the standard used in all automatic retrieval environments." "Historical Note: The Past Thirty Years in Information Retrieval," *JASIS* 38, no. 5 (1987): 375–80, at 376.

42. Luhn, "A New Method of Recording and Searching Information," 14.

43. See H. P. Luhn, "Keyword-in-Context Index for Technical Literature," *American Documentation* 11, no. 4 (1959): 288–95.

44. H. P. Luhn, "A Statistical Approach to Mechanized Encoding and Searching of Literary Information," *IBM Journal* 1, no. 4 (1957): 309–17.

45. Gerard Salton, "Associative Document Retrieval Techniques Using Bibliographic Information," *Journal of the ACM* 10, no. 4 (1963): 440–57.

46. Hinrich Schütze, "Word Space," *Advances in Neural Information Processing Systems* 5 (1993): 895–902.

47. Magnus Sahlgren, *The Word-Space Model: Using Analysis to Represent Syntagmatic and Paradigmatic Relations between Words in High-Dimensional Vector Spaces* (PhD diss., Stockholm University, 2006), 19, eprints.sics.se/437/1/TheWordSpaceModel.pdf.

48. For a review of this scholarship, see Thomas Landauer et al., eds., *Handbook of Latent Semantic Analysis* (Mahwah, NJ: Lawrence Erlbaum Associates, 2007). In particular, see essays by Landauer, "LSA as a Theory of Meaning," and Dumais, "LSA and Information Retrieval: Getting Back to Basics."

49. For a recent overview of various approaches, see Alessandro Lenci, "Distributional Models of Word Meaning," *Annual Review of Linguistics* 4, no. 1 (2018): 151–71. A more detailed discussion of fundamental concepts can be found in the survey of the field by Peter D. Turney and Patrick Pantel, "From Frequency to Meaning: Vector Space Models of Semantics," *Journal of Artificial Intelligence Research* 37, no. 1 (2010): 141–88.

50. For descriptions of topic modeling, see David Blei, "Introduction to Probabilistic Topic Models," *Communications of the ACM* 55, no. 4 (2012): 77–84; and John W. Mohr and Petko Bogdanov, "Topic Models: What They Are and Why They Matter," *Poetics* 41, no. 6 (2013): 545–69. Word-embedding models were first introduced in Tomas Mikolov et al., "Efficient Estimation of Word Representations in Vector Space," *ArXiv Preprint arXiv:1301.3781* (2013). For the relationship between these probabilistic approaches and frequency-based semantic models, see Omer Levy, Yoav Goldberg, and Ido Dagan, "Improving Distributional Similarity with Lessons Learned from Word Embeddings," *Transactions of the Association for Computational Linguistics* 3 (2015): 211–25; and Mark Steyvers and Tom Griffiths, "Probabilistic Topic Models," in *Handbook of Latent Semantic Analysis*, ed. Landauer et al. (Mahwah, NJ: Lawrence Erlbaum Associates, 2007), 427–48.

51. See Marco Baroni, Georgiana Dinu, and Germán Kruszewski, "Don't Count, Predict!: A Systematic Comparison of Context-Counting vs. Context-Predicting Semantic Vectors," *Proceedings of the 52nd Annual Meeting of the Association for Computational Linguistics* 1 (2014): 238–47.

52. For an introduction to this technique, see Katrin Erk, "Vector Space Models of Word Meaning and Phrase Meaning: A Survey," *Language and Linguistics Compass* 6, no. 10 (2012): 635–53.

53. Dominic Widdows, *Geometry and Meaning* (Stanford, CA: Center for the Study of Language and Information, 2004), 164.

54. Keyword calculations in this table are based on measurements that take the product of a normalized semantic distance and term frequency. Terms score highly as "persistently conventional" if they are both high frequency and if their vectors, when calculated in the subcorpus, are similar to the vectors of the same words when measured over the full corpus. Terms are "persistently deviant" if the vector for the term varies widely from its use in the corpus despite being used frequently. Full details about these and similar calculations can be found in this book's online supplement, *literarymathematics.org*.

55. In the field of digital humanities, studies that have attempted to combine social-network and textual analysis include David A. Smith, Ryan Cordell, and Abby Mullen, "Computational Methods for Uncovering Reprinted Texts in Antebellum Newspapers," *American Literary History* 27, no. 3 (2015): E1–E15; and Michael Gavin, "Historical Text Networks: The Sociology of Early English Criticism," *Eighteenth-Century Studies* 50, no. 1 (2016): 53–80.

56. See, for example, Ian N. Gregory and Andrew Hardie, "Visual GISting: Bringing Together Corpus Linguistics and Geographical Information Systems," *Literary and Linguistic Computing* 26, no. 3 (2011): 297–314; and Michael Gavin and Eric Gidal, "Scotland's Poetics of Space: An Experiment in Geospatial Semantics," *Journal of Cultural Analytics* 2, no. 1 (2017). See also Werner Kuhn, "Geospatial Semantics: Why, of What, and How?" *Journal on Data Semantics III* (2005): 1–24; Angela Schwering, "Approaches to Semantic Similarity Measurement for Geo-Spatial Data: A Survey," *Transactions in GIS* 12, no. 1 (2008): 5–29; and Krzysztof Janowicz et al., "Geospatial Semantics and Linked Spatiotemporal Data—Past, Present, and Future," *Semantic Web* 3, no. 4 (2012): 321–32.

57. Daniel Shore has become an important advocate in literary studies for maintaining attention to grammatical forms even as humanities computing is increasingly influenced by the intellectual tradition of information retrieval. See his *Cyberformalism: Histories of Linguistic Forms in the Digital Archive* (Baltimore: Johns Hopkins University Press, 2018). For additional background on grammatical

pattern analysis, see Susan Hunston, *Pattern Grammar: A Corpus-Driven Approach to the Lexical Grammar of English* (Amsterdam: John Benjamins Publishing, 2000).

58. Kristeva, *Kristeva Reader*, 28.

59. Hinrich Schütze, "Dimensions of Meaning," in *Proceedings of the 1992 ACM/IEEE Conference on Supercomputing* (1992): 787–96, at 795.

Chapter 3

1. Michel de Certeau, The Practice of Everyday Life, trans. Steven Rendall (Berkeley: University of California Press, 1980), 108.

2. This distinction is generally attributed to John A. Agnew, *Place and Politics: The Geographical Mediation of State and Society* (Boston: Allen and Unwin, 1987). A succinct overview of key concepts can be found in Timothy Cresswell, "Place," in *Encyclopedia of Human Geography: Volume 1*, ed. Nigel Thrift and Rob Kitchin (Amsterdam: Elsevier Science, 2009), 117–24.

3. Certeau, *Practice of Everyday Life*, 129.

4. The technique is also called "geographical text analysis." See, for example, recent studies by Catherine Porter, Ian Gregory, and others. See Catherine Porter, Paul Atkinson, and Ian Gregory, "Geographical Text Analysis: A New Approach to Understanding Nineteenth-Century Mortality," *Health and Place* 36 (2015): 25–34; and Catherine Porter, Paul Atkinson, and Ian N. Gregory, "Space and Time in 100 Million Words: Health and Disease in a Nineteenth-Century Newspaper," *International Journal of Humanities and Arts Computing* 12, no. 2 (2018): 196–216; and Ian N. Gregory and Laura L. Paterson, "Geographical Representations of Poverty in Historical Newspapers," in *The Routledge Handbook of English Language and Digital Humanities*, ed. Svenja Adolphs and Dawn Knight (London: Routledge, 2020). This newer work builds on key methodological innovations pioneered separately by Timothy Tangherlini and Ian Gregory, among others. See Ian N. Gregory and Andrew Hardie, "Visual GISting: Bringing Together Corpus Linguistics and Geographical Information Systems," *Literary and Linguistic Computing* 26, no. 3 (2011): 297–314; and Peter M. Broadwell and Timothy R. Tangherlini, "Witch-Hunter: Tools for the Geo-Semantic Exploration of a Danish Folklore Corpus," *Journal of American Folklore* 129, no. 511 (2016): 14–42.

5. Henri Lefebvre, *The Production of Space*, trans. Donald Nicholson-Smith (Oxford: Blackwell, 1974).

6. Lefebvre wrote most directly in response to Fernand Braudel, *Civilization and Capitalism, 15th–18th Century* (New York: Harper and Row, 1982). Braudel's line of inquiry was generalized to "world systems analysis" by Immanuel Wallerstein in *The Modern World-System: Capitalist Agriculture and the Origins of the European World-Economy in the Sixteenth Century* (New York: Academic Press, 1974);

and Immanuel Wallerstein, *World-Systems Analysis: An Introduction* (Durham, NC: Duke University Press, 2004).

7. Lefebvre explains: "The capitalist 'trinity' is established in space—that trinity of land-capital-labour which cannot remain abstract and which is assembled only within an equally tri-faceted institutional space: a space that is first of all global, and maintained as such—the space of sovereignty, where constraints are implemented, and hence a fetishized space, reductive of differences; a space, secondly, that is fragmented, separating, disjunctive, a space that locates specificities, places or localities, both in order to control them and in order to make them negotiable; and a space, finally, that is hierarchical, ranging from the lowliest places to the noblest, from the tabooed to the sovereign." *Production of Space*, 282.

8. See Jean-Luc Nancy, *The Sense of the World*, trans. Jeffrey S. Librett (Minneapolis: University of Minnesota Press, 1997) and Jean-Luc Nancy, *The Creation of the World; or, Globalization*, trans. François Raffoul and David Pettigrew (Albany: State University of New York Press, 2007). Nancy argues that the "unity of a world is nothing other than its diversity, and its diversity is, in turn, a diversity of worlds. A world is a multiplicity of worlds, the world is a multiplicity of worlds, and its unity is in the sharing out [partage] and the mutual exposure in this world of all its worlds." *Creation of the World*, 109.

9. The relationship between Ptolemy's *Geographia* and the development of early modern geography is described in Anthony Grafton, April Shelford, and Nancy Siraisi, *New Worlds, Ancient Texts: The Power of Tradition and the Shock of Discovery* (Cambridge, MA: Harvard University Press, 1992); and Zur Shalev and Charles Burnett, eds., *Ptolemy's Geography in the Renaissance* (London: Warburg Institute, 2011).

10. Medievalists and early modernists debate how best to characterize these developments, and in particular how we should describe the relationship between "modernity" and the "Middle Ages." In his *Origins of Capitalism and the Rise of the West* (Philadelphia: Temple University Press, 2007), Eric H. Mielants surveys different models for explaining the origins of capitalism. I hope my attempt at summary here will not seem to stake any position among these historians, nor do I presume to adjudicate their disputes.

11. My remarks on the evolution of European capitalism derive primarily from Braudel's *Civilization and Capitalism*, Lefebvre's *Production of Space*, and Mielants's *Origins of Capitalism*.

12. In addition to Joad Raymond, *The Invention of the Newspaper: English Newsbooks, 1641–1649* (Oxford: Oxford University Press, 2005); and Andrew Pettegree, *The Invention of News: How the World Came to Know about Itself* (New Haven, CT: Yale University Press, 2014); see Adam Fox, *Oral and Literate Culture in England*,

1500–1700 (Oxford: Oxford University Press, 2000) for the history of "news" as a social practice.

13. For discussions of the early modern process of territorialization, see, in addition to Braudel and Lefebvre, Saskia Sassen, *Territory, Authority, Rights: From Medieval to Global Assemblages* (Princeton, NJ: Princeton University Press, 2006).

14. In *The Invention of Improvement: Information and Material Progress in Seventeenth-Century England* (Oxford: Oxford University Press, 2015), Paul Slack provides an intellectual history of "improvement" in England.

15. The ideological reconfiguration of land as property, and therefore as a basic feature of paradigmatic citizenship, was a key feature of Whiggish political philosophy. In addition to Slack, *Invention of Improvement*, see Richard Helgerson, *Forms of Nationhood: The Elizabethan Writing of England* (Chicago: University of Chicago Press, 1992); and Jess Edwards, *Writing, Geometry, and Space in Seventeenth-Century England and America: Circles in the Sand* (London: Routledge, 2005).

16. For an overview of Renaissance travel writing, see William H. Sherman, "Stirrings and Searchings (1500–1720)," in *The Cambridge Companion to Travel Writing*, ed. Peter Hulme and Tim Youngs (Cambridge: Cambridge University Press, 2002), 17–36. A more detailed account focused on Hakluyt can be found in Helgerson, *Forms of Nationhood*, chap. 4. For the relationship between captivity narratives and British nationhood, in particular, see Linda Colley, *Captives: Britain, Empire, and the World, 1600–1850* (New York: Random House, 2010).

17. The classic study of English chorography can be found in Helgerson, *Forms of Nationhood*. In addition to Edwards and Slack, see Cynthia S. Wall, *The Prose of Things: Transformations of Description in the Eighteenth Century* (Chicago: University of Chicago Press, 2014).

18. For a detailed account of Adams's index, see William Ravenhill, "John Adams, His Map of England, Its Projection, and His *Index Villaris* of 1680," *Geographical Journal* 144, no. 3 (1978): 424–37.

19. Ayesha Ramachandran credits Mercator with initiating a "paradigmatic shift in the image of the world." *The Worldmakers: Global Imagining in Early Modern Europe* (Chicago: University of Chicago Press, 2015), 24.

20. John D. Beaumont, *The Present State of the Universe . . .* (Oxford Text Archive, 2007), http://hdl.handle.net/20.500.12024/A27210.

21. Peter Heylyn, *Cosmographie in Four Bookes . . .* (Oxford Text Archive, 2006), http://hdl.handle.net/20.500.12024/A43514.

22. For a detailed overview of globes and globe making in Europe, the classic and still-definitive account is Edward Luther Stevenson, *Terrestrial and Celestial Globes: Their History and Construction, Including a Consideration of Their Value as*

Aids in the Study of Geography and Astronomy, 2 vols. (New Haven, CT: Yale University Press, 1921). Sylvia Sumira's *Globes: 400 Years of Exploration, Navigation, and Power* (Chicago: University of Chicago Press, 2014) offers a beautifully illustrated overview of this history.

23. Roger Palmer, Earl of Castlemaine, and Joseph Moxon, Preface to *The English Globe Being a Stabil and Immobil One* . . . (Oxford Text Archive, 2007), http://hdl.handle.net/20.500.12024/A31232.

24. Patrick Gordon, *Geography Anatomiz'd* . . . (Oxford Text Archive, 2005), http://hdl.handle.net/20.500.12024/A41559.

25. Basing their analyses on a small handful of retrospectively privileged books, cultural historians almost uniformly overstate the prevalence of this global perspective to early modern writers and readers. See for example Denis Cosgrove, *Apollo's Eye: A Cartographic Genealogy of the Earth in the Western Imagination* (Baltimore: Johns Hopkins University Press, 2001); Ramachandran, *Worldmakers*; and Ayesha Ramachandran, "How to Theorize the 'World': An Early Modern Manifesto," *New Literary History* 48, no. 4 (2017): 655–84. Fredric Jameson's general assertion that "cognitive mapping in the broader sense comes to require the coordination of existential data (the empirical position of the subject) with unlived, abstract conceptions of the geographic totality" (*Postmodernism, or, The Cultural Logic of Late Capitalism*, [Durham, NC: Duke University Press, 1991], 90) is contradicted by a survey of available textual evidence. As we'll see, Nancy hits closer to the mark in *The Creation of the World* when differentiating the modern globe, as defined by geocoordinate systems and systems of international trade in commodities, from the early modern world, a fundamentally domestic space defined by divine witness and the dispensations of providence.

26. University of Oxford, *Europæ Modernæ Speculum* . . . (Oxford Text Archive, 2013), http://hdl.handle.net/20.500.12024/A38741.

27. See for example Thomas Rannew, *In This Book Is the Figure of the Dividing the Land of Israel among the Tribes of Israel* . . . (Oxford Text Archive, 2012), http://hdl.handle.net/20.500.12024/A92160.

28. For a trenchant critique of English literature as a field of study on this score, see Srinivas Aravamudan, *Tropicopolitans: Colonialism and Agency, 1688–1804* (Durham, NC: Duke University Press 1999), 233–35. In *The Language of Postcolonial Literatures: An Introduction* (London: Routledge, 2002), Ismail S. Talib argues this bias can be seen even in the field of postcolonial studies, and Roopika Risam, *New Digital Worlds* (Evanston, IL: Northwestern University Press, 2018), finds it in digital humanities as well.

29. See, most relevantly to my argument in this chapter, Helgerson's *Forms of Nationhood* and Colley's *Captives*.

30. Efforts to resist Anglocentrism in literary studies are most pronounced in the fields of comparative literature and postcolonial studies. See for example Bill Ashcroft, Gareth Griffiths, and Helen Tiffin, *The Empire Writes Back: Theory and Practice in Post-Colonial Literatures* (London: Routledge, 2003); and Charles Bernheimer, ed., *Comparative Literature in the Age of Multiculturalism* (Baltimore: Johns Hopkins University Press, 1995).

31. See Paul Gilroy, *The Black Atlantic: Modernity and Double Consciousness* (Cambridge, MA: Harvard University Press, 1993); Bryce Traister, "The Object of Study; or, Are We Being Transnational Yet?" *Journal of Transnational American Studies* 2, no. 1 (2010), https://doi.org/10.5070/T821006993; and Eve Tavor Bannet and Susan Manning, eds., *Transatlantic Literary Studies, 1660–1830* (Cambridge: Cambridge University Press, 2011).

32. Students on the team did not wish to be credited publicly by name.

33. This number may be slightly underestimated because our data-curation process worked by breaking texts down to unigrams, so compound place names like "New York" or "San Salvador" are excluded. This is not a problem for the vast majority of early modern place names, but colonies may be particularly susceptible to this naming convention and so are likely to be slightly underrepresented in the data. However, given the overall power-law distribution of place references in EEBO, it's extremely unlikely that this omission significantly affects the totals presented here.

34. If you try to check this location on a modern map, you'll think the coordinates are located somewhere in Central Europe, but keep in mind that I'm using seventeenth-century sources, which typically based the zero-degree meridian in Paris.

35. Saskia Sassen, *Territory, Authority, Rights: From Medieval to Global Assemblages* (Princeton, NJ: Princeton University Press, 2006), 81.

36. Scotland. Parliament. Committee of Estates. and England and Wales, *A Proclamation, Declaring William and Mary King and Queen of England to Be King and Queen of Scotland. Edinburgh April 11. 1689* (Oxford Text Archive, 2008), http://hdl.handle.net/20.500.12024/A92599.

37. John Owen, *Some Considerations about Union among Protestants, and the Preservation of the Interest of the Protestant Religion in This Nation* (Oxford Text Archive, 2005), http://hdl.handle.net/20.500.12024/A53728.

38. Nicolas Fontaine, *The History of the Old and New Testament Extracted out of Sacred Scripture* . . . (Oxford Text Archive, 2005), http://hdl.handle.net/20.500.12024/A39861.

39. Lefebvre, *Production of Space*, 269.

40. English Gentleman and William Carr, *An Accurate Description of the United Netherlands, and of the most considerable parts of Germany, Sweden, & Denmark* . . . (Oxford Text Archive, 2008), http://hdl.handle.net/20.500.12024/A69794.

41. Lefebvre, *Production of Space*, 269.

42. Jodocus Crull, *The Antient and Present State of Muscovy* . . . (Oxford Text Archive, 2007), http://hdl.handle.net/20.500.12024/A35310.

43. Richard Baxter, *A Paraphrase on the New Testament* . . . (Oxford Text Archive, 2006), http://hdl.handle.net/20.500.12024/A26981.

44. William Dampier, *A New Voyage Round the World* . . . (Oxford Text Archive, 2003), http://hdl.handle.net/20.500.12024/A36106.

Chapter 4

1. For the terms *distant reading, algorithmic criticism*, and *cultural analytics* as I'm using them here, see, respectively, Ted Underwood, "A Genealogy of Distant Reading," *DHQ: Digital Humanities Quarterly* 11, no. 2 (2017); Stephen Ramsay, *Reading Machines: Toward an Algorithmic Criticism* (Urbana: University of Illinois Press, 2011); and Lev Manovich, "The Science of Culture? Social Computing, Digital Humanities, and Cultural Analytics," *Journal of Cultural Analytics* 1, no. 1 (2016).

2. For overviews and examples across a variety of fields and methodologies, chosen more or less arbitrarily, see Duncan J. Watts and Steven H. Strogatz, "Collective Dynamics of 'Small-World' Networks," *Nature* 393, no. 6684 (1998): 440–42; Albert-László Barabási and Réka Albert, "Emergence of Scaling in Random Networks," *Science* 286, no. 5439 (1999): 509–12; Joshua M. Epstein, *Generative Social Science: Studies in Agent-Based Computational Modeling* (Princeton, NJ: Princeton University Press, 2006); Mark A. Pachucki and Ronald L. Breiger, "Cultural Holes: Beyond Relationality in Social Networks and Culture," *Annual Review of Sociology* 36, no. 1 (2010): 205–24; Dmitri Krioukov et al., "Hyperbolic Geometry of Complex Networks," *Physical Review E* 82, no. 3 (2010); John Mohr and Peter Bogdanov, "Topic Models: What They Are and Why They Matter?" *Poetics* 41, no. 6 (2013): 545–69; and, most recently, Alexander T. J. Barron et al., "Individuals, Institutions, and Innovation in the Debates of the French Revolution," *PNAS* 115, no. 18 (2018): 4607–12.

3. Underwood explains that the phrase *distant reading* "underlines the macroscopic scale of recent literary-historical experiments, without narrowly specifying theoretical presuppositions, methods, or objects of analysis." "Genealogy of Distant Reading."

4. I am not alone in identifying this need. See Richard Jean So, "All Models Are Wrong," *PMLA* 132, no. 3 (2017): 668–73 and Mark Algee-Hewitt, "Distributed

Character: Quantitative Models of the English Stage, 1550–1900," *New Literary History* 48, no. 4 (2017): 751–82. Algee-Hewitt expresses a view close to my own: "Establishing metrics, finding patterns, and linking these metrics and patterns with meaningful concepts of literary criticism: these are tasks that digital humanities now faces" (751).

5. By identifying distant reading's primary method with mathematical modeling rather than with visualization, I adopt a view more closely aligned with So, "All Models Are Wrong," than with Franco Moretti in *Graphs, Maps, and Trees* (London: Verso Books, 2005) or *Distant Reading* (London: Verso Books, 2013).

6. See M. A. K. Halliday, *Language as Social Semiotic: The Social Interpretation of Language and Meaning* (London: Edward Arnold, 1978), 30. This notion goes back to Bronislaw Malinowski, whose ethnographic research on indigenous language in Melanesia concluded that "primitive languages" lacked lexical and grammatical specificity; it was possible to understand the meanings of statements only for people already knowledgeable about the contexts and customs of the indigenous culture. In the 1950s and 1960s, John R. Firth argued that this principle held true for language in general, a notion that became a core assumption in the sociolinguistics of Halliday and his student, the pioneering corpus linguist John Sinclair. See Bronislaw Malinowski, "The Problem of Meaning in Primitive Languages," in *The Meaning of Meaning*, ed. C. K. Ogden and I. A. Richards (London: Kegan Paul, 1923), 296–336; J. R. Firth, *Studies in Linguistic Analysis* (Oxford: Oxford University Press, 1962); John Sinclair, *Trust the Text: Language, Corpus, and Discourse*, ed. John Sinclair and Ronald Carter (London: Routledge, 2004). This intellectual tradition overlaps with but is distinct from the tradition usually cited in computational linguistics and natural language processing, which cites Firth but often reaches back through Margaret Masterman to Ludwig Wittgenstein, whose notion of discourse as a "language game" entails very similar assumptions and implications.

7. For a comprehensive survey of these political and ethical questions from the perspective of data science, see Catherine D'Ignazio and Lauren F. Klein's *Data Feminism* (Cambridge, MA: MIT Press, 2020).

8. Some scholars might prefer to phrase these assumptions differently. In these statements, readers and authors are all taken to exist prior to the documents. Their "intentions," "concerns," and "practices" are all previously existing things somehow represented or implied by the source texts. A doctrinaire poststructuralist might say instead that commonalities across the source texts produce the illusion of a coherent readership; that unique properties of individual documents produce intention effects; and that variations inconsistent with the metadata will be labeled "errors" or "anomalies." Such a phrasing would be

perfectly consistent with the main proposition—that variation in the corpus corresponds with historical difference—because "corresponds with" is a usefully vague relation. Whether the past causes our corpus, or the corpus causes our past, doesn't really matter. Nothing in the distant reading hypothesis boxes scholars into any particular set of ontological commitments.

9. For a general overview of these topics with special emphasis on their application in computing, see Judith L. Gersting, *Mathematical Structures for Computer Science: A Modern Treatment of Discrete Mathematics*, 5th ed. (New York: W. H. Freeman, 2002). The classic introduction to set theory is Paul R. Halmos, *Naive Set Theory* (Princeton, NJ: Van Nostrand,1960). For graph theory, see Øystein Ore, *Theory of Graphs* (Providence, RI: American Mathematical Society, 1962); Claude Flament, *Applications of Graph Theory to Group Structure* (Hoboken, NJ: Prentice Hall, 1963); and Frank Harary, Robert Z. Norman, and Dorwin Cartwright, *Structural Models: An Introduction to the Theory of Directed Graphs* (New York: John Wiley and Sons, 1965). Recent introductions to graph theory oriented toward the study of networks can be found in M. E. J. Newman, *Networks: An Introduction* (Oxford: Oxford University Press, 2010), chap. 6; and Albert-László Barabási, *Network Science* (Cambridge: Cambridge University Press, 2016), chap. 2. For general topology, see Bert Mendelson, *Introduction to Topology*, 3rd ed. (1962; New York: Dover Publications, 2016); John M. Lee, *Introduction to Topological Manifolds* (New York: Springer, 2000); and Paul L. Shick, *Topology: Point-Set and Geometric* (New York: John Wiley and Sons, 2007). James R. Munkres's *Elements of Algebraic Topology* (Boston: Addison-Wesley, 1984) is the classic graduate-level textbook for algebraic topology but presupposes a mastery of basic point-set and geometric concepts.

10. Rachel Sagner Buurma briefly summarizes commentary on this point. "The Preparation of the Topic Model," *Digital Humanities Conference* (2017), https://dh2017.adho.org/abstracts/332/332.pdf.

11. Usually this challenge is described imprecisely as "interpretation" that goes into designing computer models. See, for example, Rafael C. Alvarado, "The Digital Humanities Situation," in *Debates in Digital Humanities*, ed. Matthew K. Gold (Minneapolis: University of Minnesota Press, 2012); and James J. Brown, "Crossing State Lines: Rhetoric and Software Studies," in *Rhetoric and the Digital Humanities*, ed. Jim Ridolfo and William Hart-Davidson (Chicago: University of Chicago Press, 2015), 30. The word *interpretation* is too vague to do more good than harm to a theory of distant reading, as is, for that matter, *reading*.

12. For the distinction between metric spaces and topological spaces, see Mendelson, *Introduction to Topology*, chap. 3, and Shick, *Topology*, chap. 9.

13. Many of the issues I raise here can be approached as problems in combinatorics. See Gersting, *Mathematical Structures for Computer Science*, 188–222.

14. Scholars trained in digital editing will be familiar with the "ordered hierarchy of content objects" (OHCO) model of textuality. See Charles F. Goldfarb, "A Generalized Approach to Document Markup," *ACM SIGPLAN Notices* 16, no. 6 (1981): 68–73; Steven J. DeRose et al., "What Is a Text, Really?" *Journal of Computing in Higher Education* 1, no. 2 (1990): 3–26; C. M. Sperberg-McQueen, "Text in the Electronic Age: Textual Study and Text Encoding, with Examples from Medieval Texts," *Literary and Linguistic Computing* 6, no. 1 (1991): 34–46; and Allen Renear, "Text Encoding," in *A Companion to Digital Humanities*, ed. Susan Schreibman et al. (Oxford: Blackwell, 2004). Editing with XML similarly involves devising a topological model for a corpus, but the ordinary topology of distant reading is in practice more flexible than any viable markup system, because it presumes each character to be a discrete element and relegates all categories and other structures to the status of an attribute.

15. For a succinct review of the history of network analysis within the social sciences, see John Scott, *Social Network Analysis* (Los Angeles: Sage, 2012). Barabási's *Network Science* attends more closely to developments in mathematics and physics. Geospatial topology has a much shorter history; its conceptual foundations are traced back to Max J. Egenhofer and John R. Herring, "A Mathematical Framework for the Definition of Topological Relationships," *Fourth International Symposium on Spatial Data Handling* (Zurich, Switzerland, 1990); and Max J. Egenhofer and Robert D. Franzosa, "Point-Set Topological Spatial Relations," *International Journal of Geographical Information Systems* 5, no. 2 (1991): 161–74.

16. Graphs in this technical sense are very different objects from those described in Moretti's *Graphs, Maps, and Trees*.

17. For this reason, network science shares much overlap with the study of complex systems. See Steven H. Strogatz, "Exploring Complex Networks," *Nature* 410, no. 6825 (2001): 268–76; and Albert-László Barabási, "The Network Takeover," *Nature Physics* 8, no. 1 (2011): 14–16.

18. Ulrik Brandes et al., define network science more broadly as "the study of the collection, management, analysis, interpretation, and presentation of relational data." "What Is Network Science?" *Network Science* 1, no. 1 (2013): 1–15, at 2.

19. The phrase *geographical information science* (rather than geographical information *systems*) can be traced to Michael F. Goodchild, "Geographical Information Science," *International Journal of Geographical Information Systems* 6, no. 1 (1992): 31–45.

20. For a detailed overview of research into spatial networks, see Marc Barthélemy, "Spatial Networks," *Physics Reports* 499, no. 1–3 (2011): 1–101.

21. For drama networks, see Franco Moretti, "Network Theory, Plot Analysis," *Pamphlets of the Stanford Literary Lab*, Pamphlet 2 (Stanford, CA: Stanford

Literary Lab, 2011); and Algee-Hewitt, "Distributed Character." For publishing networks see David Smith, Ryan Cordell, and Abby Mullen, "Computational Methods for Uncovering Reprinted Texts in Antebellum Newspapers," *American Literary History* 27, no. 3 (2015): E1–E15; Blaine Greteman, "Milton and the Early Modern Social Network: The Case of the *Epitaphium Damonis*," *Milton Quarterly* 49, no. 2 (2015): 79–95; and Michael Gavin, "Historical Text Networks: The Sociology of Early Criticism," *Eighteenth-Century Studies* 51, no. 3 (2016): 53–80. Epistolary networks are described in Laura Mandell, "How to Read a Literary Visualisation: Network Effects in the Lake School of Romantic Poetry," *Digital Studies / Le champ numérique* 3, no. 2 (2013); Ruth Ahnert and Sebastian E. Ahnert, "Protestant Letter Networks in the Reign of Mary I: A Quantitative Approach," *ELH* 82, no. 1 (2015): 1–33; and Dan Edelstein et al., "Historical Research in a Digital Age: Reflections from the Mapping the Republic of Letters Project," *American Historical Review* 122, no. 2 (2017): 400–424.

22. The "spatial humanities" represent one of the more vibrant subfields of digital humanities. For applications to literary study in particular, see David Cooper, Christopher Donaldson, and Patricia Murrieta-Flores, eds., *Literary Mapping in the Digital Age* (London: Routledge, 2017).

23. Research in digital humanities that bridges spatial and textual analysis includes Ian N. Gregory and Andrew Hardie, "Visual GISting: Bringing Together Corpus Linguistics and Geographical Information Systems," *Literary and Linguistic Computing* 26, no. 3 (2011): 297–314; Matthew Wilkens, "The Geographic Imagination of Civil War-Era American Fiction," *American Literary History* 25, no. 4 (2013): 803–40; Peter M. Broadwell and Timothy R. Tangherlini, "Witchhunter: Tools for the Geo-Semantic Exploration of a Danish Folklore Corpus," *Journal of American Folklore* 129, no. 511 (2016): 14–42; Michael Gavin and Eric Gidal, "Scotland's Poetics of Space: An Experiment in Geospatial Semantics," *Journal of Cultural Analytics* 2, no. 1 (2017). In the field of geospatial computing, similar lines of inquiry are pursued in Werner Kuhn, "Geospatial Semantics," *Journal on Data Semantics III* (2005): 1–24; Angela Schwering, "Approaches to Semantic Similarity Measurement for Geo-Spatial Data: A Survey," *Transactions in GIS* 12, no. 1 (2008): 5–29. Among the more imaginative extensions of GIS within literary studies is Patricia Murrieta-Flores and Naomi Howell, "Towards the Spatial Analysis of Vague and Imaginary Place and Space: Evolving the Spatial Humanities through Medieval Romance," *Journal of Map and Geography Libraries* 13, no. 1 (2017): 29–57.

24. Gunnar Carlsson emphasizes the suitability of topology for reasoning across the qualitative and quantitative domains in a range of disciplines, from image processing to neuroscience. See his "Topology and Data," *Bulletin of the AMS*, n.s., 46, no. 2 (2009): 255–308.

25. In *Mathematical Structures for Computer Science*, Gersting defines these problems in terms of set theory and combinatorics.

26. Most visibly, in the long-standing debate over the "bag-of-words" hypothesis. Writing in the last century, David D. Lewis describes the issue as already old hat: "An ongoing surprise and disappointment is that structurally simple representations produced without linguistic or domain knowledge have been as effective as any others." "Naive (Bayes) at Forty: The Independence Assumption in Information Retrieval," in *Machine Learning: ECML-98*, ed. C. Nédellec and C. Rouveirol (Berlin: Springer, 1998), 3.

27. The basics of matrix algebra are briefly reviewed in Gersting, *Mathematical Structures for Computer Science*. More comprehensive treatments are widely available. My discussion here depends most heavily on David C. Lay, *Linear Algebra and Its Applications*, 2nd ed. (Boston: Addison-Wesley, 1999); and Sheldon Axler, *Linear Algebra Done Right* (New York: Springer, 2004).

28. Often credited with introducing the term-document matrix format is Gerard A. Salton, A. Wong, and C. S. Yang, "A Vector Space Model for Automatic Indexing," *Communications of the ACM* 18, no. 11 (1975): 613–20; for a more detailed discussion see Gerard A. Salton, *Automatic Information Organization and Retrieval* (New York: McGraw-Hill, 1983); Peter D. Turney and Patrick Pantel, "From Frequency to Meaning: Vector Space Models of Semantics," *Journal of Artificial Intelligence Research* 37, no. 1 (2010): 141–88. A similar review, geared toward researchers in linguistics, is offered by Stephen Clark, "Vector Space Models of Lexical Meaning," in *The Handbook of Contemporary Semantic Theory*, ed. Shalom Lappin and Chris Fox (Oxford: John Wiley and Sons, 2015).

29. For the incidence matrix format and its projection onto univariate network models, including co-citation networks, see Newman, *Networks*. Its explanatory potential was first explored in George Homans, *The Human Group* (London: Routledge and Kegan Paul, 1951).

30. Brian J. L. Berry first described the use of matrices, stacked over a third dimension of time, to represent the changing distribution of variables over places. See his "Approaches to Regional Analysis: A Synthesis," in *Spatial Analysis: A Reader in Statistical Geography*, ed. Brian J. L. Berry and Duane F. Marble (Englewood Cliffs, NJ: Prentice Hall, 1963).

31. Matrix algebra receives strangely cursory treatment in Patrick Juola and Stephen Ramsay's *Six Septembers: Mathematics for the Humanist* (Lincoln, NE: Zea Books, 2017), which, despite its title, does not appear to have been written with any humanities applications in mind. Scholars hoping to get their feet wet with matrices should start instead with Dominic Widdows, *Geometry and Meaning* (Stanford, CA: CSLI Publications, 2004), which offers an elegant and compact

introduction to matrices in the context of semantic analysis, or with Newman, *Networks*, which introduces many of the same concepts as applied in network science.

32. Conventionally, the inner product is somewhat more general than the dot product, because it can handle complex numbers. See Axler, *Linear Algebra Done Right*, 98–99. I use the terms interchangeably.

33. For more extended examples like this, see Widdows, *Geometry and Meaning*.

34. The analogy to physical space is critiqued in Kent K. Chang and Simon DeDeo, "Divergence and the Complexity of Difference in Text and Culture," *Journal of Cultural Analytics* 5, no. 2 (2020): 1–36; and Ted Underwood and Richard Jean So, "Can We Map Culture?" *Journal of Cultural Analytics* 6, no. 3 (2021): 32–51.

35. The concept of "semantic space" is fundamental to computational studies of meaning. See Will Lowe, "Towards a Theory of Semantic Space," *Proceedings of the Annual Meeting of the Cognitive Science Society* 23, no. 23 (2001); Magnus Sahlgren, "The Word-Space Model: Using Distributional Analysis to Represent Syntagmatic and Paradigmatic Relations between Words in High-Dimensional Vector Spaces" (PhD diss., Stockholm University, 2006); and Michael Gavin et al., "Spaces of Meaning: Conceptual History, Vector Semantics, and Close Reading," in *Debates in Digital Humanities*, ed. Matthew K. Gold and Lauren Klein (Minneapolis: University of Minnesota Press, 2019).

36. For inner-product spaces, see Axler, *Linear Algebra Done Right*, chap. 6. Although the term is often used in various applications, I know of no general definition of the phrase "latent space."

37. For example, Mahalanobis distance works much like Euclidean distance but transforms each distance metric over a covariance matrix, thus adjusting the weight given to each element's difference based on its typical patterns of variation. See P. C. Mahalanobis, "On the Generalized Distance in Statistics," *Proceedings of the National Institute of Sciences of India* 2, no. 1 (1936): 49–55.

38. For a detailed discussion of principal component analysis, see I. T. Jolliffe, *Principal Component Analysis* (New York: Springer, 1986), especially chap. 7, which distinguishes PCA from factor analysis. A quick introduction can also be found in Lay, *Linear Algebra and Its Applications*.

39. LSA represents the clearest point of contact between literary theory and the information sciences. For compact introductions to its mathematical properties, see Jerome R. Bellegarda, *Latent Semantic Mapping: Principles and Applications* (San Rafael, CA: Morgan and Claypool Publishers, 2007); and Dian I. Martin and Michael W. Berry, "Mathematical Foundations behind Latent Sematic Analysis," in *Handbook of Latent Semantic Analysis*, ed. Thomas Landauer et al. (Mahwah, NJ: Lawrence Erlbaum Associates, 2007), 35–55. In that same collection,

more thorough discussion is provided in Thomas Landauer, "LSA as a Theory of Meaning" (3–34) and Susan Dumais, "LSA and Information Retrieval: Getting Back to Basics" (293–322), which describes the origins of the theory in the context of information retrieval.

40. For a compact but thorough explanation of this and other applications of spectral graph theory to network data, see Piet van Mieghem, *Graph Spectra for Complex Networks* (Cambridge: Cambridge University Press, 2011).

41. Wolf Kienzle et al., "Face Detection—Efficient and Rank Deficient," *Advances in Neural Information Processing Systems* 17 (2005): 673–80.

42. For a survey of applications of PCA to geographical problems, see Urška Demšar et al. "Principal Component Analysis on Spatial Data: An Overview," *Annals of the Association of American Geographers* 103, no. 1 (2013): 106–28.

43. The relationship between LSA and topic modeling is described in Mark Steyvers and Tom Griffiths, "Probabilistic Topic Models," in *Handbook of Latent Semantic Analysis*, ed. Thomas Landauer et al. (Mahwah, NJ: Lawrence Erlbaum Associates, 2007), 427–48. Omer Levy, Yoav Goldberg, and Ido Dagan argue that word-embedding models have mathematical properties very similar to factorized matrices; see "Improving Distributional Similarity with Lessons Learned from Word Embeddings," *Transactions of the Association for Computational Linguistics* 3 (2015): 211–25.

44. Of course, if it wasn't for the hard way, who'd get anything done? Ted Underwood seems to have followed precisely this path. See his "Topic Modeling Made Just Simple Enough," *The Stone and the Shell* (2012), https://tedunderwood.com/2012/04/07/topic-modeling-made-just-simple-enough.

45. For the formal definition of a probability space, see R. G. Laha and V. K. Rohatgi, *Probability Theory* (New York: John Wiley and Sons, 1979). The concerns of probability theory also overlap significantly with measure theory, a field of mathematics that Claude E. Shannon, in *The Mathematical Theory of Communication* (Urbana: University of Illinois Press, 1949) off-handedly refers to as providing the conceptual foundations for information theory. For measure theory and its relation to probability, see Terence Tao, *An Introduction to Measure Theory* (Providence, RI: American Mathematical Society, 2011).

46. Halmos, *Naive Set Theory*, describes complementation in the context of set theory.

47. Probability theory, like topology, is concerned primarily with the underlying premises and structures derived from set theory, while statistics are applied to specific research cases. Digital humanists are for this reason likely to find statistics, such as those introduced in Shirley Dowdy and Stanley Wearden, *Statistics for Research*, 2nd ed. (Hoboken, NJ: Wiley-Interscience, 1991) or William M.

Bolstad, *Introduction to Bayesian Statistics* (Hoboken, NJ: Wiley-Interscience, 2004), more directly applicable to their day-to-day work.

48. These concepts are succinctly defined in Thomas A. Cover and Joy Thomas, *Elements of Information Theory* (Hoboken, NJ: Wiley-Interscience, 1991), chap. 2.

49. The best account of "information" as that term is used here probably remains Shannon's discussion of discrete noiseless systems in Shannon's *Mathematical Theory of Communication*.

50. More precisely, Kullback-Leibler divergence. Like the inner product, divergence is sensitive to large differences between individual elements: the farther apart any value of p is from its corresponding q, the farther the ratio between them will deviate from 1, and therefore the larger its logarithm will be. Because at each step those logarithms are multiplied against p, the relative entropy is higher when large deviations correspond with high values of p. Essentially, relative entropy asks how much one distribution's highest, most important values deviate from another's. See Solomon Kullback and Richard A. Leibler, "On Information and Sufficiency," *Annals of Mathematical Statistics* 22, no. 1 (1951): 79–86.

51. The "expected value" E is typically the average or, when comparing two variables, the line of best fit. The "error" or "residual" is the difference between that expected value and the actual, observed value. See Dowdy and Wearden, *Statistics for Research*, 229–38.

52. In *Elements of Information Theory*, Cover and Thomas define mutual information as an extension of relative entropy. As a normalizing procedure for semantic analysis, PPMI is described in Turney and Pantel, "From Frequency to Meaning."

53. Term-frequency inverse-document frequency (TF-IDF) weighting places greater emphasis on lower frequency words and is used in many information-retrieval systems. Karen Spärck Jones is conventionally credited with its invention. See S. E. Robertson and Karen Spärck Jones, "Relevance Weighting of Search Terms," *Journal of the American Society for Information Science* 27, no. 3 (1976): 129–46. Term-weighting techniques are reviewed in Gerard Salton and Christopher Buckley, "Term-Weighting Approaches in Automatic Text Retrieval," *Information Processing and Management* 24, no. 5 (1988): 513–23.

54. In *Reading Machines: Toward an Algorithmic Criticism* (Urbana: University of Illinois Press, 2011), Stephen Ramsay uses TF-IDF weighting to creative effect in a reading of Virginia Woolf's *The Waves*. David L. Hoover critiques the method as inappropriate to Ramsay's critical goals; see "Argument, Evidence, and the Limits of Digital Literary Studies," in *Debates in Digital Humanities*, ed. Matthew K. Gold and Lauren Klein (Minneapolis: University of Minnesota Press, 2016).

55. This is the central theme of Dennis V. Lindley's *Understanding Uncertainty* (Hoboken, NJ: Wiley-Interscience, 2006), a highly accessible overview of statistics for nonmathematicians.

56. The difficulty of reasoning from samples often causes problems for anyone working with statistics. See Lindley, *Understanding Uncertainty*, 51–54; Dowdy and Wearden, *Statistics for Research*, 21–26; and Bolstad, *Introduction to Bayesian Statistics*, 13–21, for discussions of sampling errors and other kinds of interpretive dangers.

57. Dowdy and Wearden's *Statistics for Research* reflects a classical, frequentist perspective, while Bolstad's *Introduction to Bayesian Statistics* discusses the Bayesian framework.

58. Discussions of machine learning's general implications tend to be dominated by futuristic, political, and ethical considerations that are largely outside the concerns of this book, but questions of interpretation and belief are treated well in the standard textbook on machine learning and artificial intelligence, Stuart J. Russell and Peter Norvig, *Artificial Intelligence: A Modern Approach*, 2nd ed. (Upper Saddle River, NJ: Prentice Hall, 2010).

59. For example, see Ted Underwood, "Machine Learning and Human Perspective," *PMLA* 135, no. 1 (2020): 92–109.

BIBLIOGRAPHY

Adorno, Theodor W. *Prisms*. Translated by Samuel Weber and Shierry Weber. Cambridge, MA: MIT Press, 1967.

Agnew, John A. *Place and Politics: The Geographical Mediation of State and Society*. Boston: Allen and Unwin, 1987.

Ahnert, Ruth, and Sebastian E. Ahnert. "Protestant Letter Networks in the Reign of Mary I: A Quantitative Approach." *ELH* 82, no. 1 (2015): 1–33.

Algee-Hewitt, Mark. "Distributed Character: Quantitative Models of the English Stage, 1550–1900." *New Literary History* 48, no. 4 (2017): 751–82.

Allen, Graham. *Intertextuality*. New York: Routledge, 2000.

Allison, Sarah. *Reductive Reading: A Syntax of Victorian Moralizing*. Baltimore: Johns Hopkins University Press, 2018.

Alvarado, Rafael C. "The Digital Humanities Situation." In *Debates in Digital Humanities*, edited by Matthew Gold. Minneapolis: University of Minnesota Press, 2012.

Aravamudan, Srinivas. *Tropicopolitans: Colonialism and Agency, 1688–1804*. Durham, NC: Duke University Press, 1999.

Ashcroft, Bill, Gareth Griffiths, and Helen Tiffin. *The Empire Writes Back: Theory and Practice in Post-Colonial Literatures.* London: Routledge, 2003.

Axler, Sheldon. *Linear Algebra Done Right.* New York: Springer, 2004.

Baird, Ileana, ed. *Social Networks in the Long Eighteenth Century: Clubs, Literary Salons, Textual Coteries.* Newcastle upon Tyne, UK: Cambridge Scholars Publishing, 2014.

Bakhtin, M. M. *The Dialogic Imagination: Four Essays.* Translated by Caryl Emerson and Michael Holquist. Austin: University of Texas Press, 1981.

Bannet, Eve Tavor, and Susan Manning, eds. *Transatlantic Literary Studies, 1660–1830.* Cambridge: Cambridge University Press, 2011.

Bar-Hillel, Yehoshua. "The Present Status of Automatic Translation of Languages." In *Readings in Machine Translation*, edited by Sergei Nirenburg, Harold L. Somers, and Yorick Wilks. Cambridge, MA: MIT Press, 2003.

Barabási, Albert-László. *Network Science.* Cambridge: Cambridge University Press, 2016.

———. "The Network Takeover." *Nature Physics* 8, no. 1 (2011): 14–16.

Barabási, Albert-László, and Réka Albert. "Emergence of Scaling in Random Networks." *Science* 286, no. 5439 (1999): 509–12.

Baroni, Marco, Georgiana Dinu, and Germán Kruszewski. "Don't Count, Predict!: A Systematic Comparison of Context-Counting vs. Context-Predicting Semantic Vectors." *Proceedings of the 52nd Annual Meeting of the Association for Computational Linguistics* 1 (2014): 238–47.

Barron, Alexander T. J., Jenny Huang, Rebecca L. Spang, and Simon DeDeo. "Individuals, Institutions, and Innovation in the Debates of the French Revolution." *Proceedings of the National Academy of Sciences* 115, no. 18 (2018): 4607–12.

Barthélemy, Marc. "Spatial Networks." *Physics Reports* 499, no. 1–3 (2011): 1–101.

Barthes, Roland. *Image Music Text.* Translated by Stephen Heath. London: Fontana Press, 1977.

Basu, Anupam, Jonathan Hope, and Michael Witmore. "The Professional and Linguistic Communities of Early Modern Dramatists." In *Community-Making in Early Stuart Theatres: Stage and Audience*, edited by Roger D. Sell, Anthony W. Johnson, and Helen Wilcox, 63–94. London: Routledge, 2017.

Basu, Anupam, and Joseph Loewenstein. "Spenser's Spell: Archaism and Historical Stylometrics." *Spenser Studies* 33 (2019): 63–102.

Bellegarda, Jerome R. *Latent Semantic Mapping: Principles and Applications.* San Rafael, CA: Morgan and Claypool Publishers, 2007.

Bender, Emily M., and Alexander Koller. "Climbing towards NLU: On Meaning, Form, and Understanding in the Age of Data." *Proceedings of the 58th Annual Meeting of the Association for Computational Linguistics* (2020): 5185–98.

Bernheimer, Charles, ed. *Comparative Literature in the Age of Multiculturalism*. Baltimore: Johns Hopkins University Press, 1995.

Berry, Brian J. L. "Approaches to Regional Analysis: A Synthesis." In *Spatial Analysis: A Reader in Statistical Geography*, edited by Brian J. L. Berry and Duane F. Marble. Englewood Cliffs, NJ: Prentice Hall, 1968.

Biber, Douglas. "Representativeness in Corpus Design." *Literary and Linguistic Computing* 8, no. 4 (1993): 243–57.

Bisk, Yonatan, Ari Holtzman, Jesse Thomason, Jacob Andreas, Yoshua Bengio, Joyce Chai, Mirella Lapata, Angeliki Lazaridou, Jonathan May, Aleksandr Nisnevich, Nicolas Pinto, and Joseph Turian. "Experience Grounds Language." *Proceedings of the 2020 Conference on Empirical Methods in Natural Language Processing* (2020): 8718–35.

Blei, David. "Introduction to Probabilistic Topic Models." *Communications of the ACM* 55, no. 4 (2012): 77–84.

Bode, Katherine. "The Equivalence of 'Close' and 'Distant' Reading; or, Toward a New Object for Data-Rich Literary History." *Modern Language Quarterly* 78, no. 1 (2017): 77–106.

———. *A World of Fiction: Digital Collections and the Future of Literary History*. Ann Arbor: University of Michigan Press, 2019.

Bohun, Edmund. *A Geographical Dictionary Representing the Present and Ancient Names of All the Counties, Provinces, Remarkable Cities, Universities, Ports, Towns, Mountains, Seas, Streights, Fountains, and Rivers of the Whole World*. Oxford: Oxford Text Archive, 2007. http://hdl.handle.net/20.500.12024/A28561.

Bolstad, William M. *Introduction to Bayesian Statistics*. Hoboken, NJ: Wiley-Interscience, 2004.

Brady, Henry E. "The Challenge of Big Data and Data Science." *Annual Review of Political Science* 22, no. 1 (2019): 297–323.

Brandes, Ulrik, Garry Robins, Ann McCranie, and Stanley Wasserman. "What Is Network Science?" *Network Science* 1, no. 1 (2013): 1–15.

Braudel, Fernand. *Civilization and Capitalism, 15th–18th Century*. Vol. 3, *The Perspective of the World*, translated by Sian Reynolds. New York: Harper and Row, 1982.

Broido, Anna D., and Aaron Clauset. "Scale-Free Networks Are Rare." *Nature Communications* 10, no. 1 (2019): 1–10.

Broadwell, Peter M., and Timothy R. Tangherlini. "WitchHunter: Tools for the Geo-Semantic Exploration of a Danish Folklore Corpus." *Journal of American Folklore* 129, no. 511 (2016): 14–42.

Brown, James J. "Crossing State Lines: Rhetoric and Software Studies." In *Rhetoric and the Digital Humanities*, edited by Jim Ridolfo and William Hart-Davidson, 20–32. Chicago: University of Chicago Press, 2015.

Brown, Marshall. "Periods and Resistances." *Modern Language Quarterly* 62, no. 4 (2001): 309–16.

Brown, Nicole M., Ruby Mendenhall, Michael Black, Mark Van Moer, Karen Flynn, Malaika McKee, Assata Zerai, Ismini Lourentzou, and ChengXiang Zhai. "In Search of Zora / When Metadata Isn't Enough: Rescuing the Experiences of Black Women through Statistical Modeling." *Journal of Library Metadata* 19, no. 3–4 (2019): 141–62.

Brown, Nicole M., Ruby Mendenhall, Michael Black, Mark Moer, Assata Zerai, and Karen Flynn. "Mechanized Margin to Digitized Center: Black Feminism's Contributions to Combatting Erasure within the Digital Humanities." *International Journal of Humanities and Arts Computing* 10, no. 1 (2016): 110–25.

Burt, Ronald. *Structural Holes: The Social Structure of Competition*. Cambridge, MA: Harvard University Press, 1992.

Buurma, Rachel Sagner. "The Preparation of the Topic Model." *Digital Humanities Conference 2017*. https://dh2017.adho.org/abstracts/332/332.pdf.

Carlsson, Gunnar. "Topology and Data." *Bulletin of the American Mathematical Society*, n.s., 46, no. 2 (2009): 255–308.

Castells, Manuel. *The Rise of the Network Society*. Malden, MA: Blackwell Publishers, 1996.

Certeau, Michel de. *The Practice of Everyday Life*. Translated by Steven Rendall. Berkeley: University of California Press, 1980.

Chang, Kent K., and Simon DeDeo. "Divergence and the Complexity of Difference in Text and Culture." *Journal of Cultural Analytics* 5, no. 2 (2020): 1–36.

Church, Kenneth W., and Robert L. Mercer. "Introduction to the Special Issue on Computational Linguistics Using Large Corpora." *Computational Linguistics* 19, no. 1 (1993): 1–24.

Clark, Stephen. "Vector Space Models of Lexical Meaning." In *The Handbook of Contemporary Semantic Theory*, edited by Shalom Lappin and Chris Fox. Oxford: John Wiley and Sons, 2015.

Clauset, Aaron, Cosma Rohilla Shalizi, and M. E. J. Newman. "Power-Law Distributions in Empirical Data." *SIAM Review* 51, no. 4 (2009): 661–703.

Colley, Linda. *Captives: Britain, Empire, and the World, 1600–1850*. New York: Random House, 2010.

Cooper, David, Christopher Donaldson, and Patricia Murrieta-Flores, eds. *Literary Mapping in the Digital Age*. London: Routledge, 2017.

Cosgrove, Denis. *Apollo's Eye: A Cartographic Genealogy of the Earth in the Western Imagination*. Baltimore: Johns Hopkins University Press, 2001.

Cover, Thomas A., and Joy A. Thomas. *Elements of Information Theory*. Hoboken, NJ: Wiley-Interscience, 1991.

Cresswell, Timothy. "Place." In *Encyclopedia of Human Geography: Volume 1*, edited by Nigel Thrift and Rob Kitchin, 117–24. Amsterdam: Elsevier Science, 2009.

Davison, Kate. "Early Modern Social Networks: Antecedents, Opportunities, and Challenges." *American Historical Review* 124, no. 2 (2019): 456–82.

De Bolla, Peter. *The Architecture of Concepts: The Historical Formation of Human Rights*. New York: Fordham University Press, 2013.

De Bolla, Peter, Ewan Jones, Paul Nulty, Gabriel Recchia, and John Regan. "Distributional Concept Analysis." *Contributions to the History of Concepts* 14, no. 1 (2019): 66–92.

Demšar, Urška, Paul Harris, Chris Brunsdon, A. Stewart Fotheringham, and Sean McLoone. "Principal Component Analysis on Spatial Data: An Overview." *Annals of the Association of American Geographers* 103, no. 1 (2013): 106–28.

DeRose, Steven J., David G. Durand, Elli Mylonas, and Allen Renear. "What Is a Text, Really?" *Journal of Computing in Higher Education* 1, no. 2 (1990): 3–26.

Dowdy, Shirley, and Stanley Wearden. *Statistics for Research*. 2nd ed. Hoboken, NJ: Wiley-Interscience, 1991.

Dumais, Susan T. "LSA and Information Retrieval: Getting Back to Basics." In *Handbook of Latent Semantic Analysis*, edited by Thomas Landauer, Danielle S. McNamara, Simon Dennis, and Walter Kintsch, 293–322. Mahwah, NJ: Lawrence Erlbaum Associates, 2007.

Edelstein, Dan, Paula Findlen, Giovanna Ceserani, Caroline Winterer, and Nicole Coleman. "Historical Research in a Digital Age: Reflections from the Mapping the Republic of Letters Project." *American Historical Review* 122, no. 2 (2017): 400–424.

Edwards, Jess. *Writing, Geometry, and Space in Seventeenth-Century England and America: Circles in the Sand*. London: Routledge, 2005.

Egenhofer, Max J., and Robert D. Franzosa. "Point-Set Topological Spatial Relations." *International Journal of Geographical Information Systems* 5, no. 2 (1991): 161–74.

Egenhofer, Max J., and John R. Herring. "A Mathematical Framework for the Definition of Topological Relationships." *Fourth International Symposium on Spatial Data Handling*. Zurich: Switzerland, 1990.

Epstein, Joshua M. *Generative Social Science: Studies in Agent-Based Computational Modeling*. Princeton, NJ: Princeton University Press, 2006.

Erickson, Mark. "Network as Metaphor." *International Journal of Criminology and Sociological Theory* 5, no. 2 (2012): 912–21.

Erk, Katrin. "Vector Space Models of Word Meaning and Phrase Meaning: A Survey." *Language and Linguistics Compass* 6, no. 10 (2012): 635–53.

Eve, Martin Paul. *Close Reading with Computers: Textual Scholarship, Computational Formalism, and David Mitchell's Cloud Atlas.* Stanford, CA: Stanford University Press, 2019.

Fagan, Frank. "Big Data Legal Scholarship: Toward a Research Program and Practitioner's Guide." *Virginia Journal of Law and Technology* 20, no. 1 (2016): 1–81.

Firth, J. R. *Studies in Linguistic Analysis.* Oxford: Oxford University Press, 1962.

Fish, Stanley. *Professional Correctness: Literary Studies and Political Change.* Oxford: Clarendon Press, 1995.

———. "What Is Stylistics and Why Are They Saying Such Terrible Things about It?" Chap. 2 in *Is There a Text in This Class?: The Authority of Interpretive Communities.* Cambridge, MA: Harvard University Press, 1980.

Flament, Claude. *Applications of Graph Theory to Group Structure.* Hoboken, NJ: Prentice Hall, 1963.

Fotheringham, A. Stewart, Chris Brunsdon, and Martin Charlton. *Quantitative Geography: Perspectives on Spatial Data Analysis.* Thousand Oaks, CA: Sage Publications, 2000.

Fox, Adam. *Oral and Literate Culture in England, 1500–1700.* Oxford: Oxford University Press, 2000.

Froehlich, Heather. "Dramatic Structure and Social Status in Shakespeare's Plays." *Journal of Cultural Analytics* 5, no. 1 (2020).

Gadd, Ian. "The Use and Misuse of Early English Books Online." *Literature Compass* 6, no. 3 (2009): 680–92.

Gallon, Kim. "Making a Case for the Black Digital Humanities." In *Debates in the Digital Humanities*, edited by Matthew K. Gold and Lauren F. Klein, 42–49. Minneapolis: University of Minnesota Press, 2016.

Gastaldi, Juan Luis. "Why Can Computers Understand Natural Language?: The Structuralist Image of Language behind Word Embeddings." *Philosophy and Technology* 34, no. 1 (2020): 1–66.

Gavin, Michael. "Historical Text Networks: The Sociology of Early Criticism." *Eighteenth-Century Studies* 51, no. 3 (2016): 53–80.

———. "How to Think about EEBO." *Textual Cultures* 11, no. 2 (2017): 70–105.

———. *The Invention of English Criticism, 1650–1760.* Cambridge: Cambridge University Press, 2015.

———. "Is There a Text in My Data? (Part 1): On Counting Words." *Journal of Cultural Analytics: Debates* 5, no. 1 (2020).

Gavin, Michael, and Eric Gidal. "Scotland's Poetics of Space: An Experiment in Geospatial Semantics." *Journal of Cultural Analytics* 2, no. 1 (2017). doi:10.22148/16.017.

Gavin, Michael, Collin Jennings, Lauren Kersey, and Brad Pasanek. "Spaces of Meaning: Conceptual History, Vector Semantics, and Close Reading." In *Debates in Digital Humanities*, edited by Matthew K. Gold and Lauren Klein. Minneapolis: University of Minnesota Press, 2019.

Geeraerts, Dirk. *Theories of Lexical Semantics*. Oxford: Oxford University Press, 2009.

Genette, Gérard. *Palimpsests: Literature in the Second Degree*. Translated by Channa Newman and Claude Doubinsky. Lincoln: University of Nebraska Press, 1977.

Gersting, Judith L. *Mathematical Structures for Computer Science: A Modern Treatment of Discrete Mathematics*. 5th ed. New York: W. H. Freeman, 2002.

Ghosh, Debarchana, and Rajarshi Guha. "What Are We 'Tweeting' about Obesity? Mapping Tweets with Topic Modeling and Geographic Information System." *Cartography and Geographic Information Science* 40, no. 2 (2013): 90–102.

Gilroy, Paul. *The Black Atlantic: Modernity and Double Consciousness*. Cambridge, MA: Harvard University Press, 1993.

Goldfarb, Charles. "A Generalized Approach to Document Markup." *ACM SIGPLAN Notices* 16, no. 6 (1981): 68–73.

Goodchild, Michael F. "Geographical Information Science." *International Journal of Geographical Information Systems* 6, no. 1 (1992): 31–45.

Grafton, Anthony, with April Shelford and Nancy Siraisi. *New Worlds, Ancient Texts: The Power of Tradition and the Shock of Discovery*. Cambridge, MA: Harvard University Press, 1992.

Grand, Gabriel, Idan Blank, Francisco Pereira, and Evelina Fedorenko. "Semantic Projection: Recovering Human Knowledge of Multiple, Distinct Object Features from Word Embeddings." arXiv preprint arXiv:1802.01241, 2018.

Granovetter, Mark S. "The Strength of Weak Ties." *American Journal of Sociology* 78, no. 6 (1973): 1360–80.

Gregory, Ian N., and Andrew Hardie. "Visual GISting: Bringing Together Corpus Linguistics and Geographical Information Systems." *Literary and Linguistic Computing* 26, no. 3 (2011): 297–314.

Gregory, Ian N., and Laura L. Paterson. "Geographical Representations of Poverty in Historical Newspapers." In *The Routledge Handbook of English Language and Digital Humanities*, edited by Svenja Adolphs and Dawn Knight. London: Routledge, 2020.

Greteman, Blaine. "Milton and the Early Modern Social Network: The Case of the *Epitaphium Damonis*." *Milton Quarterly* 49, no. 2 (2015): 79–95.

Griffiths, Devin. *The Age of Analogy Science and Literature between the Darwins*. Baltimore: Johns Hopkins University Press, 2016.

Grimmer, Justin, and Brandon M. Stewart. "Text as Data: The Promise and Pitfalls of Automatic Content Analysis Methods for Political Texts." *Political Analysis* 21, no. 3 (2013): 267–97.

Guldi, Jo, and David Armitage. *The History Manifesto*. Cambridge: Cambridge University Press, 2014.

Haig, Robert L. "New Light on the King's Printing Office, 1680–1730." *Studies in Bibliography* 8 (1956): 157–67.

Halliday, M. A. K. *Language as Social Semiotic: The Social Interpretation of Language and Meaning*. London: Edward Arnold, 1978.

Halmos, Paul R. *Naive Set Theory*. Princeton, NJ: D. Van Nostrand, 1960.

Harary, Frank, Robert Z. Norman, and Dorwin Cartwright. *Structural Models: An Introduction to the Theory of Directed Graphs*. New York: John Wiley and Sons, 1965.

Harris, Zellig. "Distributional Structure." *Mind* 10 (1954): 146–62.

———. *Methods in Structural Linguistics*. Chicago: University of Chicago Press, 1951.

Helgerson, Richard. *Forms of Nationhood: The Elizabethan Writing of England*. Chicago: University of Chicago Press, 1992.

Hesse, Mary. *Models and Analogies in Science*. Notre Dame, IN: University of Notre Dame Press, 1966.

Hill, Alexandra. "Lost Print in England: Entries in the Stationers' Company Register, 1557–1640." In *Lost Books: Reconstructing the Print World of Pre-Industrial Europe*, edited by Flavia Bruni and Andrew Pettegree, 144–59. Leiden: Brill, 2016.

Hirshfeld, Heather. "Early Modern Collaboration and Theories of Authorship." *PMLA* 116, no. 3 (2001): 609–22.

Homans, George. *The Human Group*. London: Routledge and Kegan Paul, 1951.

Hoover, David L. "Argument, Evidence, and the Limits of Digital Literary Studies." In *Debates in Digital Humanities*, edited by Matthew K. Gold and Lauren Klein. Minneapolis: University of Minnesota Press, 2016.

Hüllen, Werner. *Networks and Knowledge in "Roget's Thesaurus."* Oxford: Oxford University Press, 2009.

Hunston, Susan. *Pattern Grammar: A Corpus-Driven Approach to the Lexical Grammar of English*. Amsterdam: John Benjamins Publishing, 2000.

Hutchins, W. John. *Machine Translation: Past, Present, Future*. Chichester, UK: Ellis Horwood, 1986.

Ide, Nancy, and Jean Véronis. "Introduction to the Special Issue on Word Sense Disambiguation: The State of the Art." *Computational Linguistics* 24, no. 1 (1998): 1–40.

Ide, Nancy, and Donald Walker. "Introduction: Common Methodologies in Humanities Computing and Computational Linguistics." *Computers and the Humanities* 26, no. 5-6 (1992): 327-30.
D'Ignazio, Catherine, and Lauren F. Klein. *Data Feminism*. Cambridge, MA: MIT Press, 2020.
Jackson, MacDonald P. "The Printer of the First Quarto of 'Astrophil and Stella' (1591)." *Studies in Bibliography* 31 (1978): 201-3.
Janowicz, Krzysztof, Simon Scheider, Todd Pehle, and Glen Hart. "Geospatial Semantics and Linked Spatiotemporal Data—Past, Present, and Future." *Semantic Web* 3, no. 4 (2012): 321-32.
Jockers, Matthew L. *Macroanalysis: Digital Methods and Literary History*. Urbana: University of Illinois Press, 2013.
Jolliffe, I. T. *Principal Component Analysis*. New York: Springer, 1986.
Juola, Patrick, and Stephen Ramsay. *Six Septembers: Mathematics for the Humanist*. Lincoln, NE: Zea Books, 2017.
Kadushin, Charles. *Understanding Social Networks: Theories, Concepts, and Findings*. Oxford: Oxford University Press, 2012.
Kastan, David Scott. "Humphrey Moseley and the Invention of English Literature." In *Agent of Change: Print Culture Studies after Elizabeth L. Eisenstein*, edited by Sabrina Alcorn Baron, Eric N. Lindquist, and Eleanor F. Shevlin, 105-24. Amherst: University of Massachusetts Press, 2007.
Kienzle, Wolf, Gökhan Bakir, Matthias Franz, and Bernhard Schölkopf. "Face Detection—Efficient and Rank Deficient." *Advances in Neural Information Processing Systems* 17 (2005): 673-80.
Kilgarriff, Adam. "Language Is Never, Ever, Ever, Random." *Corpus Linguistics and Linguistic Theory* 1, no. 2 (2005): 263-75.
Kilgore, Christopher D. "Rhetoric of the Network: Toward a New Metaphor." *Mosaic: A Journal for the Interdisciplinary Study of Literature* 46, no. 4 (2013): 37-58.
Kim, Kyung Hye. "Examining US News Media Discourses about North Korea: A Corpus-Based Critical Discourse Analysis." *Discourse and Society* 25, no. 2 (2014): 221-44.
Knights, Mark. "John Starkey and Ideological Networks in Late Seventeenth-Century England." *Media History* 11, no. 1-2 (2005): 127-45.
Krioukov, Dmitri, Fragkiskos Papadopoulos, Maksim Kitsak, Amin Vahdat, and Marián Boguñá. "Hyperbolic Geometry of Complex Networks." *Physical Review E* 82, no. 3 (2010).
Kristeva, Julia. *Julia Kristeva Interviews*, edited by Ross Mitchell Guberman. New York: Columbia University Press, 1996.

———. "Le Lieu Sémiotique." In *Essays in Semiotics / Essais de Sémiotique*, edited by Julia Kristeva, Josette Ray-Debove, and Donna Jean Umiker, 1–7. The Hague: Mouton, 1971.

———. Σημειωτική: *Recherches pour une sémanalyse*. Paris: Edition du Seuil, 1969.

———. "Word, Dialogue, and Novel." In *The Kristeva Reader*, edited by Toril Moi, 34–61. New York: Columbia University Press, 1986.

Kuhn, Werner. "Geospatial Semantics." *Journal on Data Semantics III* (2005): 1–24.

Kullback, Solomon, and Richard A. Leibler. "On Information and Sufficiency." *Annals of Mathematical Statistics* 22, no. 1 (1951): 79–86.

Kytö, Merja, and Päivi Pahta. "Evidence from Historical Corpora up to the Twentieth Century." In *The Oxford Handbook of the History of English*, edited by Terttu Nevalainen and Elizabeth Closs Traugott, 123–33. Oxford: Oxford University Press, 2012.

Ladd, John R. "Network Poetics: Studies in Early Modern Literary Collaboration." PhD thesis, Washington University, 2019.

Laha, R. G., and V. K. Rohatgi. *Probability Theory*. New York: John Wiley and Sons, 1979.

Lahti, Leo, Jani Marjanen, Hege Roivainen, and Mikko Tolonen. "Bibliographic Data Science and the History of the Book (c. 1500–1800)." *Cataloging and Classification Quarterly* 57, no. 1 (2019): 5–23.

Landauer, Thomas K. "LSA as a Theory of Meaning." In *Handbook of Latent Semantic Analysis*, edited by Thomas Landauer, Danielle S. McNamara, Simon Dennis, and Walter Kintsch, 3–34. Mahwah, NJ: Lawrence Erlbaum Associates, 2007.

Landauer, Thomas, K., Danielle S. McNamara, Simon Dennis, and Walter Kintsch, eds. *Handbook of Latent Semantic Analysis*. Mahwah, NJ: Lawrence Erlbaum Associates, 2007.

Lang, Anouk. "Visual Provocations: Using GIS Mapping to Explore Witi Ihimaera's *Dear Miss Mansfield*." *English Language Notes* 52, no. 1 (2014): 67–80.

Laver, Michael, Kenneth Benoit, and John Garry. "Extracting Policy Positions from Political Texts Using Words as Data." *American Political Science Review* 97, no. 2 (2003): 311–31.

Lavin, J. A. "The First Two Printers of Sidney's *Astrophil and Stella*." *The Library* 5, no. 3 (1971): 249–55.

Lay, David C. *Linear Algebra and Its Applications*. 2nd ed. Boston: Addison-Wesley, 1999.

Lazarsfeld, Paul F., and Robert K. Merton. "Friendship as a Social Process: A Substantive and Methodological Analysis." In *Freedom and Control in Modern Society*, edited by Morroe Berger, 18–66. New York: Van Nostrand, 1954.

Lee, Nancy Howell. *The Search for an Abortionist*. Chicago: University of Chicago Press, 1969.

Lee, James Jaehoon, Blaine Greteman, Jason Lee, and David Eichmann. "Linked Reading: Digital Historicism and Early Modern Discourses of Race around Shakespeare's *Othello*." *Journal of Cultural Analytics* 3, no. 1 (2018).

Lee, John M. *Introduction to Topological Manifolds*. New York: Springer, 2000.

Lefebvre, Henri. *The Production of Space*. Translated by Donald Nicholson-Smith. Oxford: Blackwell, 1974.

Lenci, Alessandro. "Distributional Models of Word Meaning." *Annual Review of Linguistics* 4, no. 1 (2018): 151–71.

Levine, Caroline. *Forms: Whole, Rhythm, Hierarchy, Network*. Princeton, NJ: Princeton University Press, 2017.

Levy, Omer, Yoav Goldberg, and Ido Dagan. "Improving Distributional Similarity with Lessons Learned from Word Embeddings." *Transactions of the Association for Computational Linguistics* 3 (2015): 211–25.

Lewis, David D. "Naive (Bayes) at Forty: The Independence Assumption in Information Retrieval." In *Machine Learning: ECML-98*, edited by C. Nédellec and C. Rouveirol, 4–15. Berlin: Springer, 1998.

Lindley, Dennis V. *Understanding Uncertainty*. Hoboken, NJ: Wiley-Interscience, 2006.

Long, Hoyt, and Richard Jean So. "Literary Pattern Recognition: Modernism between Close Reading and Machine Learning." *Critical Inquiry* 42, no. 2 (2016): 235–67.

———. "Turbulent Flow: A Computational Model of World Literature." *Modern Language Quarterly* 77, no. 3 (2016): 345–67.

Lowe, Will. "Towards a Theory of Semantic Space." *Proceedings of the Annual Meeting of the Cognitive Science Society* 23, no. 23 (2001).

Luhn, H. P. "Keyword-in-Context Index for Technical Literature." *American Documentation* 11, no. 4 (1959): 288–95.

———. "A New Method of Recording and Searching Information." *American Documentation* 4, no. 1 (1953): 14–16.

———. "A Statistical Approach to Mechanized Encoding and Searching of Literary Information." *IBM Journal* 1, no. 4 (1957): 309–17.

Mahalanobis, P. C. "On the Generalized Distance in Statistics." *Proceedings of the National Institute of Sciences of India* 2, no. 1 (1936): 49–55.

Mak, Bonnie. "Archaeology of a Digitization." *Journal of the Association for Information Science and Technology* 65, no. 8 (2014): 1515–26.

Malinowski, Bronislaw. "The Problem of Meaning in Primitive Languages." In *The Meaning of Meaning*, edited by . C. K. Ogden and I. A. Richards, 296–336. London: Kegan Paul, 1923.

Mandell, Laura. "How to Read a Literary Visualisation: Network Effects in the Lake School of Romantic Poetry." *Digital Studies / Le champ numérique* 3, no. 2 (2013).

Manovich, Lev. "The Science of Culture? Social Computing, Digital Humanities, and Cultural Analytics." *Journal of Cultural Analytics* 1, no. 1 (2016).

Martin, Dian I., and Michael W. Berry. "Mathematical Foundations behind Latent Sematic Analysis." In *Handbook of Latent Semantic Analysis*, edited by Thomas Landauer, Danielle S. McNamara, Simon Dennis, and Walter Kintsch, 35–55. Mahwah, NJ: Lawrence Erlbaum Associates, 2007

Masten, Jeffery. *Textual Intercourse: Collaboration, Authorship, and Sexualities in Renaissance Drama*. Cambridge: Cambridge University Press, 2007.

Masterman, Margaret. "Computerized Haiku." In *Cybernetics, Art, and Ideas*, edited by Jasia Reichardt, 175–83. Greenwich, CT: New York Graphic Society, 1971.

———. *Language, Cohesion, Form*, edited by Yorick Wilks. Cambridge: Cambridge University Press, 2005.

———. "Mechanical Pidgin Translation." In *Readings in Machine Translation*, edited by Sergei Nirenburg, Harold L. Somers, and Yorick Wilks. Cambridge, MA: MIT Press, 2003.

———. "What Is a Thesaurus?" Cambridge: Cambridge Language Research Unit, 1959.

Masterman, Margaret, R. M. Neeham, and Karen Spärck Jones. "The Analogy between Mechanical Translation and Library Retrieval." In *Proceedings of the International Conference on Scientific Information*. Washington, DC: National Academy of Sciences, 1959: 917–35.

Mattix, Micah. "Periodization and Difference." *New Literary History* 35, no. 4 (2004): 685–97.

McEnery, Tony, and Andrew Hardie. *Corpus Linguistics: Method, Theory, and Practice*. Cambridge: Cambridge University Press, 2012.

Medici, Catherine. "Using Network Analysis to Understand Early Modern Women." *Early Modern Women* 13, no. 1 (2018): 153–62.

Mendelson, Bert. *Introduction to Topology*. 3rd ed. New York: Dover, 1962. Reprinted in 2016.

Midura, Rachel. "Conceptualizing Knowledge Networks: Agents and Patterns of 'Flow.'" In *Empires of Knowledge: Scientific Networks in the Early Modern World*, edited by Paula Findlen, 373–77. New York: Routledge, 2018.

Mielants, Eric H. *Origins of Capitalism and the Rise of the West*. Philadelphia: Temple University Press, 2007.

Mikolov, Tomas, Kai Chen, Greg Corrado, and Jeffrey Dean. "Efficient Estimation of Word Representations in Vector Space." *ArXiv Preprint arXiv:1301.3781*, 2013.

Miller, John H., and Scott E. Page. *Complex Adaptive Systems: An Introduction to Computational Models of Social Life.* Princeton, NJ: Princeton University Press, 2007.

Mitts, Tamar. "From Isolation to Radicalization: Anti-Muslim Hostility and Support for ISIS in the West." *American Political Science Review* 113, no. 1 (2019): 173–94.

Mohr, John W., and Peter Bogdanov. "Topic Models: What They Are and Why They Matter?" *Poetics* 41, no. 6 (2013): 545–69.

Mohr, John W., Christopher A. Bail, Margaret Frye, Jennifer C. Lena, Omar Lizardo, Terence E. McDonnell, Ann Mische, Iddo Tavory, and Frederick F. Wherry. *Measuring Culture.* New York: Columbia University Press, 2020.

Moretti, Franco. *Distant Reading.* London: Verso Books, 2013.

———. *Graphs, Maps, and Trees.* London: Verso Books, 2005.

———. *Network Theory, Plot Analysis.* Pamphlets of the Stanford Literary Lab, Pamphlet 2. Stanford, CA: Stanford Literary Lab, 2011.

Munkres, James R. *Elements of Algebraic Topology.* Boston: Addison-Wesley, 1984.

Murrieta-Flores, Patricia, and Naomi Howell. "Towards the Spatial Analysis of Vague and Imaginary Place and Space: Evolving the Spatial Humanities through Medieval Romance." *Journal of Map and Geography Libraries* 13, no. 1 (2017): 29–57.

Nancy, Jean-Luc. *The Creation of the World; or, Globalization.* Translated by François Raffoul and David Pettigrew. Albany: State University of New York Press, 2007.

———. *The Sense of the World.* Translated by Jeffrey S. Librett. Minneapolis: University of Minnesota Press, 1997.

Newman, M. E. J. *Networks: An Introduction.* Oxford: Oxford University Press, 2010.

———. "Power Laws, Pareto Distributions, and Zipf's Law." *Contemporary Physics* 46, no. 5 (2005): 323–51.

Obradovich, Nick, Ömer Özak, Ignacio Martín, Edmond Awad, Manuel Cebrián, Rubén Cuevas, Klaus Desmet, Iyad Rahwan, and Ángel Cuevas. "Expanding the Measurement of Culture with a Sample of Two Billion Humans." NBER Working Paper Series. Cambridge: National Bureau of Economic Research, 2020.

Olsen, Mark. "Signs, Symbols and Discourses: A New Direction for Computer-Aided Literature Studies." *Computers and the Humanities* 27, no. 5 (1993): 309–14.

Ore, Øystein. *Theory of Graphs.* Providence, RI: American Mathematical Society, 1962.

Orr, Mary. *Intertextuality: Debates and Contexts.* Malden, MA: Polity, 2003.

Osgood, Charles E. "The Nature and Measurement of Meaning." *Psychological Bulletin* 49, no. 3 (1952): 197–237.

Pachucki, Mark A., and Ronald L. Breiger. "Cultural Holes: Beyond Relationality in Social Networks and Culture." *Annual Review of Sociology* 36, no. 1 (2010): 205–24. http://dx.doi.org/10.1146/annurev.soc.012809.102615.

Peacy, Jason. "Cromwellian England: A Propaganda State?" *History* 91, no. 2 (2006): 176–99.

Pettegree, Andrew. *The Invention of News: How the World Came to Know about Itself.* New Haven, CT: Yale University Press, 2014.

Pincus, Steve. *1688: The First Modern Revolution.* New Haven, CT: Yale University Press, 2009.

Piper, Andrew. *Enumerations: Data and Literary Study.* Chicago: University of Chicago Press, 2018.

———. "There Will Be Numbers." *Journal of Cultural Analytics* 1, no. 1 (2016).

Porter, Catherine, Paul Atkinson, and Ian N. Gregory. "Geographical Text Analysis: A New Approach to Understanding Nineteenth-Century Mortality." *Health and Place* 36 (2015): 25–34.

———. "Space and Time in 100 Million Words: Health and Disease in a Nineteenth-Century Newspaper." *International Journal of Humanities and Arts Computing* 12, no. 2 (2018): 196–216.

Proksch, Sven-Oliver, Will Lowe, Jens Wäckerle, and Stuart Soroka. "Multilingual Sentiment Analysis: A New Approach to Measuring Conflict in Legislative Speeches." *Legislative Studies Quarterly* 44, no. 1 (2019): 97–131.

Ramachandran, Ayesha. "How to Theorize the 'World': An Early Modern Manifesto." *New Literary History* 48, no. 4 (2017): 655–84.

———. *The Worldmakers: Global Imagining in Early Modern Europe.* Chicago: University of Chicago Press, 2015.

Ramsay, Stephen. *Reading Machines: Toward an Algorithmic Criticism.* Urbana: University of Illinois Press, 2011.

Ravenhill, William. "John Adams, His Map of England, Its Projection, and His *Index Villaris* of 1680." *Geographical Journal* 144, no. 3 (1978): 424–37.

Raymond, Joad. *The Invention of the Newspaper: English Newsbooks, 1641–1649.* Oxford: Oxford University Press, 2005.

Rehder, Robert. "Periodization and the Theory of History." *Colloquium Helveticum* 22 (1995): 117–36.

Reifler, Erwin. "The Mechanical Determination of Meaning." In *Readings in Machine Translation*, edited by Sergei Nirenburg, Harold Somers, and Yorick Wilks, 21–36. Cambridge: MIT Press, 2003.

Renear, Allen. "Text Encoding." In *A Companion to Digital Humanities*, edited by Susan Schreibman, Ray Siemens, and John Unsworth. Oxford: Blackwell, 2004.

Riffaterre, Michael. "Compulsory Reader Response: The Intertextual Drive." In *Intertextuality: Theories and Practices*, edited by Michael Worton and Judith Still, 56–78. New York: Manchester University Press, 1990.

———. *Semiotics of Poetry*. Bloomington: Indiana University Press, 1978.

Risam, Roopika. *New Digital Worlds: Postcolonial Digital Humanities in Theory, Praxis, and Pedagogy*. Evanston, IL: Northwestern University Press, 2018.

Robertson, S. E., and Karen Spärck Jones. "Relevance Weighting of Search Terms." *Journal of the American Society for Information Science* 27, no. 3 (1976): 129–46.

Russell, Stuart J., and Peter Norvig. *Artificial Intelligence: A Modern Approach*. 2nd ed. Upper Saddle River, NJ: Prentice Hall, 2010.

Sahlgren, Magnus. "The Word-Space Model: Using Analysis to Represent Syntagmatic and Paradigmatic Relations between Words in High-Dimensional Vector Spaces." PhD diss., Stockholm University, 2006.

Sahlgren, Magnus, and Fredrik Carlsson. "The Singleton Fallacy: Why Current Critiques of Language Models Miss the Point." *arXiv preprint arXiv:2102.04310*, 2021.

Salton, Gerard. "Associative Document Retrieval Techniques Using Bibliographic Information." *Journal of the ACM* 10, no. 4 (1963): 440–57.

———. *Automatic Information Organization and Retrieval*. New York: McGraw-Hill, 1983.

———. "Historical Note: The Past Thirty Years in Information Retrieval." *JASIS* 38, no. 5 (1987): 375–80.

Salton, Gerard, and Christopher Buckley. "Term-Weighting Approaches in Automatic Text Retrieval." *Information Processing and Management* 24, no. 5 (1988): 513–23.

Salton, Gerard, A. Wong, and C. S. Yang. "A Vector Space Model for Automatic Indexing." *Communications of the ACM* 18, no. 11 (1975): 613–20.

Sassen, Saskia. *Territory, Authority, Rights: From Medieval to Global Assemblages*. Princeton, NJ: Princeton University Press, 2006.

Schwering, Angela. "Approaches to Semantic Similarity Measurement for Geo-Spatial Data: A Survey." *Transactions in GIS* 12, no. 1 (2008): 5–29.

Schütze, Hinrich. "Dimensions of Meaning." *Proceedings of the 1992 ACM/IEEE Conference on Supercomputing* (1992): 787–96.

———. "Word Space." *Advances in Neural Information Processing Systems* 5 (1993): 895–902.

Scott, John. *Social Network Analysis*. 3rd ed. Los Angeles: Sage, 2012.

Scott-Warren, Jason. "Reconstructing Manuscript Networks: The Textual Transactions of Sir Stephen Powle." In *Communities in Early Modern England*, edited by Alexandra Shepard and Phil Withington, 18–37. Manchester: Manchester University Press, 2000.

Shalev, Zur, and Charles Burnett, eds. *Ptolemy's Geography in the Renaissance*. London: Warburg Institute, 2011.

Shannon, Claude E., and Warren Weaver. *The Mathematical Theory of Communication*. Urbana: University of Illinois Press, 1949.

Sherman, William H. "Stirrings and Searchings (1500–1720)." In *The Cambridge Companion to Travel Writing*, edited by Peter Hulme and Tim Youngs, 17–36. Cambridge: Cambridge University Press, 2002.

Shick, Paul L. *Topology: Point-Set and Geometric*. New York: John Wiley and Sons, 2007.

Shore, Daniel. *Cyberformalism: Histories of Linguistic Forms in the Digital Archive*. Baltimore: Johns Hopkins University Press, 2018.

Sinclair, John. *Trust the Text: Language, Corpus, and Discourse*, edited by John Sinclair and Ronald Carter. New York: Routledge, 2004.

Slack, Paul. *The Invention of Improvement: Information and Material Progress in Seventeenth-Century England*. Oxford: Oxford University Press, 2015.

Slapin, Jonathan B., and Sven-Oliver Proksch. "A Scaling Model for Estimating Time-Series Party Positions from Texts." *American Journal of Political Science* 52, no. 3 (2008): 705–22.

Smith, David A., Ryan Cordell, and Abby Mullen. "Computational Methods for Uncovering Reprinted Texts in Antebellum Newspapers." *American Literary History* 27, no. 3 (2015): E1–E15.

So, Richard Jean. "All Models Are Wrong." *Publications of the Modern Language Association of America* 132, no. 3 (2017): 668–73.

Sokal, Alan, and Jean Bricmont. *Fashionable Nonsense: Postmodern Intellectual's Abuse of Science*. New York: Picador, 1998.

Spärck Jones, Karen. *Automatic Keyword Classification for Information Retrieval*. London: Butterworths, 1971.

Sperberg-McQueen, C. M. "Text in the Electronic Age: Textual Study and Text Encoding, with Examples from Medieval Texts." *Literary and Linguistic Computing* 6, no. 1 (1991): 34–46.

Stevenson, Edward Luther. *Terrestrial and Celestial Globes: Their History and Construction, Including a Consideration of Their Value as Aids in the Study of Geography and Astronomy*. 2 vols. New Haven, CT: Yale University Press, 1921.

Steyvers, Mark, and Tom Griffiths. "Probabilistic Topic Models." In *Handbook of Latent Semantic Analysis*, edited by Thomas Landauer, Danielle S. McNamara, Simon Dennis, and Walter Kintsch, 427–48. Mahwah, NJ: Lawrence Erlbaum Associates, 2007.

Strogatz, Steven H. "Exploring Complex Networks." *Nature* 410, no. 6825 (2001): 268–76.

Suarez, Michael F. "Book History from Descriptive Bibliographies." In *The Cambridge Companion to the History of the Book*, edited by Leslie Howsam, 199–218. Cambridge: Cambridge University Press: 2014.

———. "Historiographical Problems and Possibilities in Book History and National Histories of the Book." *Studies in Bibliography* 56, no. 1 (2003-4): 140–70.

———. "Towards a Bibliometric Analysis of the Surviving Record, 1701–1800." In *The Cambridge History of the Book in Britain*, edited by Michael F. Suarez and Michael L. Turner, 37–65. Cambridge: Cambridge University Press, 2009.

Sumira, Sylvia. *Globes: 400 Years of Exploration, Navigation, and Power*. Chicago: University of Chicago Press, 2014.

Talib, Ismail S. *The Language of Postcolonial Literatures: An Introduction*. London: Routledge, 2002.

Tao, Terence. *An Introduction to Measure Theory*. Providence, RI: American Mathematical Society, 2011.

Tedder, H. R., and Joyce Boro. "Jugge, Richard (c. 1514–1577), Bookseller and Printer." *Oxford Dictionary of National Biography*, 2008. https://doi.org/10.1093/ref:odnb/15160.

Tenen, Dennis Yi. "Toward a Computational Archaeology of Fictional Space." *New Literary History* 49, no. 1 (2018): 119–47.

Tobler, Waldo. "A Computer Movie Simulating Urban Growth in the Detroit Region." *Economic Geography* 46, no. sup1 (1970): 234–40.

Traister, Bryce. "The Object of Study; or, Are We Being Transnational Yet?" *Journal of Transnational American Studies* 2, no. 1 (2010). https://doi.org/10.5070/T821006993.

Trott, Sean, Tiago Timponi Torrent, Nancy Chang, and Nathan Schneider. "(Re)Construing Meaning in NLP." *Proceedings of the 58th Annual Meeting of the Association for Computational Linguistics* (2020): 5170–84.

Turney, Peter D., and Patrick Pantel. "From Frequency to Meaning: Vector Space Models of Semantics." *Journal of Artificial Intelligence Research* 37, no. 1 (2010): 141–88.

Underwood, Ted. *Distant Horizons: Digital Evidence and Literary Change*. Chicago: University of Chicago Press, 2019.

———. "A Genealogy of Distant Reading." *Digital Humanities Quarterly* 11, no. 2 (2017).

———. "Machine Learning and Human Perspective." *PMLA* 135, no. 1 (2020): 92–109.

———. "Topic Modeling Made Just Simple Enough." *The Stone and the Shell*, 2012. https://tedunderwood.com/2012/04/07/topic-modeling-made-just-simple-enough/.

———. *Why Literary Periods Mattered: Historical Contrast and the Prestige of English Studies*. Stanford, CA: Stanford University Press, 2013.

Underwood, Ted, and Richard Jean So. "Can We Map Culture?" *Journal of Cultural Analytics* 6, no. 3 (2021): 32–51.

Van Mieghem, Piet. *Graph Spectra for Complex Networks*. Cambridge: Cambridge University Press, 2011.

Van Vugt, Ingeborg. "Using Multi-Layered Networks to Disclose Books in the Republic of Letters." *Journal of Historical Network Research* 1, no. 1 (2017): 25–51.

Wakely, Maria. "Printing and Double-Dealing in Jacobean England: Robert Barker, John Bill, and Bonham Norton." *The Library* 8, no. 2 (2007): 119–53.

Wall, Cynthia S. *The Prose of Things: Transformations of Description in the Eighteenth Century*. Chicago: University of Chicago Press, 2014.

Wallerstein, Immanuel. *The Modern World-System: Capitalist Agriculture and the Origins of the European World-Economy in the Sixteenth Century*. New York: Academic Press, 1974.

———. *World-Systems Analysis: An Introduction*. Durham, NC: Duke University Press, 2004.

Watts, Duncan J. *Small Worlds: The Dynamics of Networks between Order and Randomness*. Princeton, NJ: Princeton University Press, 2000.

Watts, Duncan J., and Steven H. Strogatz. "Collective Dynamics of 'Small-World' Networks." *Nature* 393, no. 6684 (1998): 440–42.

Weaver, Warren. "Machine Translation." In *Readings in Machine Translation*, edited by Sergei Nirenburg, Harold L. Somers, and Yorick Wilks, 13–18. Cambridge, MA: MIT Press, 2003.

Weedon, Alexis. "The Uses of Quantification." In *A Companion to the History of the Book*, edited by Simon Eliot and Jonathan Rose, 33–49. London: Blackwell Publishing, 2008.

Widdows, Dominic. *Geometry and Meaning*. Stanford, CA: Center for the Study of Language and Information, 2004.

Wilkens, Matthew. "The Geographic Imagination of Civil War-Era American Fiction." *American Literary History* 25, no. 4 (2013): 803–40.

Wilkerson, John, and Andreu Casas. "Large-Scale Computerized Text Analysis in Political Science: Opportunities and Challenges." *Annual Review of Political Science* 20, no. 1 (2017): 529–44.

Wilks, Yorick, Brian M. Santor, and Louise M. Guthrie. *Electric Words: Dictionaries, Computers, and Meanings.* Cambridge, MA: MIT Press, 1996.

Yarowsky, David. "Unsupervised Word Sense Disambiguation Rivaling Supervised Methods." *Proceedings of the 33rd Annual Meeting on Association for Computational Linguistics.* Cambridge, MA: Association for Computational Linguistics, 1995.

Yngve, Victor H. "Early Research at M.I.T.: In Search of Adequate Theory." In *Early Years in Machine Translation: Memoirs and Biographies of Pioneers*, edited by W. John Hutchins. Amsterdam: John Benjamins Publishing, 2000.

Zwicker, Steven N. "Is There Such a Thing as Restoration Literature?" *Huntington Library Quarterly* 69, no. 3 (2006): 425–50.

INDEX

Adorno, Theodor, 9
Ahmed, Manan, 3
Ahnert, Ruth, 3
Ahnert, Sebastian, 3
Algee-Hewitt, 3, 232n4
Allison, Sarah, 3
Atkinson, Paul, 3
authorship, 16, 24–26, 34–35, 38, 41, 47, 50, 52–56, 217n29

Bakhtin, Mikhail, 19, 61, 68
   dialogism, 64–65, 77, 89, 109–10, 220n7
Bar-Hillel, Yehoshua, 61, 71, 74
Barabási, Albert-László, 28–30, 32, 39
Barthes, Roland, 66–67, 110, 221n20
Basu, Anupam, 3
Behn, Aphra, 43, 53, 54, 97, 102–05, 109

Benoit, Kenneth, 1–2
bibliographical metadata. *See* metadata
big data, 1, 3
Bode, Katherine, 3
Bolla, Peter de, 3
book history. *See* authorship; booksellers; printers
booksellers, 16, 24–26, 41, 50, 52, 57
Brady, Henry E., 1
Braudel, Fernand, 116, 150, 154
Broadwell, Peter, M. 3
Brown, Nicole M., 3
Burt, Roland S., 218n32, 219n44

Carlsson, Fredrik, 59
Cartwright, Dorwin, 31
Castells, Manuel, 28, 32

Certeau, Michel de, 113–14
Chomsky, Noam, 71–72
complexity, 18, 26–30, 57–58, 82–83, 109–10, 180
  versus complication, 30, 66
  world systems, 21, 116–18, 123, 148–50
computational linguistics, 2, 7, 10, 69, 71, 76, 81, 111–12, 169, 192–93, 203. *See also* distributional hypothesis
computational literary studies. *See* corpus-based inquiry; distant reading
concepts, 19–20, 61–62, 64, 70, 77–78, 82, 93
  computational analyses of:
    affect, 91–93, 102–04, 158–59
    architecture, 88
    anatomy, 90
    animality, 20, 93–95
    authority, 101–02, 108
    biblicality, 94–95, 115–16, 150–51, 154, 156–59
    body (human), 20, 85–87, 90–93, 97, 155–57, 162
    books and print culture, 148
    capitalism (trade), 95–98, 115–19, 123–24, 148, 154, 159–62
    colonialism, 95–98, 124, 160–61
    color, 19, 90, 92
    ecology, 94–95
    gender, 20, 95–97, 102–104, 155–56, 159
    geography, 94, 113–64
    measurement, 88
    mind, 91–92, 98–99
    money, 97–98
    nationalism, 115, 144–51, 158–59
    navigation, 95–96, 115
    personhood, 92–93, 97–100, 104
    slavery, 20, 96–97
    spatiality, 88
    world, 156–59, 162
  conceptual nonstationarity, 100–08.
  See also vector semantics
  conceptual topography. *See* geospatial semantics
corpus-based inquiry, 1–4, 6–13, 23, 197–99
  importance of heterogeneous data, 16, 100, 108–09
  mathematical structure of, 7, 68–69, 180–86, 203
  metaphysical considerations of, 8, 11, 22, 27, 171–72, 202, 232n8
  outliers, 9
  purpose of, 2, 7–8, 9
  theory of, 6–12, 22–23, 164–78.
  See also distant reading
corpus linguistics. *See* computational linguistics
cultural analytics. *See* distant reading

Davison, Kate, 30, 33
distant reading, 1–4, 6, 22, 109, 166–71, 183, 186, 195, 197–98, 203
  distant reading hypothesis, 168–69
  early modern studies, 2, 14–16
  interdisciplinary character of, 1–4, 10–11, 13, 23, 57–58, 110–12, 165–66, 202, 205–07
  literary studies, 2–5, 165–66, 180, 186, 205–06
  misunderstandings of 3–5, 9, 12, 166, 191, 212n21, 212n23
  skepticism of 3, 57–58, 60–61, 109, 212n23
  success of 4, 8–10, 59–61, 109, 112

theoretical grounds for 167–72
versus close reading 9, 97, 112, 121–22, 163, 177, 212n21
See also concepts; corpus-based inquiry; geographical text analysis; vector semantics
distribution of difference. *See* variation
distributional hypothesis, 10, 22, 59–61, 72–73, 76, 174–75, 202–07
Dumais, Susan, 2, 61, 81

Early English Books Online (EEBO), 13–20, 24–25, 28, 33–41, 43–46, 50–53, 58, 61–62, 85, 115, 134, 163, 173, 184–85, 217n29, 217n30, 218n31, 230n33
bibliographical metadata, 24–26, 34, 43, 57–58, 217n31
copublication network, 33–37
exclusions from, 15
geographical structure, 115–16, 121–22, 125–42, 162–63
history of, 14
keyword-in-context (KWIC) matrix, 83–84, 223n41
markup of, 14, 127–29, 173–74, 234n14
as topological model, 234n14
representativeness of, 16
semantic analyses of, (*see under* concepts)
England, 15–16, 21, 37, 48, 97, 115–26, 132–37, 140–51, 162

Firth, J. R., 11, 61, 73, 232n6
Flament, Claude, 31
Froehlich, Heather, 3

Gallon, Kim, 3
Garry, John, 1–2
Gastaldi, Juan Luis, 60, 62
geographical text analysis, 2, 20–22, 108, 115–16, 129–30. *See also* geospatial semantics
geography
agricultural, 118
biblical, 115–16, 122–25, 135, 138–39, 156–59, 162
cartography, 119, 121, 162–3, 186
celestial, 120, 123, 162–63, 228n22
classical, 117, 119, 122, 125
colonialism, 95–98, 117–19, 162
fantastical, 120
geographical dictionaries, 119–20, 122, 126–28
geospatial topology, 125–26, 162, 185–86
global, 31, 42, 120–21, 125–27, 131, 134–35, 146, 152, 159–62, 164, 170–73
history of, 117–25, 162–63
misunderstandings of, 121–22, 124, 163
nationalism, 31, 133–34, 144–51, 154, 162, 166, 168–69
quantitative, 7, 120–21
centroid, 20, 139–142
latitude and longitude, 20–21, 121, 123, 126, 129–30, 138–39, 159–62
range, 139–40
spatial autocorrelation, 11, 176
Tobler's First Law, 11
travel guides, 121
travel narratives, 118
world geography, 117–30, 134, 138–39, 156–59, 227n8, 229n25.
See also geospatial semantics; place; space
geospatial semantics, 22, 108, 114, 162–63

INDEX 263

geospatial semantics (*continued*)
    semantic footprint, 20–21, 114–15, 139–40, 142, 151
Genette, Gérard, 67
Gil, Alex, 3
Granovetter, Mark, 31
graph theory. *See* network theory
Gregory, Ian, 3
Greteman, Blaine, 3

Halliday, M. A. K., 232n6
Harary, Frank, 31
Hardie, Andrew, 3
Harris, Zellig, 10, 61, 70–73, 80, 83, 174
Helgerson, Richard, 124
Homans, George, 30–31
Hope, Jonathan, 3
Howell, Naomi, 3

information retrieval, 19, 59, 69–70, 76–82, 87
information science, 178, 195–97
    Kullback-Leibler divergence, 239n50
    positive pointwise mutual information (PPMI), 84–86, 195
    term frequency inverse document frequency (TF-IDF), 239n53
intertextuality, 19, 60–61, 65–69, 82–83, 109–12, 177

Jehlen, Myra, 124
Jennings, Helen, 30, 31
Jockers, Matthew, 3

Kilgore, Christopher D., 29
Kristeva, Julia, 19–20, 61–69, 82, 109–112

Landauer, Thomas K., 1, 81
Lang, Anouk, 3

latent semantic analysis. *See* vector semantics
Laver, Michael, 1–2
Lazarsfeld, Paul F., 10, 30
Lee, James Jaehoon, 3
Lee, Nancy Howell, 31
Lefebvre, Henri, 115, 153–54, 227n7
Levine, Caroline, 30, 33
Lewin, Kurt, 30
literary mathematics, 22–23
    definition of, 12, 22, 167
    purpose of, 12–13, 165–66
Locke, John, 100–02
Long, Hoyt, 3
Lowe, W., 1
Luhn, H.P., 19, 61, 76–78, 109

machine learning, 81, 196–97
machine translation, 19, 59, 69–76, 82, 222n34
markup, 14, 129, 173–74, 234n14
Malinowski, Bronislaw, 232n6
Manovich, Lev, 2
Massey, Doreen, 154
Masterman, Margaret, 19, 71–72, 74–76, 109
matrix algebra, 12, 31, 83–84, 186–91
    dot product, 187–89, 193
    matrix decomposition, 189–90
    matrix multiplication, 35–36
meaning, 9, 18–19, 22, 60
Merton, Robert K., 10, 30
metadata, 7, 24–25, 57–58, 100–09, 125–29, 172, 201
    relation to variation, 8, 100, 108, 171–77, 201–02
Mitts, Tamar, 1
Moreno, Jacob L., 30, 31
Moreno, Zerka T., 30
Moretti, Franco, 2–3, 43, 167, 212n21
Murrieta-Flores, Patricia, 3

Nancy, Jean-Luc, 116, 227n8, 229n25
network theory, 7, 10, 12, 26–31, 175–76, 185–86
  abstraction, 29–30
  adjacency matrix, 35
  betweenness, 35–36
  bipartite networks, 34–35, 57, 187
  community detection, 17–19
  degree, 35, 37–38, 41–42
  degree (mean), 43–48
  degree distribution, 39–40
  group dynamics, 30–31
  homophily, 10, 30–31, 175–76
  incidence matrix, 35, 187
  mathematical formalization of, 31
  metaphorical use of, 29
  projection, 35–36, 57
  "real-world," 17, 32, 39–41
  relation to corpus metadata, 17, 108
  "scale-free," 32, 39–41
  "small-world," 32
  social psychology, 30–32
  sociometry, 26
  "structural holes," 17–18, 38, 50–51, 177
  temporality, 43–48
  "weak ties" 26, 31–32.
  See also complex systems theory
Newman, M. E. J., 28
Norman, Robert, 31

Oettinger, Anthony, 71
Osgood, Charles E., 2

periodization, 17–18, 43–57, 108, 134–38
Piper, Andrew, 2–3
place, 8, 11–12, 20–22, 31, 100, 113–17.
  See also geospatial semantics
Porter, Catherine, 3

printers, 34–38, 41, 47–48, 50–54
Proksch, Sven-Oliver, 1
Reifler, Erwin, 71, 73
Riffaterre, Michael, 67, 221n20
Risam, Roopika, 3

quantitative text analysis. *See* corpus-based inquiry
Sá Pereira, Moacir P. de, 2

Sahlgren, Magnus, 59, 80
Salton, Gerard, 19, 61, 76, 109–10, 175
Sassen, Saskia, 145
Schütze, Hinrich, 80, 111–12
semantic space. *See* vector semantics
Shannon, Claude, 61, 70
Shore, Daniel, 3
Sinclair, John, 232n6
Slapin, Jonathan, 1
Sokal, Alan, 69, 112
Spärck Jones, Karen, 61, 75–76, 175
So, Richard Jean, 3
space, 7, 113–15
  celestial, 120, 123
  domestic, 123, 154
  environmental, 146, 151, 154, 157–58
  geographical, 108, 113–64
  global, 159–161
  latent, 189, 237n36
  lexical production of, 115
  social production of, 115–16, 153, 227n7
  topological ,7, 33–34, 60, 117, 125–26, 145–47, 154, 179–80, 188–89
statistics, 12, 191–97, 238n47

Tangherlini, Timothy, 3
Tenen, Dennis Yi, 3

Text Creation Partnership, 14 44, 127, 214n1
Text Encoding Initiative, 173
textuality, 3-4, 57, 60, 68, 180, 197, 202-03. *See also* intertextuality
topic modeling, 4, 12, 81, 191
topological space. *See* space (topological)
topology, 178-86, 203. *See also* markup, metadata, space (topological)
type-token distinction, 7, 82, 110, 180-86, 203

Underwood, Ted, 3, 49, 231n3

variation, 6-8, 22-23, 45, 49, 74, 77, 81, 100, 108-09, 142, 167-80, 184, 187-99, 203-06
vector semantics, 18
    cosine similarity, 84, 88-89
    disambiguation, 71-73, 80, 86-87
    intertextuality (similarity to), 19-20, 61-63, 68-69, 74, 77, 81-83, 89
    latent semantic analysis, 190
    meaning modeled by, 61-63, 70, 77-83, 84, 89-108, 110
    networks (similarity to), 18-19, 61, 82, 109
    semantic decomposition, 20, 62, 87-89, 93-100
    semantic similarity, 80, 86, 88-89, 110, 190, 200-01, 204
    semantic space, 62, 76, 80-82, 88-89, 101-2, 189, 237n35
    vector composition, 87-89, 108
See also matrix algebra

Wallerstein, Immanuel, 116, 150, 154
Warner, Michael, 124
Watts, Duncan, 28, 32
Weaver, Warren, 10, 61, 70-71, 73-74
White, Harrison, 31
Widdows, Dominic, 88
Witmore, Michael, 3
Wong, Andrew, 78
word embeddings, 12, 81, 224n50, 238n43

Yang, Chungshu, 78
Yngve, Victor, 71

Zipf, George, 70

STANFORD
TEXT TECHNOLOGIES

Series Editors
Elaine Treharne
Ruth Ahnert

Michelle Warren
Holy Digital Grail: A Medieval Book on the Internet

Blaine Greteman
Networking Print in Shakespeare's England: Influence, Agency, and Revolutionary Change

Simon Reader
Notework: Victorian Literature and Nonlinear Style

Yohei Igarashi
The Connected Condition: Romanticism and the Dream of Communication

Elaine Treharne and Claude Willan
Text Technologies: A History

The authorized representative in the EU for product safety and compliance is:
Mare Nostrum Group
B.V Doelen 72
4831 GR Breda
The Netherlands

www.ingramcontent.com/pod-product-compliance
Lightning Source LLC
Chambersburg PA
CBHW022002220426
43663CB00007B/929